The Media City

Theory, Culture & Society

*Theory, Culture & Society* caters for the resurgence of interest in culture within contemporary social science and the humanities. Building on the heritage of classical social theory, the book series examines ways in which this tradition has been reshaped by a new generation of theorists. It also publishes theoretically informed analyses of everyday life, popular culture and new intellectual movements.

EDITOR: Mike Featherstone, *Nottingham Trent University*

SERIES EDITORIAL BOARD
Roy Boyne, *University of Durham*
Mike Hepworth, *University of Aberdeen*
Scott Lash, *Goldsmiths College, University of London*
Roland Robertson, *University of Aberdeen*
Bryan S. Turner, *National University of Singapore*

THE TCS CENTRE
The Theory, Culture & Society book series, the journals *Theory, Culture & Society* and *Body & Society*, and related conference, seminar and postgraduate programmes operate from the TCS Centre at Nottingham Trent University. For further details of the TCS Centre's activities please contact:

The TCS Centre
School of Arts and Humanities
Nottingham Trent University
Clifton Lane, Nottingham NG11 8NS, UK
email: tcs@ntu.ac.uk
web: http://sagepub.net/tcs/

*Recent volumes include:*

Informalization: Manners and Emotions Since 1890
*Cas Wouters*

The Culture of Speed: The Coming of Immediacy
*John Tomlinson*

The Dressed Society: Clothing, the Body and Some Meanings of the World
*Peter Corrigan*

Advertising in Modern and Postmodern Times
*Pamela Odih*

# The Media City

## Media, Architecture and Urban Space

Scott McQuire

Los Angeles | London | New Delhi
Singapore | Washington DC

First published 2008
Reprinted 2011

SAGE Publications Ltd
1 Oliver's Yard

London EC1Y 1SP
55 City Road
SAGE Publications Inc.
2455 Teller Road
Thousand Oaks, California 91320

SAGE Publications India Pvt Ltd
B 1/I 1 Mohan Cooperative Industrial Area
Mathura Road
New Delhi 110 044

SAGE Publications Asia-Pacific Pte Ltd
33 Pekin Street #02-01
Far East Square
Singapore 048763

**Library of Congress Control Number: 2007927662**

**British Library Cataloguing in Publication data**

A catalogue record for this book is available from the British Library

ISBN 978–1–4129–0793–4
ISBN 978–0–85702–537–1 (pbk)

Typeset by Newgen Imaging Systems (P) Ltd, Chennai, India
Printed and bound in Great Britain by the MPG Books Group
Printed on paper from sustainable resources

# Contents

# List of illustrations

# Preface

Social life in the 21st century is increasingly life lived in media cities. This statement suggests two things simultaneously. First, that the spaces and rhythms of contemporary cities are radically different to those described in classic theories of urbanism; and second, as much as the city has changed, so have media. The broad argument I unfold in this book is that the convergence of media which is increasingly mobile, instantaneous and pervasive with urban space has become a constitutive frame for a distinctive mode of social experience. Rather than treating media as something separate from the city – the medium which 'represents' urban phenomena by turning it into an image – I argue that the spatial experience of modern social life emerges through a complex process of co-constitution between architectural structures and urban territories, social practices and media feedback. The contemporary city is a *media-architecture complex* resulting from the proliferation of spatialized media platforms and the production of hybrid spatial ensembles. While this process has been underway at least since the development of technological images in the context of urban 'modernization' in the mid-19th century, its full implications are only coming to the fore with the extension of digital networks. In this respect, the term media city is designed to foreground the role of media technologies in the dynamic production of contemporary urban space, in Lefebvre's (1991) sense of binding affect and cognition to space.

While terms such as 'informational city' or 'digital city' are more established, media city is my strategic choice for three related reasons. First, I think it is vital to recognize a longer and more diverse history of the mediated production of urban space than a tight concentration on contemporary ICTs enables. In other words, the 'media city' has been a long time in the making, and has moved through a number of different iterations in the process. Part of my argument is that distinct instantiations of modern urban space have been articulated with specific media platforms, beginning with photography in the mid-19th century, shifting to cinema in the early 20th century, and more recently to electronic and digital media. While this is by no means a linear succession in which one format simply replaces another, these broad thresholds are nevertheless useful in articulating key transformations affecting the social production of urban space. Second, my interest is more the transformation of spatial experience, rather than the economic forces shaping urbanism through corporate organization and workforce composition on which writers such as Castells, Harvey and Sassen have concentrated. For this reason, I find it more useful to think of 'media' as an environment in McLuhan's sense, but also to think of the city as a 'medium' in Kittler's (1996) sense. My particular concern here is the social relations of space and time generated in the distinctive nexus of technology, architecture and emergent social relationships which characterizes the modern city. Third, I want to emphasize the increasing convergence of computing and telecommunications with older media such as photography, cinema and television. This merging, which is uneven rather than monolithic, has transformed the sites and social functions of media. In the process, it has catalyzed new means of producing social space and created new forms of social agency, and these potentials are fast becoming integral dimensions of 21st-century cities.

The book is structured around three major parts supplemented by an introduction. The introduction offers some conceptual markers for thinking about the transformation of social space in contemporary cities. The remaining chapters attempt not so much to 'apply' these approaches as to insinuate their logic into different historical situations. The dominant theme of Part 1 is the link between 'big city life' and new media at specific historical thresholds; Part 2 explores the transformation of public space, while Part 3 concerns the reconstruction of private space. Clearly these are overlapping rather than mutually distinctive orientations. While each chapter has its own trajectory and coherence, it is my hope that they establish a collective resonance capable of revealing different facets of the complex social life of modern and contemporary cities. While this book has a substantial historical focus, it is worth noting that its genesis was the spatio-temporal impact of digital media in the present. In my endeavour to theorize this condition I have been guided by a number of writers, including Georg Simmel, Siegfried Kracauer, Henri Lefebvre, Paul Virilio and Scott Lash. But the pivotal figure in this story is Walter Benjamin. Benjamin's pioneering approach to the relation between new media and big-city life developed in the 1920s and 1930s remains instructive: in particular his attention to the ambivalent political currents of what he calls phenomena 'at the crossroads'.

In the 1980s and into the 1990s the proliferation of digital media gave rise to a pervasive 'cyber' rhetoric characterized by sweeping forecasts that time and space would 'disappear'. In Chapter 1, I contextualize this outbreak of what I call the rhetoric of the 'annihilation of space and time' as a recurrent reaction to the roll-out of new media technologies. However, while I want to move beyond idealistic responses to new media, I don't want to move so far beyond them that emergent phenomena generated by interactions between media and urbanism disappear into 'the taken-for-granted'. Rather, following Benjamin's concern for phenomena 'at the crossroads', each chapter in the book is organized around a particular threshold in the nexus between media technology and urban form; a liminal period in which the social relations for inhabiting that space-time are not yet fully in place, but are instead subject to slippage, contradiction and contestation. My case studies include the photographing of Haussmann's 'modernized' Paris beginning in the 1850s (Chapter 2) and the electric lighting of urban space beginning in the 1880s (Chapter 5); the modernist glass house (Chapter 7) and the city-symphony film of the 1920s

(Chapter 3); and finally the transformative effect of computers and digital media on the city (Chapter 4), public space (Chapter 6) and the private dwelling (Chapter 8) in the present. The timing of these different snapshots was chosen partly to register key socio-economic transformations across the period; namely, the initial emergence of mass commodity production, the rise of the Fordist-Taylorist logic of industrial production, and the transition to a post-industrial, global information society. But assembling these different moments is primarily intended to index the emergence of the media-architecture complex: what I am calling the media city. It is also designed to sketch out the ambivalence of this new formation, stretched between utopian aspirations and mundane, if not malignant, actualities.

Attention to ambivalence also structures the conceptual framework I develop through these case studies. In particular, ambivalence informs the concept of 'relational space' which I argue is the characteristic frame for the spatial experience of contemporary urban life. Relational space names the ambivalent spatial configuration which emerges as the taken-for-granted nature of social space is withdrawn in favour of the active constitution of heterogeneous spatial connections linking the intimate to the global. Relational space is the experience of subjectivity remade through the expanded demand on individuals to make life choices in the apparent absence of traditional social collectivities. The concept of relational space situates the double role that media technologies have played in the reconstruction of the city as modernity's uncanny home. A 'crisis' in urban space has been announced regularly since the rapid expansion of industrial cities in the second half of the 19th century. Media have been an integral part of modern urbanism, seized as a 'solution' to urban crisis even as they actively undermine traditional regimes of space-time. Changes in urban form that have diminished the coherence of traditional means of urban representation have also levied increased demands on technological images to 'map' the city, and thereby make it available to perception, cognition and action. In the mid-19th century, photography was seized as a solution to the emerging crisis of urban representation. In Chapter 2, I describe the way *serial photography* offered a novel means of responding to the upheavals of modern urbanism, and registering the growing contingency of modern social relationships exemplified by fleeting public encounters on the street. By the 1920s such hopes were increasingly projected onto cinema, most strikingly manifested by the flowering of the 'city-symphony' film. In Chapter 3, I explore the manner in which the city-symphony exemplified the growing influence of industrial production on aesthetic and cultural sensibilities. More recently, hopes for 'mapping' urban space have been progressively transferred to high-speed data processing and computer imaging. Chapter 4 analyses the way in which such investment repeats the paradoxical reliance on media as key spatio-temporal frameworks capable of 'grounding' contemporary social relations in a radically ungrounded milieu. Flows of digital data are integral to the transformation of contemporary urban space, but are also critical tools for apprehending the complex patterns and dynamic forces of contemporary urban life.

The second and third sections of the book dealing with public space and private space respectively are each organized around chapters contrasting key modern and contemporary phenomena. Chapter 5 concerns the impact of electric lighting in producing a fluid and ephemeral urban space, while Chapter 6 explores current trajectories towards 'performative' space underpinned by public screens, mobile media and interactive networks. Chapter 7 delves into the revolutionary political ambitions invested in modernist glass construction, while the final chapter explores the contradictory psycho-social forces mobilized by the transposition of the modern desire for 'openness' onto the contemporary digitally networked home.

My ambition in this book is to suggest new ways of discerning the 'logic' expressed by the transformation of the industrial city of factory production into the media city of pervasive communication flows. The imbrication of media and urban space does not produce a one-way street of negative effects, but a complex series of possibilities and potentials whose outcomes are not yet wholly given. If the ambivalence of relational space is partly the result of the erosion of the certitudes of an earlier era of progress, its positive face is the increased demand to discriminate between differences, and to understand phenomena in terms of relations between different positions or states which are not mutually exclusive. Ambivalence in this sense is not indecision, lack of certainty or the weakening of moral fibre, but recognition that the complexity of intricately related, cascading consequences render all choices problematic in some way or to some degree. Ambivalence is the predicament of contemporary social life in the media city.

This is the critical paradox of the media city which informs my starting point in this book: as much as developments in telematics have been constitutive of the 'crisis' of urban space, they are also an essential part of any meaningful response to that crisis. In many respects, the media city of the digital age is currently 'at the crossroads'. The image of digital 'flow' as the harbinger of new freedom is everywhere contradicted by the pervasive use of digital technologies for enhanced forms of instrumental mastery over space. Yet, alongside the trajectory epitomized by the extension of panopticism in the name of state surveillance and corporate practice, other possibilities remain. My aim in this book is to provide a critical political analysis of the new social spaces created by the imbrication of media platforms and urban terrains. This might help to identify some of the fault lines which would enable the media city to be reconstructed on more inclusive terms and thereby realize the promises so often made in its name.

# Acknowledgements

Some books get written faster than others. This has been a slow book about a process of acceleration. I first began to develop the idea around 1998, although substantial work didn't begin until 2004. Along the way I have been sidetracked by a number of things – other research projects, other books, a couple of new jobs, the birth of two children, the death of my much-loved father. This extended genesis has allowed me to observe the intensification of the process I began thinking about. It also means I owe thanks to many people who have helped with this project *en route*. In particular, I would like to acknowledge Peter Lyssiotis and Don Miller with whom I began watching city films so many years ago. I would also like to thank students and staff at various seminars and conferences where parts of this work has been rehearsed, including Victoria Lynn for the 'Space Odysseys' symposium at Art Gallery of New South Wales and 'Deep Space' at the Australian Centre for the Moving Image; Colin Langridge at the Hobart Art School, University of Tasmania; Suzie Attiwill and Pia Ednie-Brown at RMIT University; John Hutnyk at Goldsmiths College; James Donald at the University of New South Wales; Mirjam Struppek and Geert Lovink for the 'Urban Screens' conference in Amsterdam. Thanks also to Rafael Lozano-Hemmer, David Shephard and Eva Riehl for permission to reproduce images. Extended passages are reprinted by permission of the publisher from WALTER BENJAMIN: SELECTED WRITINGS, VOLUME 4, 1938–40, edited by Howard Eiland and Michael W. Jennings, translated by Edmund Jephcott and Others, Cambridge, Mass.: The Belknap Press of Harvard University Press, Copyright © 2003 by the President and Fellows of Harvard College. I owe a significant debt to my colleagues and postgraduate students from the University of Melbourne. I am especially grateful to Meredith Martin for her unstinting, good-humoured and innovative research assistance, and to Nikos Papastergiadis with whom I have shared so many things. Thanks also to Mike Featherstone for his interest in this project from the beginning. Some parts of this research has appeared in earlier versions in the *Space Odysseys* exhibition catalogue, *Cultural Studies Review*, *Scan*, *Space and Culture*, and *First Monday*. Funding from the Australian Research Council has assisted this project, as has study leave provided by the University of Melbourne. On a personal level, my deep gratitude to the Brunswick mothers, especially Bec, Mary-Anne and Maja who pitched in when desperately needed. Special thanks to my mother for her extraordinarily generous practical support in caring for Lachie and Alistair. My biggest hugs go to Lachie and Alistair who have immeasurably enriched this journey. And finally, to my darling Sarah, who has lived with this project through all its stages – this book is dedicated to you.

# 1

## Introduction: The Uncanny Home

> There will be a road. It will not connect two points. It will connect all points. Its speed limit will be the speed of light. It will not go from here to there. There will be no more there. We will all only be here.
>
> (TV ad 1993)

> [T]he dream of a completely fluid and passable world-space may be the last utopia of the 20th century.
>
> (Multiplicity 2005)[1]

### The house that Gates built

In the mid-1990s, as the dotcom boom ramped up in velocity, media reports circulated about the house Bill Gates was constructing in Seattle. Conceived as a state-of-the-art merging of computer technology with architecture, Gates' multi-million dollar residence boasted all the standard automated functions such as climate control and electronic security systems, as well as a few extras like a hot tub which switched itself on as soon as the master's car entered the grounds. But the most striking feature of the Gates' house was its walls. Gates' original plan called for interior walls consisting of a series of massive floor to ceiling video screens. In some cases, like the trampoline room, the 360-degree panorama would be supplemented by an additional screen in the ceiling. All these screens could be programmed, according to his guests' wishes, with works of art selected from their host's virtual collection (the largest in the world). The duration of the displayed images could be tailored to each guest's attention span, while the different rooms they entered, accessed via electronic security PINs, would never repeat the same picture.

These chameleon-like walls gripped the imagination of many commentators, including leading proselytizers of 'digital architecture' such as William Mitchell (1995: 33):

> The interior wall panels are not what they seem. They turn out to be huge, flat video screens. In repose they simulate the surfaces of standard architectural materials, but activated they become electronic windows opening onto anything at all.

Penz and Thomas (1997: 3) soon envisaged the democratization of such possibilities:

> What Bill Gates has in his domestic environment today, we will all be able to have in our homes the day after tomorrow, or the day after that. Our digital windows will be able to provide a screen version of the world offering anywhere, anytime, any reality [ ... ].

A similar vision was evident in the 'Digital House' designed by New York-based architects Hariri and Hariri for *House Beautiful* magazine in 1998. The design was an adaptation of the 'plug-in' logic developed by Archigram's Peter Cook in the 1960s, comprising a central core onto which additional factory-built rooms could be joined, as one might connect new electrical appliances. The main walls were to be made from LCD screens, dubbed 'the building blocks of the future' by the architects (quoted in Riley 1999: 56).

Of course, wall-size screens were familiar creations of 20th-century science fiction. In *Tomorrow Revealed* (1955), author John Atkins envisaged walls that were not only screens, but interactive devices enabling the house to become a conscious entity capable of speech, thought, listening, acting and entertaining:

> The walls could dissolve into a three-dimensional scene of jungle or veldt, anything you liked, a scene from a fairy-tale or from a romance, with animals and vegetation to match, smells, sounds, hot sun, cold snow. The walls were not quite alive, but they were at the next remove: made of crystal, played on with dimensional, super-reactionary, super-sensitive colour film behind glass screens, plus odorophonics and sonics. (Atkins 1955: 180)

Wall-size screens have also featured in numerous science fiction films, including landmark productions such as Fritz Lang's *Metropolis* (1927), William Cameron Menzies' *Things To Come* (1936), Francois Truffaut's *Fahrenheit 451* (1966) and Paul Verhoeven's *Total Recall* (1990). What is immediately noticeable from such films is the wall-screen's political versatility. In *Metropolis*, the wall-screen is both a symbol and a practical technique of technocratic power; a unique device located in the top floor office of the city's patriarch. In *Things To Come*, the screen facilitates a more democratic form of technocracy, distributed throughout the populace to serve an apparently benign educational and communicational function, while in *Fahrenheit 451*, made in the era of broadcast television, the wall-screen is figured as a propaganda device for pacifying the general population. In *Total Recall* the range of imagery that the wall-screen pro-vides, from live news feeds to ambient images, is used to dramatize the split consciousness of the protagonist.

As it turned out, wall-screens were much easier to propose in literature or simulate in films, than they were to produce materially and architec-turally. Lamenting the fact that the hardware for producing large-scale screens with sufficiently high definition had not been perfected in the mid-1990s, Bill Gates was forced to scale down his ambitious plans. Nevertheless, as Penz and Thomas forecast, spin-off technology from digital cinema systems meant that wall-size images were soon becoming a familiar experience in the home.[2] Walls that have become electronic windows construct a novel point of view which is no longer continuous with site, but instead establish variable sightlines apparently capable of opening 'anywhere, any time, any reality'. Such window-walls offer to radically renovate the home, displacing its customary interiority, while also disturbing the spatiality of the world at large.

## Technological nature

There are several points we might note in relation to this scenario. The first is the way that imagination and desire continually outstrip technology, despite – or perhaps because of – extraordinarily rapid technological development. To give one point of reference, it is well-known that the field of computing has undergone a period of exponential growth lasting several decades. In the first issue of *Wired* in 1993, Frederic Davis (1993: 30) commented:

> [H]ad automobile technology advanced at a similar pace over the last 20 years, your car would travel at 500 000 miles an hour, get a million miles to the gallon, and only cost a measly $1000.

Yet, even this dizzying velocity of technological change in a realm where many of the changes are themselves mostly about speed (measured in processing power and bandwidth), leaves many impatient and frustrated that things don't move even faster. The 'world wide web' was soon ironically dubbed the 'world wide wait' as bandwidth limitations – and the cost of addressing them – became apparent in the mid-1990s. Like Bill Gates, we often find ourselves waiting for technology to catch up to where our imagination – fuelled by corporate advertising – has already taken us. A striking example was the wave of enthusiasm, crossed by a frisson of fear, that surrounded Virtual Reality technologies from the mid-1980s to the early 1990s, as 'cyberspace' became the new frontier for millennial fantasies. As anyone who was actually able to get access to a pair of EyePhones or some other VR system soon discovered, the experience fell a long way short of the total perceptual hallucination promised in films like *The Lawnmower Man* (1992). While there was certainly industry hype in the service of commercial agendas at work here, there was also a kind of longing – a technological *yearning* – which we need to recognize as part of the motor driving the ideology of progress. The deep-seated aspirations for the mastery of nature and the transcendence of bodily limits which have long underpinned faith in progress have found themselves increasingly invested in new waves of technology, culminating in the emergence of 'technoculture' in which the place of 'nature' and the delineation of 'human nature' have become problematic in new ways.[3]

If fantasies of mastery and transcendence constitute a general premise of modern technological development, they have found particularly fertile ground in the field of media and communication. Because media and communication technologies have the capacity to reconfigure the spatial and temporal parameters of perception and experience, enabling us to see, hear and even act 'at-a-distance', they alter frames of existence previously taken for granted as natural, if not immutable. The ability to span space and compress time through different generations of media from telegraph to satellite television and the internet has not only exerted a powerful fascination over modern imagination, but has fundamentally shaped the economic and social relations of modernity. As Giddens (1991: 17) observes:

> Modern social organization presumes the precise co-ordination of actions of many human beings physically absent from one another; the 'when' of these actions is directly connected to the 'where', but not, as in pre-modern epochs, via the mediation of place.

The widening of the gap between ways of life primarily grounded in place, and emergent ways of life in which spatial experience is increasingly opened to events occurring elsewhere has been a primary characteristic since industrial modernity. The capacity of new steam-powered vehicles such as trains and ships to traverse space more rapidly and consistently in the second half of the 19th century fed the massive extension of colonial empire and international trade in that period. In the 21st century, the increased capacity of new media technologies to generate 'real time' action-at-a-distance has underpinned the post-industrial phase of globalization characterized by the heightened penetration of transnational economic and cultural exchanges into the 'local' interstices of everyday life. Lash (2002a: 15) argues the centrality of new communication forms underpins a general shift to 'technological forms of life' characterized by the pervasiveness of human-machine interfaces. Insofar as technological culture is 'constitutively *culture-at a-distance*', social bonds assume technological forms:

> I operate as a man-machine interface – that is, as a technological form of natural life – because I must necessarily navigate through technological forms of social life. [...] Because my forms of social life are so normally and chronically at-a-distance, I cannot navigate these distances, I cannot achieve sociality apart from my machine interface. (Lash 2002a: 15)

Since these developments collectively redefine not only the speed of economic exchange but the spatio-temporal frameworks of human experience, it is not surprising that cultural responses often seem to simultaneously reach backwards and forwards in time: on the one hand, towards creation myths and the sort of omnipresence traditionally attributed to the gods, and on the other to a future in which all material coordinates, including the body, are dissolved to unimaginable ends. This broad spectrum underlines the extent to which responses to technological transformation have long been marked by ambivalence. The desire for technological transcendence has been intimately linked to the cultural production of what might be called the technological unconscious – a theme cogently explored in modern art and literature, perhaps most notably in the modern genre of science fiction. Atkins' 'telepathic house' of the 1950s is both distant and yet recognizable at the dawn of the 21st century. The walls 'which were not quite alive' evoke the distinctly modern myth of the technological creation of life – an ur-narrative which enters modern consciousness precociously with Mary Shelley's *Frankenstein* (1818), in which the all-too-human 'monster' comprises a collection of body parts animated by electricity.

If Shelley's monster is an assemblage which serves to index the growing uncertainty about the boundaries of the human in a society subject to new forces such as steam power and electricity, the vastness of industrial transformation over the next century demanded the invention of a new primal scene. This need was memorably fulfilled by the famous scene of the creation of the robot in Fritz Lang's *Metropolis* (1927). While Lang's fantasy robot was also enervated by electricity, it was quite a different entity to Shelley's patchwork monster. Instead of a crude copy, the technological double could now be imagined as visually indistinguishable from the organic human being – a shift paralleling the uncanny doubling of the visible world by the technological images of cinema.

Following World War II, and the emergence of the cybernetic paradigm, the encounter of human and machine was increasingly figured through the enigma of the cyborg.[4] The cyborg is neither human nor machine as these terms have been traditionally defined, but depends instead upon their merging as informational and communicational *systems* to produce a hybrid entity. In her influential 'Cyborg Manifesto' of 1984, Donna Haraway (1991: 150) appropriated the term to stress the conditions of identity in cultures which were rapidly being computerized: 'By the late twentieth century, our time, a mythic time, we are all chimeras, theorized and fabricated hybrids of machine and organism; in short we are cyborgs.' The cybernetic paradigm has exercised a major influence over the trajectory of scientific research, notably in underwriting developments in biotechnology. The success of the Human Genome Project in garnering massive research funding, which led to the earlier than expected completion of its mapping phase in mid-2000, depended on a cybernetic understanding of the lived body as a computational system running on a genetic programme in which DNA figures as 'the code of codes'. In this vein, Walter Gilbert (1992: 96) conjures a digital primal scene, looking forward to the day when 'one can pull a CD out of one's pocket and say, "Here's a human being; it's me".' This is a new conception of personal media; the person *as* media.

These three narratives of technological birth, spread across almost two centuries, can be read as distinct moments in the rewriting of Nature by technology, as industrial machines are supplemented by informational machines – media – and the horizon of programmed and patented life forms beckons. Lash (2002a: xi) underlines this trajectory when he links the emergence of genetic engineering to a broader shift in the operation of power, and argues that the transition from a discursive to informational mode of power-knowledge means that '[ ... ] "life" becomes a question no longer of organic systems but technological systems.'

## Unsettling the home

Because of the radical uncertainty affecting what was once taken for granted as the 'ground' of social experience, I want to try to dislodge my response to the Gates' house from the familiar trajectory in which yesterday's science fiction becomes today's reality. The issue is more complex than the neat succession this kind of narrative promotes. Instead, I want to read the Gates' house as a metaphor for the *generally* unsettling effect exercised by electronic and digital media on the production of public and private space in contemporary cities. The transformation of the individual home is paralleled on a metropolitan scale by the reconstruction of urban spaces, and on a global scale by the spread of digital networks which are reshaping the vectors of economic and political power, as well as the matrices of cultural affiliation. In fact, the most significant change is that where these fronts or frontiers – domestic, local, urban, regional, national, transnational – were once distinct, or, at least, were believed to be – they now seem to be irreducibly imbricated in one another. The globalization of media flows goes hand in hand with the reorganization of the space of domestic life, including the micro-politics of the family.

The home itself now contains a wide array of media forms. Many of these are in the process of shifting from predominantly one-way broadcast systems with regional or national reach, to interactive global networks in which each node of consumption is also capable of production. As Beatriz Colomina (1994: 210) notes: 'The house is now a media centre, a reality that will forever transform our understanding of both public and private.' If the boundaries of the home have become more porous in an era of ubiquitous media, so have the borders of the nation-state. Contemporary cultural identity is consequentially less defined by an 'imagined community' based on the geographical borders of a single national territory, but increasingly assumes the mosaic pattern adumbrated by the overlapping footprints of satellites and the flows of digital networks. At the same time, media devices have become ubiquitous elements shaping the public space of contemporary cities, embedded in urban infrastructure in a wide variety of locations and forms from informational kiosks, large public screens, digital surveillance cameras and computerized traffic systems. The development of new generations of mobile media which are carried in the course of everyday life has further intensified the challenge to established boundaries of public and private space. The transformation of the spatial relations supported by the telephone is symptomatic. For the best part of a century, a phone call was made to a fixed site such as a house or office, and the caller asked whether or not a certain person was 'there'. In contrast, the customary greeting on a mobile phone is 'where are you?' In an era in which media have become mobile, ubiquitous and personalized, technology and person have merged, and this merging is fast becoming taken for granted.

The wall-screen of the Gates' house can thus be read as symptomatic of the ways in which a broad array of new media technologies and platforms are not only redefining architecture and urbanism, but the social life sustained within their domain. The image of the city, and the ways of imagining existence within its bounds, are in flux. If the function of the wall as an architectural staple has been increasingly drawn into question, so have the private space of the home and the public space of the street. Thinking through this condition, which produces effects reaching from the interior subjectivity characteristic of modern identity to the role of public space as the forum for collective interaction and political contestation, demands our departure from the theoretical paradigm of media representation. By 'representation', I mean the varied discourse built on the underlying, if often unarticulated, assumption that the role of media is to provide representations – faithful or otherwise – of the world outside. This understanding that media are ultimately separate from the 'real world' informs the bulk of modern media analysis, as well as the 'postmodern' discourse about the blurring or collapse of the real in face of the media onslaught. While the issue of *how* the world is constructed in and through media remains critically important, it is equally critical to fully accept that media can no longer be set apart from the social; nor, for that matter, from the political, the economic and the cultural. Acceptance of the heightened role of media in the production of contemporary experience demands the critical embrace of McLuhan's insight that media constitute an *environment*. This aspect has become more manifest as media technologies have extended beyond fixed sites and specialized places of consumption such as home, office or cinema. Moving through the world at large now involves the ongoing negotiation of, and participation in, diverse media flows. Neither home nor street nor city can now be thought apart from the media apparatus which redistributes the scale and speed of social interaction in their domains.

Of course, 'home' needs to be heard here as more than a physical structure, but also as designating a sense of cultural belonging and existential shelter. However, it is important to try and hold the physical and the psychical together, without simply collapsing one into the other. There is a sense in which the spatial mutations affecting contemporary architecture and urbanism – the way in which we gain access to buildings, the passage between rooms, the proximity of separate sites, and so on – are critically linked to transformations in contemporary thought and experience which affect the social relations of subjectivity and meaning. The crisis of 'Grand Narratives', which Lyotard (1984) posed as the fundamental condition of postmodernity, can be at least partly understood as conditioned by a crisis of boundary, reference and dimension. How do we demarcate inside and outside? What are the coordinates of the near and the far? What happens when 'here' and 'there' are no longer held apart, but threaten to collapse into one another.

Questions such as these exert a profound impact on the way in which we can define 'home' in the present, whether at the level of the private dwelling, the post-industrial city or the radically dispersed communities that make up the heterogeneous 'homelands' of contemporary nation-states. The older *geographical* question 'where is your home?' has been displaced by a newer imperative: what is the *meaning* of home? Do contemporary urban forms, with their unprecedented scale and dispersion, still correspond to what was historically called the city? Can cities accommodate the ascendancy of the new forms of technological mobility characteristic of 'real time' media? Suspended between the resurgent promise of technological ubiquity and the recurrent threat of technological alienation, there is an urgent need to investigate what it means today to be 'at home'. Does this still correspond to a particular location, site or territory – or rather, to a particular sense of situation, of locatedness, of cultural belonging? More to the point, how might we plot the coordinates or demarcate the boundaries of our homes in the present?

### The technological uncanny

In his well-known essay 'The "Uncanny"' published in 1919, Freud (1955) traces the etymology of the German word *unheimlich*, which is often translated into English as 'uncanny' but is more literally rendered as *unhomely*. For Freud, the sensation of the uncanny is not caused by what is strange or unfamiliar. Rather, it arises when the known and the familiar are *made* strange. Uncanniness is a *disturbed* domesticity, the return of the familiar in an apparently unfamiliar form. Elsewhere in his essay, Freud approvingly quotes Schelling who defines the uncanny as the bringing to light of that which ought to have remained hidden. Uncanniness thus belongs to a complex scene of veiling and unveiling, of secrecy, revelation and improper exposure.

In his discussion, Freud continually links the uncanny to the experience of *ambivalence*, and he offers a number of suggestive examples. The first is uncertainty as to whether an animate being is alive, or, conversely, whether an object is really inanimate; the second concerns the enigma of the *doppelgänger* or double (here Freud narrates a personal experience in which he saw but did not recognize his own reflection, recalling that he thoroughly disliked what he saw); the third concerns the experience in which the distinction between imagination and reality is effaced. As Anthony Vidler (1994) has pointed out, even though Freud developed his concept of the uncanny in the context of Romantic literature and the 19th-century discovery of buried cities such as Pompeii and Troy, the categories he deploys seem peculiarly suited to exploring the way contemporary media technologies can rearrange bodies, times and spaces, seemingly at will.

As writ large in the Gates' house, the solidity of our walls has increasingly given way to the restless luminosity of electronic screens. Looking through these strange windows we are invited to perceive the world as if divorced from bodily constraints. We see the world from where we are *not*, from where we have *never been*. Despite its everyday familiarity, this mode of disembodied perception – which can be equated in psychoanalytic terms with the fantasy of seeing from the place of the 'other' – retains a strong sense of the uncanny. One of Freud's primary reference points in his essay was the 19th-century story of the 'The Sandman' by E.T.A. Hoffmann. In Hoffmann's story, the Sandman is a quasi-mythical figure used by adults to persuade children to go to sleep. At one point, the young protagonist's Nurse tells him:

> He's a wicked man who comes when children won't go to bed, and throws handfuls of sand in their eyes so that they jump out of their heads all bleeding. (Quoted in Freud 1955: 237)

In his analysis of the story, Freud (1955: 230) relates the experience of the uncanny 'to the idea of being robbed of one's eyes'. The deeper Freudian analogy is, of course, the ubiquitous spectre of castration. But, before proceeding too rapidly to this destination, it may pay to read Hoffmann more literally. In many respects, the fear of being 'robbed of one's eyes' is akin to the spectre which has haunted modern consciousness ever since the invention of the camera. While technological images were readily inserted into the Enlightenment discourse associating light and transparency with reason and truth, enabling a direct relation to be plotted between the transparency desired in political representation and the transparency invested in photographic representation, the other side of this discourse has been the threat that photographic prostheses will in fact *replace* the organ they were meant to merely supplement. In other words, the media will effectively rob us of our eyes, of our capacity to see for ourselves.

As early as the 1880s, when photography was first industrialized and public images began to proliferate in newspapers and on postcards, the camera's prodigious capacity to hijack visual appearances and to transport them into new contexts highlighted an unnerving instability in the bond between image and referent. What was inaugurated was the growing recognition of the inability of modern signs to *secure* meaning, an instability which opened a rift at the centre of the positivist model of knowledge. The scientific vision which had enthusiastically acclaimed photography as objective truth in the mid-19th century found itself increasingly outflanked by the radical promiscuity of what Kracauer (1995: 58) aptly called the 'blizzard' of modern images. The ambivalence of photorealism is central to the instability of what Habermas (1989) calls the 'publicness' which forms a key plank in modern forms of political legitimation. Faith in the capacity of visual images to bring us close to the real has been counterpointed by a growing suspicion that media form a screen blocking the real. This tension between the factual pull of technological images and the semantic instability arising from their capacity to be manipulated and reproduced in different contexts has never been resolved. Instead, it has been systematically displaced onto each new wave of image technology – photography, cinema, television, VR – triggering recurrent fears about the capacity of images to *replace* the real. This ambivalence has been magnified in the brave new era of digital imaging. From the moment that we began to see Michael Jackson morph into a panther in front of our eyes, or Sam Neil run from a herd of dinosaurs in *Jurassic Park* (1993) – in other words, when we could *see* photorealistic moving images of things we knew didn't exist – the knot linking technological images, realism and embodied perception has become subject to new exigencies.[5]

My interest here is not so much trying to disentangle the residues of 'photorealism' from 'manipulation', nor to demarcate truth and ideology, as if such gestures are feasible on more than a limited, situated basis. Rather, I am more concerned with exploring the ambivalence which currently affects all of us who live with media technology as an integral part of our daily lives. As Virilio (1995: 99) points out: 'The technology question is inseparable from the question of *where* technology occurs.' Inserted directly into the heart of domestic space, devices such as the telephone, radio, television and computer, punch right through the physical threshold of the private residence. Instead of being defined primarily by the passage of material bodies, access to a residence increasingly depends upon the activation of an electrical circuit. Conceiving the home as an interactive *node* permanently on-line to vast information flows radically alters the division and dynamics of public and private space. One result is a profound *de-territorialization* of the home, insofar as what we see and experience within its walls is no longer contained by their limits. At the same time, and as a result of the same forces, public space also undergoes profound changes, as the immediacy of various forms of action-at-a-distance dislodge the social primacy of embodied presence. The intersection between modern media and modern urbanism transforms the nexus between place and experience, familiar and foreign, self and stranger. The blurring of boundaries between human perception and technological vision asks us to rethink the space of consciousness, as the models of autonomy and interior subjectivity which have dominated modernity become increasingly difficult to reconcile with everyday experience.

Instead of the presumption of spatial continuity which has been the historical 'ground' of social relations, the immediacy of the continuous space surrounding our bodies is increasingly overlaid with a matrix that is intermittent, discontinuous and fluctuating. In the screen window, spaces appear and disappear abruptly. We can activate links between physically discontinuous sites at a moment's notice but these conjunctions are transient and inherently unstable. Dwelling in a space-time framed by a proliferation of media technologies fundamentally alters human sensory and perceptual parameters, sustaining a range of encounters which question the limits of the body and the authority of embodied perception. It is the tendency for technology to displace the body as the privileged measure of human experience which induces what I referred to above as a crisis of boundary, reference and dimension. Events happening in one place have instantaneous effects in another, or in a multiplicity of others, potentially impacting on sites distributed across the entire globe. With live television and 'real time' networked media, the classical definition of 'the event' as a singular occurrence is brought increasingly into question. In this context, concepts such as distance, proximity and locality, as well as interiority and exteriority, take on a range of new meanings. This transformation of the relation between sites, boundaries, and systems of access and enclosure, points to a critical aspect of contemporary experience which I want to call the *technological uncanny*.

The 19th-century uncanny was frequently linked to dark, hidden spaces. A classic literary example was Poe's *The Fall of the House of Usher* (1839) in which the narrator encounters the horror of a living being who has been walled up, buried alive in a house which itself assumes frightful organic qualities. It was precisely this 'unhealthy' profusion of dank cellars, hidden recesses and musty attics which modern architects such as Le Corbusier sought to abolish with flat-roofed residences, elevated above ground on thin pilotis, surrounded by verdure, with their terraces and windows open to the endless flow of light and air. Exposure of the hidden, the bringing to light of the repressed was thought to have a healing function. It offered a way of exorcising the demons. In contrast, the technological uncanny is less a function of hidden space or invisibility than of what Virilio aptly calls the *overexposure* of space. For Virilio (1991a: 19): 'This overexposure attracts our attention to the extent that it offers a world without antipodes and without hidden aspects, a world in which opacity is but a momentary interlude.' Borrowing Freud's sense of 'improper unveiling' – the exposure of something which ought to remain hidden – I will argue that the con-temporary drive towards technological visibility and social transparency is producing a range of effects which depart the forms of truth and knowledge once imagined as the mark of the rational subject. The Enlightenment dream of subjecting the exercise of power to rational control through public scrutiny has been parlayed into the progressive mediatization of the home, and the reconstruction of urban space along the twin axes of surveillance and spectacle. If, on the one hand, the extension of media throughout urban space has supported strategies of instrumental control, it is becoming increasingly clear that visibility can no longer be correlated to security. As Peter Weibel (2002: 214) argues: 'The more the state attempts to make its citizens become transparent people and the community a transparent community, the more insecurity is created.' Vastly exceeding the effects of State surveillance is the way new media platforms – media which are always on and always available – support the extension of market relations and commodity values into more and more areas of everyday life.

Yet, even while acknowledging the reach and extent of these headings, it is important to recognize they are neither inevitable nor yet total. In this sense, the concept of the technological uncanny has a strategic aim.

Foregrounding the ambivalence created by technological transformation of the city and the private dwelling as 'home' offers a way of reading emergent signs of social contradiction and political contestation. Realizing this ambition demands the detachment of the uncanny from its Romantic origins in the Burkean sublime.[6] It also demands adding a critical historical context to Freud's usage, to interpret the spatial ambivalence generated by media technologies as symptoms of unarticulated and often repressed political contradictions.[7] Focusing on the ambivalence of the socio-cultural experiences generated by new media technologies is helpful in thinking the spatiality of the media city as one of doubling and displacement, but also for emphasizing different media temporalities – the belated, delayed or deferred effects – which are routinely obscured beneath, or actively repressed by the current drive towards 'real time' networks.

### The 'annihilation' of space and time

In a television advertisement for telecommunications company MCI screened in the 1993, the much-heralded 'information superhighway' was presented in the following terms:

> There will be a road. It will not connect two points. It will connect all points. Its speed limit will be the speed of light. It will not go from here to there. There will be no more there. We will all only be here.

While the ad starts out with the familiar metaphor of a road, it is soon evident that it envisaged less a traditional linear thoroughfare than a *network* in which infinite speed overcomes distance to generate a technological form of perpetual presence. In a world in which 'There will only be here', MCI propose not so much a journey with an identifiable destination as the triumph of technology over the margins, over marginality as such. The ad invites us to imagine a future in which we will never be 'outside', never 'there' but permanently 'here'. Less clear are the social and political ramifications of this putative transcendence. If there is no more *there*, does this imply – at least in fantasy – the disappearance of the place of the other, the final solution to colonial strategies of territorial domination and assimilation, what Paul Virilio (1986: 135) has called the geostrategic homogenization of the globe? Or is a different heading indicated? Once the *here* has been generalized and universalized – dare one say *democratized* – can colonial hierarchies between metropole and periphery, self and other still assume the same authority? To pose this question another way, does being propelled on a journey bereft of familiar coordinates operate to problematize mastery and overthrow entrenched relations of power, or does it simply accentuate an existing state of generalized disorientation and alienation?

MCI's image of a ubiquitous network connected at light-speed drew on prevailing *fin-de- siècle* rhetoric prophesying that the internet would – finally – produce the technological annihilation of time and space. Such rhetoric drew a utopian energy from the legacy of *Wired*'s adopted patron saint Marshall McLuhan (1974: 11), who had famously proclaimed in the mid-1960s that electronic media 'have extended our central nervous system itself in a global embrace, abolishing space and time as far as our planet is concerned'. However, if one looks back further, similar pronouncements can be traced right across the 20th century. Marinetti's 'Founding Manifesto of Futurism', published in *Le Figaro* in 1909, extolled the victory of technological speed to boldly assert 'Time and Space died yesterday' (Apollonio 1973: 22). Corbusier's (1971: 187) vision of modern offices presented in his 1924 book *Urbanisme* (later translated as *City of Tomorrow*), stressed that 'Everything is concentrated within them: apparatus for abolishing time and space, telephones, cables and wireless [...].' Dziga Vertov's (1984: 18) famed 1923 'Kino-eye' manifesto proclaimed cinema as a machine capable of abolishing space and time: 'free of the limits of time and space, I put together any given points in the universe.' When Howard Hughes completed his continuous circumnavigation of the globe by air in 1938, the *News of the Day* newsreel acclaimed him as 'The world's no. 1 annihilator of time and space'. It would be easy to multiply these examples.

In fact, as Schivelbusch (1986) has pointed out, similar rhetoric first emerged as long ago as the 1820s, when the invention of steam-powered trains radically transformed the way that people saw and experienced the landscape. Mechanically powered motion, in conjunction with the increased speed of travel, the relatively smooth transit offered by engineered and embanked tracks, and the closeting of train travellers in glass-windowed carriages, all combined to alter spatial perception. According to Schivelbusch (1986: 10):

> 'Annihilation of time and space' was the *topos* which the early nineteenth century used to describe the new situation into which the railroad placed natural space after depriving it of its hitherto absolute powers. Motion was no longer dependent on the conditions of natural space, but on a mechanical power that created its own spatiality.

In his pioneering work on the technological sublime, Leo Marx (2000: 194) observed similar responses to the emerging machine culture of the 19th-century United States:

> No stock phrase in the entire lexicon of progress appears more often than the 'annihilation of space and time', borrowed from one of Pope's relatively obscure poems [...]. The extravagance of his sentiment is apparently felt to match the sublimity of technological progress.

The reappearance of similar sentiments surrounding the 1980s invention of 'cyberspace' indicates the need to interpret them as a particular *rhetoric*. Such a stance is a necessary first step towards a richer understanding of emergent relationships between technology, territory and social experience. One of the major problems with simply accepting the claims of 'annihilation' at face value is that it positions the present as the apex of the historic process, leaving little room for conceptualizing further change. Time and space have not yet *disappeared*, nearly two centuries after this fate was first widely pronounced. However, the ways in which time and space are individually and collectively experienced have certainly undergone dramatic and far-reaching changes.

Once we recognize that pronouncements of the 'annihilation of time and space' form a *recurrent* theme in the technological transformation of modern life, we can begin to plot the specific thresholds – particularly those concerning the emergence of new transport and media technologies – at which this theme is deployed. We can also begin to map a cyclical process in which the rhetoric of annihilation constitutes a specific moment in the assimilation of novel and potentially disjunctive spatio-temporal experiences. In this respect, it is important to appreciate that the longevity of the rhetoric is partly a function of its adaptability. Marinetti's account was dominated by the automobile; Corbusier's by telephone and radio; Vertov's by cinema; Hughes' by air travel; McLuhan's by television; MCI looked to the internet.

Positioning the rhetoric of the 'annihilation of time and space' as a particular moment in a dynamic cycle of rupture and recuperation enables a deliberate focus on the process of transition. If the rhetoric of 'annihilation' generally corresponds to the initial roll-out of a new technology, and 'assimilation' to the moment in which that technology has entered the dominant social habitus to such an extent that it can ground new forms of abstract knowledge and social practice, what separates these two poles is the passage of negotiation.[8] It is this in-between or transitional phase that I want to particularly focus on in this book. As Walter Benjamin (1999b: 857) pointed out long ago, there is a strategic value in analysing phenomena 'at the crossroads': 'namely, the new view on the historical world at the point where a decision is forthcoming as to its reactionary or revolutionary application'. At the crossroads, the contradictory tendencies and ambivalent currents of new phenomena can often assume a marked *political* tenor. What may in retrospect seem the 'logical' pathway of future development is not yet inevitable; other possibilities remain open.

The railway is itself a prime example of this dialectic. As Schivelbusch (1986: 10) demonstrates, initial responses to steam power tended to focus on its profound disruption to established patterns of geography and mobility. Accelerated mechanical motion broke up the customary space-time of embodied human experience, and it was this profound sense of rupture which generated the modern rhetoric of the annihilation of time and space, establishing the template for apprehending many future technological developments. The fact that the process was grasped largely through the rhetoric of 'annihilation' is by no means an indication that reactions were uniformly negative. Rather, the predominance of 'annihilation' signals that the experience of discontinuity with the past was the primary register for processing technological change. In the rhetoric of annihilation, technology is generally positioned as an autonomous agent, enabling extravagant claims to be made concerning its transformative powers. But this phase does not last forever. While the railway's impact was widely described in terms of the 'annihilation of time and space' for several decades from the 1820s, such claims began to recede as the new mode of travel became more habitual, and people were able to contemplate travel at 30 miles an hour with greater equanimity. Schivelbusch (1986: 14) argues the outcome was the formation of the new perceptual habitus which he dubs 'panoramic perception'. By the new century, the once novel space-time of train travel had become such a common experience that Albert Einstein (1920) could draw on it as a way of explaining relativity theory to general readers.[9] The familiarity of train travel meant that it could form a 'ground' from which to explain the radical new concept of field theory.

Positioning shifting social responses to new technologies in terms of this dialectic of rupture and recuperation can be regarded as a specific example of the broader process of the 'dis-embedding' and 're-embedding' of tradition that Featherstone and Lash (1995: 4) argue is characteristic of modernity. What I am seeking to give greater emphasis to here is the extent to which any 're-embedding' enabling the social assimilation of new media technologies has been dependent on paradigmatic shifts in the social relations of space and time. In the process, initial experiences of discontinuity and rupture have given way to new continuities established at a more abstract level. Clearly, a term such as 'abstract' cannot assume an absolute value, since what is experienced as more abstract for one generation – for example, rail travel between cities – may well become 'natural' to another. Once naturalized, experience can become the basis for further 'abstractions' affecting both knowledge and social practice. This underlines the fact that 'assimilation' is neither inherently conservative, nor simply directed towards functional integration in the interests of social cohesion. Assimilation does not imply social stasis, but simply a lessening of the initial experience of rupture surrounding the new technology, as certain uses become routinized while others are gradually closed off or remain latent. In fact, the social assimilation of technological media has produced profoundly ambivalent outcomes, underpinning the general shift from social 'structures' to the 'flows' of increasingly open systems. In this respect, assimilation accentuates latent social contradictions and generates further pressures for social transformation, resulting in the generalization of media-architecture complexes: what I am calling the media city.

## The city as home

It is remarkably easy to forget how recent the phenomenon of mass urbanization is, and therefore to ignore to what extent it constitutes an *experimental* mode of living. As Mumford (1973: 40) notes in his magisterial account of urban history: 'until the present period of urbanization, cities contained only a small fraction of mankind.' Kasinitz (1994: 8) points out that: 'As late as 1850 there was no predominantly urban society on the planet. In 1900 there was only one, Great Britain.' This was despite the rapid expansion of cities during the first half of the 19th century, when many European cities were subject to phenomenal rates of growth. However, it was only during the 20th century that cities became the dominant form of dwelling for entire national populations. The fall in rural population was most dramatic in the United States, from over 90 per cent of total population in 1810 to below the 50 per cent threshold around 1920 to below 3 per cent in 1980 (Short 1991: 104). While this decline has been less extreme in other nations, the general trajectory from country to city remains dominant. Moreover, on a global basis, it is still accelerating. Since 1950, the proportion of urban dwellers worldwide has tripled (Ferrarotti 1994: 462). According to estimates from the United Nations (2004: 3), 2007 will be the threshold at which more than 50 per cent of the world's population live in cities, rising to 61 per cent by 2030. Perhaps most significantly, the fastest urban growth is no longer in developed, industrialized nations, but in poorer nations where industrialization is uneven or marginal.[10]

Not only are more people living in cities, but cities have themselves increased enormously in scale over this period. In the 19th century, cities of more than one hundred thousand people were rare. Even by 1920, only 1 in a 100 people lived in cities with populations of more than 1 million. As Soja (2002: 95) has pointed out: 'In a few years the majority of the world's population are going to be living in these megacities of more than a million inhabitants.' Cities of far larger scale are also multiplying rapidly. In the mid-20th century, only London and New York possessed populations of more than 8 million; in 2002 there were 22 'megalopolises' of at least this size.

The rapid growth in the scale and density of cities from the mid-19th century occurred in close concert with the development of new transport and communication technologies, which, paradoxically, fed both centripetal and centrifugal pressures. The horizontal extension of the modern city was directly dependent on the emergence of new vehicles such as trains, bicycles, trams and automobiles which provided the infrastructure for the suburban dispersion of populations, while also enabling new forms of linkage between cities and surrounding regions. Urban extrusion was also facilitated by new communication technologies such as the telephone, which supported the coordination of spatially separated production and retail sites in the factory system. Conversely, the dense concentration of workers in office buildings and factories demanded mass transit networks capable of delivering peak loads to central sites, while the logistics of office work demanded communication networks such as telephones capable of servicing multiple cells aggregated in monolithic structures such as the high-rise tower.

Even in the mid-19th century, it was becoming evident that the growth of the city challenged its historical coherence. London seemed vast and apparently limitless to Friedrich Engels (1971: 30), who wrote in 1844 of 'a city in which one can roam for hours without reaching the beginning of the end'. Here Engels announces two recurrent themes of modern metropolitan discourse: the image of the city as a labyrinth, and the implicit annexation of its public space to the male *flâneur* whose mobile gaze would soon be elevated by Baudelaire to a privileged mode of modern experience. As Benjamin pointed out, the modern city assumed a labyrinthine quality *in spite of* the rationalization of urban space advocated by those such as Haussmann in mid-19th-century Paris:

> Most hidden aspect of the big cities: this historical object, the new metropolis, with its uniform streets and endless rows of houses, has given material existence to those architectures of which the ancients dreamed – the labyrinths. (1999b: 839)[11]

In retrospect, it can be more clearly appreciated that, rather than establishing a stable system capable of anchoring the new social order, the modern industrial city introduced a new set of variables which altered the nexus between urban space and the reproduction of cultural identity. In the traditional city, whether antique, medieval or Renaissance, the stable disposition of buildings, monuments and public spaces formed a network which held the lives of its citizens in relatively tight rein. The city was both the concrete expression of the hierarchy of social and political relationships, and the material structure of a collective memory which ensured the maintenance of those relationships. Dominated by a cathedral or castle, bounded by a wall with secure gates, the city constituted a protected environment in which movement was controlled and the appearance of strangers – particularly foreigners – was a noticeable event. In contrast, as Simmel emphasized, the modern metropolis is characterized by an influx of strangers and the experience of 'shock'.[12] The displacement of rural workers into urban factories was accompanied by the increasing depersonalization of social relations under the market system of capitalism. Growing anonymity from one's neighbours was double-edged. If anonymity brought new opportunities for self-invention, as old social hierarchies were eroded by the pursuit of individual advancement, it also carried the price tag of increasing alienation and estrangement.

In Mumford's (1973: 41) account, the 'invention' of the city was originally the result of spatial implosion:

> [T]he city may be described as a structure specially equipped to store and transmit the goods of civilization, sufficiently condensed to afford the maximum amount of facilities in the minimum space, but also capable of structural enlargement [ ... ].

The ancient city developed its competitive advantage over surrounding regions by condensing things in a concentrated space: people, capital, technology and access to natural resources produced the fecund urban mixture 'which resulted in an enormous expansion of human capabilities in every direction' (Mumford 1973: 40). The modern industrial city replaced medieval walls with new forms of circulation: boulevards, railway tracks, telegraph wires and telephone lines. But even as late as the 19th century, industrial cities still followed the ancient model in many respects. Major cities tended to be located at significant transportation junctions, most commonly ports. The growth of railroads served to amplify the older natural advantages of port cities like London, New York and Chicago. However, by the end of the 19th century, the growing networks of tram and suburban rail lines had created the characteristic wheel-spoke pattern of the industrial metropolis comprising an inner core or central business district, a middle production zone of factories and crowded working-class housing, and an outer ring of more affluent middle-class suburbs.[13] While many, including Mumford, regarded these cities as horrific, they 'worked', at least according to their own logic. The clustering of businesses in the city centre multiplied opportunities for face-to-face contacts and the exchange of information, creating advantages over small town competitors. Mass transit to the city centre enabled large-scale patronage to support new forms of shopping and entertainment.[14]

In many respects, the 1920s stands as the zenith of the industrial city. After this time, the dominant model of concentric urban rings began to wane. If the modernist *avant-garde* of the 1920s tended to represent urban space as decentred and decentring, more recent developments have made the city's 'loss of centre' even more radical. With the rise of automobile culture after World War II, the dependence of the suburbs on the city centre declined rapidly. Fishman (1994: 394) notes that in the United States the suburban population doubled as a proportion of the total, from 23 per cent in 1950 to 45 per cent in 1990. At the same time, twice as many suburban workers commuted to another suburb rather than to the city centre. The result, according to Fishman (1994: 398), is that 'the peripheries have replaced the urban cores as the heartlands of our civilization.' In his landmark essay, 'The Overexposed City', Paul Virilio (1991: 12) underlined the role of transport and communication technologies in this transformation:

> The phrase 'to go into town', which replaced the nineteenth century's 'to go to town', indicates the uncertainty of the encounter, as if we could no longer stand before the city but rather abide forever within. If the metropolis is still a place, a geographic site, it no longer has anything to do with the classic oppositions of city/country nor centre/periphery. The city is no longer organized into a localized and axial estate. While the suburbs contributed to this dissolution, in fact the intramural-extramural opposition collapsed with the transport revolutions and the development of communication and telecommunications technologies. These promoted the merger of disconnected metropolitan fringes into a single urban mass.

At the beginning of the 21st century, urban form is no longer typified by the highly concentrated and vertically stratified city of Lang's *Metropolis* (modelled on Manhattan), but by the sprawling, ex-centric agglomeration of suburb, mall and freeway covering vast tracts of land. The basic urban unit is no longer the street measured in blocks but the *growth corridor* measured in hundreds of square kilometres. This city is symbolized less by a skyline of iconic skyscrapers than by networks of superhighways whose logic can best be understood from the air, or, increasingly, by invisible digital networks which demand to be mapped in new ways.

## Cities without centres

As Sassen (1991: 13) notes: 'Cities have historically provided national economies, polities and societies with something we can think of as centrality.' Of equal significance to the sheer size of the new conurbations is their lack of identifiable centres. Mumford (1973: 45) highlighted this tendency more than half a century ago, adopting a language McLuhan would soon popularize:

> We live in fact in an exploding universe of mechanical and electronic invention [ ... ]. This technological explosion has produced a similar explosion of the city itself: the city has burst open and scattered its complex organs over the entire landscape. The walled urban container indeed has not been merely broken open: it has also been largely demagnetised, with the result that we are witnessing a sort of devolution of urban power into a state of randomness and unpredictability.

This 'technological explosion' represents a profound reversal of the historic rationale for urbanism. For Fishman (1994: 398): 'The new city [ ... ] lacks what gave shape and meaning to every urban form of the past: a dominant single core and definable boundaries.' The result is something that still lacks a recognized name. Fishman (1994: 400) argues: 'Not urban, not rural, not suburban, but possessing elements of all three, the new city eludes all the conventional terminology of the urban planner and the historian.' Similarly, Ferrarotti (1994: 463) argues: 'We are moving towards an urban-rural continuum [ ... ]. Here, the city is deprived of its natural center of attraction, its core.' Sorkin (1992: xi) talks about 'the emergence of a wholly new kind of city, a city without a place attached to it' which he terms an 'ageographical city'.[15] Soja (2000, 2002: 95) uses the term 'postmetropolis' and elsewhere '*exopolis*' to describe the new urban landscapes 'to stress their oxymoronic ambiguity, their city-full non-cityness'. Rem Koolhaas (2004: 161, 166) sums up the transformation with the appellation *junk space*:

> Junkspace is what remains after modernization has run its course, or, more precisely, what coagulates while modernism is in progress, its fallout. Modernization had a rational program: to share the blessings of science, universally. Junkspace is its apotheosis or meltdown [ ... ] Junkspace pretends to unite but it actually splinters. It creates communities not of shared interest or free association, but of identical statistics and unavoidable demographics [ ... ]. Each man, woman and child is individually targeted, tracked, split off from the rest [ ... ].

The loss of urban centre is not total.[16] But it has clearly generated what Boyer (1999: 138) terms a 'crisis' of urban representation as what Lynch (1960) once called the 'legible city' has become increasingly unreadable. Virilio (1991a: 30) posits successive thresholds in this growing urban illegibility, as the city loses historic coherence, productive functions and, finally, the geometric space on which urbanism was predicated:

> With the decay of urban centrality and axiality, the symbolic and historical reference points go first. Then, when the industrial apparatus and the monuments lose their meanings, the architectonic references vanish. Most decisively, the demise of the ancient categorization and partition of the physical dimension leads to the loss of the geometric reference points

It is the displacement of 'substantive, continuous and homogeneous space inherited from classical geometry' in favour of what Virilio (1991a: 35) calls 'the relativity of an accidental, discontinuous and heterogeneous space' of electronic media which deals the final blow to the spatial paradigms of classical architecture and urbanism. In this context, Virilio (1991a: 30) argues that we are forced to 'find other, electronic means of evaluating time and space, ones which share no common ground with the measuring systems of the past'. Unfortunately, in practice, Virilio has tended to ignore this task, preferring to interpret the transformation of urban space overwhelmingly in terms of loss and disorientation. The rhetoric of the 'annihilation of time and space' becomes his stock lexicon.[17] But the exhaustion of classical geometry or humanist architecture cannot be equated with the end of space and time. Rather than continuing to lament an absolute loss, I am more interested in exploring new ways of conceptualizing the space-time of social experience and agency in a context in which the older boundaries of both territory and media are in flux.

## Relational space

The trend towards statistical and probabilistic forms of knowledge and meaning, which emerged in the mid-19th century, was consolidated in the formal elaboration of cybernetics towards the end of World War II. By the 1960s, electronic information processing machines had begun to change both work practices and social organization to such an extent that futurologists such as Daniel Bell (1968: 4) saw networked computers as a key element of post-industrialism. The new nexus between technology, economic production and social relations also inspired Archigram's futuristic visions of information-based dwellings and 'plug-in' cities.[18] If, as Mumford (1973) and Kittler (1996) argue, there is a sense in which the city has always been a *medium*, the interlacing of urban space with high-speed interactive networks nevertheless constitutes a critical change in urban experience. The intermeshing of digital technology with urban terrain has produced a new set of pressures with both centripetal and centrifugal trajectories. On the one hand, digital networks have promoted the dispersal of economic activities across geographical space, increasingly on a global scale, while, on the other hand, they also produce increasing concentrations of power, as command and control centres for the global economy are consolidated in relatively few 'global cities'.[19] These trajectories increasingly interpenetrate and shape the context of personal life. As Sussman (1997: 36) points out, while many ordinary people, particularly in affluent societies, have more 'opportunities for distant association' than did their parents, the same technological infrastructure has 'helped to normalize a degree of industrial, commercial, social and familial separation that was also unknown to earlier generations'. The consequences for the less affluent are even starker. As Nikos Papastergiadis (2000) has argued, the cross-border move-ment of people in the face of poverty, environmental degradation or war has become a defining characteristic of the present.

The paradoxical combination of dispersion and concentration arising from the growing importance of information and communication networks to economic, social and political organization, manifested in the simultane-ous abolition of distance and the inscription of new forms of distancing and exclusion, has accentuated awareness of the growing dislocation of 'place' from 'space'. Castells (1989: 6) influentially defined the 'informational city' in terms of 'the emergence of a *space of flows* which dominates the historically constructed space of places'. Despite his use of 'domination', Castells clearly recognized that informational flows do not simply obliterate existing geographical and urban space, but are articulated with it in complex ways. Sassen (1991) similarly stressed that, while cross-border economic processes lead to a 'partial unbundling' of the nation-state in favour of the ascendancy of other units and scales of organization such as cities and regions, the communication and information infrastructure underpinning such flows is itself materially located.

This emphasis provided a useful corrective to the tendency to either lav-ishly celebrate or lament the emergence of 'cyberspace' for displacing 'real' social space.[20] Now that such hyperbole has subsided from its dotcom heights, it is increasingly recognized – even by some who once confidently prophesied the replacement of bricks by bytes – that, instead of the 'annihilation of space and time', we are experiencing the emergence of new spatial ensembles. This new conjunction of media and architecture has been variously described in terms of 'augmented reality', 'mixed reality', 'augmented space' and 'stereo reality' – descriptions which all seek to emphasize the heterogeneous spatial regimes of what I call the media city.[21] While descriptors such as 'informational city' or 'digital city' are more established, I find media city more useful in encompassing both the historical dimensions of the relation between media and modern urban space, and in connecting this history to the changes driven by digital convergence in the present.

As media become increasingly mobile, scalable and interactive, the new mode of social experience in the media city is characterized by what I term *relational space*. I want this concept to carry a particular load here. Of course, there is a sense in which spacing – setting things apart – always implies relation. However, by relational space I am referring to the contemporary condition in which the horizon of social relationships has become radically open. As Lash (2002a: 16) puts it: 'In technological forms of life, what were more or less closed systems, my body, the social body, becomes more or less open constellations.' This openness brings with it a new freedom to construct social relationships across space and time. The flipside of this freedom is that it cannot be refused. As Beck (1994: 46) argued when defining the 'reflexive modernity' which characterizes risk society, the conundrum of reflexive modernity is that the reflexive subject cannot refuse to choose.[22] The heightened contingency and fluidity of space in the media city is a manifestation of this condition. Relational space names the spatial experience characteristic of 'reflexive modernity', as the pre-given nature of social space and the taken-for-granted contours of subjectivity are increasingly withdrawn in favour of the ambivalence of mobile spatial configurations and ephemeral individual choices.

The openness of relational space is a condition which has been most often defined in merely negative terms, focusing on what has been lost as social space has been stripped of inherent qualities, such as stable dimensions, persistent appearances and secure meanings. If such stripping has a productive element, summed up by the 'creative destruction' that Marx identified as the progressive force of capitalism, it can all too easily tip into what Harvey (1990: 105) calls 'destructive creation' in which tradition and territory are levelled in the name of the total market rather than recast in more inclusive and democratic forms. Yet, resistance to market fundamentalism can no longer simply appeal to classical notions of spatial stability with enduring forms and secure boundaries as the frame for supposedly homogeneous identities. If the process of dis-embedding tradition and de-territorializing locality which characterizes modernity has created the conditions for space to be increasingly experienced as shifting, variable and contingent, contemporary politics must begin from the possibilities produced by this unstable dynamism. As Beck (1994: 11–12) argues:

> In a political and existential sense, the fundamental question and decision that opens up here is, will the new manufactured incalculability and disorder be opposed according to the pattern of instrumental rational control, that is by recourse to the old industrial society (more technology, market, government, and so on). Or is a rethinking and a new way of acting beginning here, which accepts and affirm the ambivalence – but then with far-reaching consequences for all areas of social action?

The first theoretical intimations of spatial relativity in a modern sense appeared with Maxwell's equations for electromagnetic field theory published in 1864. The spatial consequences of field theory were extended and finally consolidated by Einstein's relativity theory in 1905, which confirmed the break with the Cartesian–Newtonian universe in favour of a radically differential perception of time and space irrevocably dependent upon the observer's frame of reference. However, while relativity became a hallmark of *avant-garde* theory and practice in the early 20th century, most notably in the visual arts with the Cubist-inspired break with geometric perspective, it is only with the intensive development of media and communication technologies in the second half of the century that relational space has become dominant in everyday experience. This shift from abstract theoretical construct to the dominant condition of social space is a function of the increasing social primacy assumed by technological speed. As Virilio (1995: 141) reminds us, speed is a consequence of the relation between different phenomena. Relational space is the condition of social space shaped by the simultaneous experience of radically different velocities: the overlapping of what Virilio (1995: 144) calls the 'metabolic' speed of the body, the relative mechanical speed of vehicles, and the 'absolute' light-speed of media and communication technologies. Relational space comes to the fore when the primacy once accorded to the stability of material objects is reframed by the variable relations established between different velocities. In this respect, the light-speed of electronic media is critical. If relational space began to be conceptualized with Nietzsche's (1998) radical 'perspectivism' proposed in 1887 – the fact that all phenomena must be observed from somewhere – it comes to fruition when the extension of network logic demands recognition that every point of observation is *connected* to innumerable others. Relational space is the social space created by the contemporary imperative to actively establish social relations 'on the fly' across heterogeneous dimensions in which the global is inextricably imbricated with the face-to-face. It is a condition defined by the growing demand to recognize the unique position of each social actor and the situated context of every experience, coupled to the simultaneous recognition that context eludes exhaustive definition, or 'saturation' as Derrida (1982) puts it.

The media city achieves critical mass once relational space begins to emerge as a cultural dominant. Since relational space cannot be defined by essential attributes or inherent and stable qualities, it assumes significance primarily through the interconnections established between different nodes and sectors. Such interconnections are characterized above all by their variability and impermanence. As Lash (2002a: 206) argues, older social bonds organized on the basis of spatial proximity are being displaced by communicational bonds which are 'at-a-distance' – either communication coming from a distance, or people coming from a distance in order to meet face-to-face. Communicational bonds exhibit different durations and velocities to older forms of social bonds embedded in spatial proximity: in Lash's terms, they are brief, intense, discontinuous and no longer governed by narrative continuity.[23] Thus, while certain connections may endure over time or even assume a sense of relative permanence, the general context is one of growing susceptibility to rapid and volatile realignments.

This heightened volatility has increasingly become an operative factor in the exercise of power. In Deleuze's (1992) terms, the fixed and stable spatial 'moulds' of disciplinary society have given way to the continual processes of digital modulation. For Kittler (1996: 726), the loss of stable spatial hierarchies, such as those which once defined the notion of 'the capital', means that political power often springs up in 'less obvious tangents'. Exercising power may be less a matter of occupying a traditional spatial centre such as a city square than making tactical assessments of communicational possibilities:

> Power thus means occupying at the right moment the channels for technological data processing. And centrality becomes a variable dependent on media functions, rather than vice versa.

Relational space is characterized by the frustration or complication of all simple or direct relations between 'inside' and 'outside'. While this corresponds to what Deleuze (1992) described as a general attack on established systems of enclosure, this tendency towards more open constellations is not characterized by a simple expansion of 'freedom'. In practice, contemporary social space also manifests what the architectural collective Multiplicity (2005: 173) describe as 'a proliferation of borders, walls, fences, thresholds, signposted areas, security systems and checkpoints, virtual frontiers, specialized zones, protected areas under control'. The porosity of boundaries at some levels has been counterpointed by new forms of friction and the proliferation of new mechanisms of policing and border control at others.

While relational space is often experienced as contingent, the versatility of networks and connections means it can also be made into a space of belonging – a 'home'. The reconfiguration of 'home' in modernity is the product of *both* the loss of stable coordinates, *and* the invention of new continuities and new processes of cultural affiliation across interlinked domains. Once again, it is important to emphasize the ambivalent and contradictory currents of such a process. As Guattari (1984: 36) argues: 'The more capitalism follows its tendency to "de-code" and "de-territorialize," the more does it seek to awaken or to re-awaken artificial territorialities and residual encodings, thus moving to counter-act its own tendency.'[24] There is no absolute and final 'loss of centre' in the de-territorializing tendencies of modernity. New 'centres' can be – and are – formed. However, such centres lack the aura of permanence that was integral to them in the past. Instead, each 'centre' now has to be situated in relation to – and legitimated against – a multitude of others. This condition has propelled nostalgia for a general *loss of centre* to a recurrent theme. Derrida (2002: 79–80) notes the way that global media feed a desire for being at home:

> [T]oday, we are witnessing such a radical expropriation, deterritorialization, delocalization, dissociation of the political and the local, of the national, of the nation-state and the local, that the response, or rather the reaction, becomes: 'I want to be *at home* , I want finally to be at home, with my own, close to my friends and family.' [ ... ] The more powerful and violent the technological expropriation, the delocalization, the more powerful, naturally, the recourse to the at-home, the return toward home.

While de-territorialization can produce nostalgic and parochial responses, it is also the condition for rethinking social relations and cultural affiliations around more complex patterns than the model of the nation-state allowed. Relational space is necessarily more *other*-oriented, insofar as the 'here' becomes open and porous. As Giddens (1991: 96–97) expresses it:

> A world where no one is 'outside' is one where pre-existing traditions cannot avoid contact with others, but also with many alternative ways of life. By the same token, it is one where the 'other' cannot any longer be treated as inert. The point is not only that the other 'answers back', but that mutual interrogation is possible.

If Giddens' optimism demands qualification, his analysis highlights the new social context created by 'instantaneous global electronic communication' in which every situation is increasingly experienced as lacking 'full' presence and is instead conditioned by the fluctuating and discontinuous pressure of the generalized 'elsewhere'. Relational space is space suffused with 'uncanny' experiences of doubling and displacement, as the pulsions of events in other spaces interrupt and recontextualize immediate experience.

From the preceding discussion, it should be evident that the concept of relational space is not premised on elevating space over time, or vice-versa. Rather, relational space expands the modern recognition of the inextricability of time and space to foreground the existence of heterogeneous temporalities which coexist, intersect and overlap. In this sense, it is not simply the 'space of flows' but also the *pace of flows* which is critical to power and political change in the present. As Lash (2002b: 58–59) notes: 'there's a form of inhabiting in something like an informational environment. And how does that work, when it's not all shock experience and mere operationality? Well, I would say it just has to organize itself differently.' Learning to inhabit mediated space *differently* is as much a question of speed as it is one of ownership or content. It demands the creation of media ecologies with the capacity to sustain a far more varied range of informational velocities than the current imperative of instant response allows.

Rather than opposing space to time, the most productive way of understanding Virilio's *chronopolitics* is in terms of the new sense of simultaneity which informs relational space. As Nowotny (1994) points out, the experience of simultaneity emerged in the early 20th century with the growth of electronic media. But it is only with ubiquitous 'real time' media that global simultaneity becomes culturally dominant. As Latour (2005: 40) notes, one effect of the new simultaneity is that the temporal hierarchies of colonial modernity become unsustainable: '*everything becomes contemporary.*' When everything is contemporary, contradictions can no longer be displaced onto the supposed slowness, backwardness or belatedness of the periphery according to the logic of historical progress. Instead contradictions are forced to coexist, and actively impinge on each other.

Latour argues that this novel situation demands an entirely new set of political questions revolving around the politics of cohabitation.

If the all-too evident contradictions of contemporary globalization dominated by a neo-liberal economic agenda are to become susceptible to new political currents, there is an urgent need for the articulation of new forms of social collectivity and collective interaction. This is undoubtedly a difficult task. It demands ways of thinking and acting collectively while respecting multiple levels of difference. It demands recognition of the uniqueness of individuals without exacerbating prevailing tendencies towards social atomization and solipsism. It demands the articulation of a new basis for collective projects and the constitution of new public spaces at the historical moment when collectivity has to be expanded beyond the geography of national borders. The extension of what Papastergiadis (2005) calls collaborative networks and clusters across older geographical and cultural borders, and their deepening to include new forms of dialogue and co-operation, is a vital manifestation of the role media might play in determining spatial ambience and social agency. If relational space grows out of the modern understanding that spatial surroundings can no longer be taken for granted as an inert container, the contemporary media city is the social milieu in which social agency comes to be routinely defined by feedback from other sites and other speeds. In the radical *openness* of relational space, we can feel the ambiguous headings which today affects the homeliness of our homes, the urbanity of our cities and the identity of our selves.

## Notes

1  The ad was made for US telecom MCI, and the words spoken by child star Anna Paquin; Multiplicity 2005: 169.
2  Texas Instrument's Digital Light Processing (DLP) technology, originally developed for theatrical projection has become the dominant platform for the consumer roll-out of video projection systems. See McQuire 2004.
3  Once 'nature' is no longer opposed to 'culture', but subsumed within it, the two spheres increasingly merge into techno-nature and techno-culture. Beck (1994: 27) positions such a shift as the point of entry to 'risk society': 'The abstraction of nature leads into industrial society. The integration of nature into society leads beyond industrial society.'
4  The term cyborg, a contraction of 'cybernetic organism', was coined by Clynes and Kline (1960: 27) in 1960, under the influence of Norbert Wiener's (1948) work on cybernetics. See McQuire 2006.
5  This is not to suggest that the digital threshold 'caused' the crisis of photographic authority; rather that it intensified concerns, particularly in institutions such as news organizations and police forces with a high investment in photographic evidence, which had already been broadly articulated in photographic theory.
6  As Sean Cubitt (2004: 9–10) points out, sublime experience tends to exist outside history, time and the social. Technology has been related to the sublime by Marx (1965) and more recently Nye (1994), Carey (1989) and Mosco (2004).
7  Benjamin's example in the 1930s is suggestive, when he drew loosely on Freud to create his concept of the 'optical unconscious' as a means of theorizing the

changing relation between technological images and urban experience. See Chapter 3.

8   It is important to appreciate that these phases are overlapping rather than linear, and that each stage assumes only relative permanence. Spatio-temporal frameworks, considered as social settings for particular forms of life, are not transformed overnight according to the high velocity vicissitudes of fashion. Nor are they immutable. The decline of what Gurvitch (1964) calls 'enduring time' as a regulative social force is itself a key index of the difference of contemporary understandings of space and time to those held by many earlier societies.

9   See his *Relativity: The Special and General Theory. A Popular Exposition* (1920), where Einstein makes numerous references to train travel as a way of conceptualizing differential spatio-temporal frames of reference in order to explain relativity theory to readers lacking advanced knowledge of mathematics and theoretical physics.

10  Koolhaas et al. (2001: 2–7) note that, of the 33 'megalopolises' with populations of 8 million or more predicted to exist by 2015, 27 will be in the least developed countries. The only 'rich' city remaining among the world's ten largest in terms of population will be Tokyo.

11  In a 1938 letter to Horkheimer, Benjamin (1994: 557) adds: 'the crowd is the latest and most unfathomable labyrinth in the labyrinth of the city.' The crowd and the *flâneur* will be discussed further in Chapter 2.

12  This theme will be elaborated in Chapter 3.

13  While this pattern belongs more to cities built on the US model with a high-rise central core, it is also applicable to 'modernized' European cities.

14  As Fishman (1994: 401) points out, the rewards were not evenly shared: the best-served group of this city model were the middle-class who 'enjoyed all the economic benefits of the great city while living in a quite, leafy-green, smoke free environment at its edge'.

15  Sorkin (1992: xii) adds: 'Whether agora, castle, piazza, or downtown, the idea of a city of centres stands, at a minimum, for the idea of a spatial city, a city in which order is a function of proximity.' With regard to the 'ageographical city', he concludes: 'In fact, the structure of this city is a lot like television.'

16  Sassen (1991) points out that face-to-face contacts continue to play a vital role in business, buttressing the emergence of 'global cities' which exercise command and control functions in the global economy. However, core city prosperity rests on a much narrower base than previously, with declining retailing dominance and loss of corporate employment to dispersed 'back-offices' providing outsourced functions such as computing and call centres. Instead, the traditional 'city centre' is increasingly defined by its role housing major cultural institutions such as museums, concert halls and art galleries. Possession of this infrastructure, which fuelled the recent wave of inner city gentrification, has become subject to national and international competition.

17  See McQuire 1999.

18  See Chapter 4.

19  Sassen (1991:24) notes:

> Economic globalization and the new ICTs have contributed to produce a spatiality for the urban that pivots in cross-border networks as well as territorial locations with massive concentration of resources. This is not a completely new feature. Over the centuries cities have been at the crossroads of major, often worldwide processes. What is different today is the intensity, complexity and global span of these networks, the extent to which significant proportions of economies are now de-materialized and digitised, hence the extent to which they can travel at great speeds

through some of these networks, and the number of cities that are part of cross-border networks operating at vast geographic scales.

20 The rhetoric of 'cyberspace' will be discussed further in Chapters 4 and 5.

21 See for example Azuma 1997, Benford et al. 1999, Ranaulo 2001, Manovich 2006.

22 Beck, Giddens and Lash (1994) all used the concept of 'reflexive modernity' to periodize a shift from 'simple' to 'full' modernity in the second half of the 20th century. However, while Beck stresses that 'risk society' demands responses from subjects who, in having no choice but to choose, are often reduced to mere 'reflex' reactions; Giddens offered a more optimistic picture of heightened individual agency emerging as personal relations fully 'de-traditionalized'. Lash's argument, which treats reflexivity as an ambivalent gift, is more useful for my purposes, insofar as he contends that it is not social structures which underpin reflexive modernity but an 'articulated web of global and local networks of *information and communication structures*' (1994: 121).

23 Lash (2002a: 75) makes his debt to Benjamin's contrast between 'storytelling' and 'information' explicit elsewhere, arguing: 'Social relations themselves are becoming less a question of sociality than informationality.'

24 Lash (2002a: 205) similarly argues for the need to understand the society of 'flows' dialectically: 'These flows gain hegemony in the grand "de-territorialization" of structures and institutions. But there is never the pure indifference of flows. The de-territorialized flows wind up "solidifying" in a group of new re-territorializations, some of which become infrastructure for the flows themselves.'

## Part One

Thresholds of the Media City

# 2

## The Territory of Images

I am a stranger to what is coming and to what is here, as for example to these new boulevards without turnings, without perspectives, implacable in their straight lines [ ... ].

(Edmond de Goncourt 1860)

Haussmann [ ... ] estranges Parisians from their city. They no longer feel at home there and start to become conscious of the inhuman character of the metropolis.

(Walter Benjamin 1935)[1]

Daguerre's photographic process was announced to the public in 1839, coinciding with a period of phenomenal urban growth. Between 1801 and 1851, the population of Paris doubled, while that of London tripled (Blau 1989: 36). To call the parallel development of technological images and the industrial reconstruction of the city a 'coincidence' stretches that term beyond its usual bounds. Both processes belonged to the broader transformation of modern life in which the market system and commodity production were vastly extended in scale and velocity. Integral to the modern condition is the fact that photographs of the city often outlast the buildings and urban settings they depict. This inversion situates the point at which Susan Sontag's (1979: 52) observation that photography constructs the ultimate Surrealist universe meets Walter Benjamin's (1999a: 211) dictum that 'no face is as surrealistic to the same degree as the true face of a city.'

One of the earliest and best-known photographic surveys of a city was the work of Charles Marville, commissioned by Baron von Haussmann's Prefecture of the Seine in 1856.[2] For the next 15 years Marville worked as 'Photographer of the City of Paris' documenting the process by which medieval Paris was progressively 'modernized'. The two projects enjoyed a close relationship. Haussmann's reconstruction of Paris was the first attempt to modernize an existing medieval city, and it became the model for many similar undertakings.[3] Marville's work also inspired a multitude of similar projects – Annan in Glasgow, Bool and Dixon in London, Koppmann in Hamburg, Burgoyne in Birmingham to name a few which followed soon after. Its deeper significance was the way it embodied a new relationship between image and urban space.

In this chapter, I want to explore the convergence between the 'regularization' of the streets of Paris under Haussmann and the photographic mapping of this new territory by Marville. I want to read Marville's project as more than a repository of historical data about 19th-century Paris.[4] Instead I will argue that his body of work exemplifies a critical shift in media practice, as the sense of self-contained meaning pertaining to the individual image begins to drift towards a new logic in which meaning is established through the cumulative flow of the series or set. Technological reproduction results in the formation of what Sekula (1989: 116) has termed a 'territory of images'. In this territory, new forms of urban knowledge crystallized, laying the uncertain foundations for the construction of the media city. Paris, which Benjamin famously dubbed the 'capital of the 19th century', pioneered this new relation between technological images and urban space.

### Photographing the street

Alongside landscape and portraiture, architecture is one of the classic photographic genres. With its ability to translate the Renaissance optic of geometric perspective into a mechanical image, the camera seemed ideally suited to depicting the built environment. Architecture in its turn was an ideal subject which 'sat' patiently – a great advantage since the slow speed of early photographic emulsions necessitated exposure times of up to half an hour. Unlike people, buildings didn't have to be strapped into a neck brace in order to register a solid image. However, this meant that prior to 1851, when Archer's wet collodion process opened the way to 'instantaneous photography', urban photography was distinguished by the emptiness of the streets. If this emptiness seems striking today, it was even stranger for 19th-century viewers to see usually crowded thoroughfares bereft of pedestrians and traffic. In a letter written to his brother in 1839, telegraphy pioneer Samuel B. Morse was transfixed by a solitary figure in an image made by Louis Daguerre in 1838:

> The Boulevard, so constantly filled with a moving throng of pedestrians and carriages, was perfectly solitary, except an individual who was having his boots brushed. (Quoted in Gernsheim 1968: 89–90)

Morse makes us pause and appreciate that this visual effect was less a deliberate choice, as it would be later for Atget, than a direct consequence of slow film speeds and camera lenses. It was only because this individual was 'compelled, of course, to be stationary for some time' that his figure appeared in the image. In fact, this outcome was only half-achieved: while 'his boots and legs were well-defined, [ ... ] he is without body or head, because these were in motion.'

While technological limitations played a significant role in effectively *editing* people out of the city, there were other reasons that early photographers tended to avoid the street. Frontal elevations, which were the most common form of architectural photography into the 1850s, were usually taken from above street level. In a practical sense, this positioning helped to overcome the problem of converging vertical lines, enabling camera images to conform more closely to the established conventions of orthographic projection. But such a stance also played a significant ideological role, enabling viewers to dominate the scenes depicted. The popularity of elevated points of view underlines the extent to which street life, as distinct from architecture, was not yet seen as a proper subject for photography. In this respect, most early photographers followed other visual artists by ignoring aspects of city life they saw as unaesthetic. While the impact of industrialization on the city was largely absent, the growing market for architectural photographs which emerged in the 1850s instead clung to the established categories of urban topography derived from lithography. The usual menu of images consisted of the principal churches, civic buildings and palaces, major streets, bridges, parks, clubs and monuments – the ingredients of what would soon be called a *tourist* itinerary. In summation, as much as street life was technically difficult to photograph in the 1850s, the avoidance of street photography was not simply a technical question. The potential rupture produced by the invention of modern technological images was still largely contained by making them conform to established modes of vision. While an audience prepared to consume social life as a collection of reproducible images was beginning to emerge in the 1850s, it was not yet in place.

When photography did descend to the streets, this move was closely linked to the reconstruction of urban space. The phenomenal growth in European cities in the first half of the 19th century was felt most acutely in Paris. After doubling between 1801 and 1851, the population grew a further 30 per cent between 1851 and 1861. Moreover, as Choay (1969: 15) notes, in contrast to London, it was difficult for Paris to expand beyond its medieval walls. For Maxime Du Camp, Paris of the 1850s seemed poised to burst:

> Paris, as we find it in the period following the revolution of 1848, was about to become uninhabitable. Its population had become greatly enlarged and unsettled by the incessant activity of the railroad (whose rails extended further each day and linked up with those of neighboring countries), and now this population was suffocating in the narrow, tangled, putrid alleyways in which it was forcibly confined. (Quoted in Benjamin 1999b: 122)

Rapid increases in urban population were accompanied by sharpening class divisions. Writing in 1840s London, Charles Dickens noted the coexistence of different worlds, each of which 'has its own inhabitants; each is distinct from and almost unconscious of the existence of the other' (quoted in Blau 1989: 36). The complex divisions of urban space inspired new modes of investigation. Journalists borrowed the language of travel writers to describe journeys into the urban slums, creating a popular non-fiction form, while social reformist photographers such as Henry Mayhew presented their work in similar terms to the exploits of early anthropologists. Others such as Alexander Dumas borrowed colonial frontier metaphors: regarding his *Les Mohicans de Paris*, Roger Caillois commented: 'the title says all.'[5]

Harvey (2003: 41) positions Balzac's novels as pivotal to mapping the change in urban space, in which the correspondence between specific sectors and distinct class 'character' was subjected to a greater dynamism:

> The spatial rigidities that play a deterministic role in *The History of the Thirteen* become malleable in later works. [ ... ] The spatiality of the city is increasingly appreciated as dialectical, constructed and consequential rather than passive or merely reflective. [ ... ] We learn to understand the city from multiple perspectives.[6]

This shift to 'multiple perspectives' indicates the new conditions for visualizing the city which emerged in mid-19th-century Paris, as an earlier, more limited form of capitalism was displaced by an expanded economy gearing up for mass production. Class solidarities based on ways of life rooted in the *quartier* were becoming subject to new forms of turbulence. By the 1850s, the industrial city was feeling the effects of the contradictory temporality generated by the ideology of progress, stretched between unlimited aspirations for future development and the growing sense that the past was threatening to disappear. The traditional mnemonic function of the city itself was increasingly problematic. As Marshall Berman (1982: 99) observes, the dynamic forces of capitalism produce a crisis in urban monumentality:

> The pathos of all bourgeois monuments is that their material strength and solidity actually count for nothing and carry no weight at all, that they are blown away like frail reeds by the very forces of capitalist development that they celebrate.

Photography, with its speed, relative low cost, capacity for wide circulation, and air of objectivity, offered an important placebo to this looming problem of cultural memory. Projects to document architectural heritage formed an integral part of the State-supported museological armature which developed at the time. The Mission Héliographique was established in France by the Commission of Historical Monuments in 1851 to record French architectural and archaeological heritage. It was soon followed by other projects to document urban sites slated for demolition in the name of modernization. This was the context of Marville's employment as 'Photographer of the City of Paris', documenting the explosive force known as 'Haussmannization'.

### Haussmannization: or the urbanization of regularization

While there is some dispute over the extent to which the reconstruction of Paris can be directly attributed to Haussmann, the fact that 'Haussmannization' constitutes a crucial threshold in modern urbanism is beyond question.[7] For Engels (1970: 69) writing in 1872, Haussmann's reconstruction of Paris had already assumed an exemplary role:

> By 'Haussmann' I mean the practice which has now become general, of making breaches in the working class neighbourhoods of our big cities, particularly in those which are centrally situated [ ... ].[8]

The historic importance of 'Haussmannization' lies in the way it pioneered a different conception of urban space. If Haussmannization departed all previous attempts to 'modernize' a city in terms of its enormous scale and resources, its most important break was its ambition to treat the city as a unified space in which the relation between local parts was to be subordinated to the coordination of the whole.[9] This stance, which underpinned the emergence of modern urban planning, undoubtedly situates Haussmann's enduring appeal to Le Corbusier, who concluded his *La Ville Radiuese* of 1935 (1964: 209) by declaring: 'My respect and admiration for Haussmann'.

The sheer scale of Haussmann's undertaking ensures that it remains emblematic of the 'creative destruction' that Berman (1982) posits as the ambivalent essence of modernization. By the time of his dismissal in 1870, one-fifth of the streets of central Paris had been newly created, while, at the height of reconstruction in the mid-1860s, fully 20 per cent of the Parisian work force was employed in building trades. The social disruption caused by the demolitions was immense: on Haussmann's own reckoning the new boulevards displaced 350 000 people. But the process involved far more than simply building new streets. It also meant virtually doubling the area of the old city, providing new services such as aqueducts and sewers, gas street lighting and public lavatories, instituting forms of zoning for industry and designing new spaces such as public parklands for entertainment and leisure, constructing a rail ring to connect the core to outlying areas, and, finally, organizing a professional police force to supervise the new terrain. As Vidler (1978: 93) points out, following Haussmann: 'The very word for urban reconstruction, once "embellishment," was changed to "transformation." ' To both his detractors and his supporters, the result was the tantamount to the disappearance of the old city.

The unprecedented scope and ambition of the redevelopment make it difficult to explain in terms of a single cause. Siegfried Kracauer (2002: 158) placed the Emperor's desire for immortality at the forefront, suggesting 'like all dictators, his dread of perishability led him to erect monuments.' However, Kracauer (2002: 158), who was writing under the shadow of Hitler, adds:

> [H]e was also actuated by purely practical aims, such as the combating of unemployment, the improvement of hygiene, and the betterment of traffic conditions; and last but not least, broad, straight streets made insurrections more difficult, because they could be swept away by artillery, and macadamized roads increased the difficulty of putting up barricades.

This last reason appealed also to Walter Benjamin, who titled one section of his Arcades project 'Haussmann or the Barricades' (1999b: 12, 23):

> The true goal of Haussmann's projects was to secure the city against civil war. [ . . . ] Widening the streets is designed to make the erection of barricades impossible, and new streets are to furnish the shortest route between the barracks and the workers' districts. Contemporaries christen the operation 'strategic embellishment'.

Haussmann himself had acknowledged as much in his *Mémoires*, when describing the benefits of the new Boulevard de Sebastopol:

> It meant the disemboweling of the old Paris, the *quartier* of uprisings and barricades, by a wide central street piercing through and through this almost impossible maze, and provided with communicating side streets, whose continuation would be bound to complete the work thus begun. The subsequent completion of the Rue de Turbigo made the Rue Transonian [symbolic capital of the barricades] disappear from the map of Paris! (Quoted in Clark 1999: 39)

Others such as Frampton (1982: 24) give more credit to Haussmann's desire to improve hygiene in the city by sanitizing the water supply and building a sewage system to cope with the booming population. Paris had long been described as filthy and unhygienic.[10] Even in 1850, most streets had central gutters which still functioned as the main sewers – a feature revealed in many of Marville's photographs. Of course, improving health outcomes was not necessarily opposed to class warfare: Hambourg (1981: 8) notes that the most militant working-class districts frequently had the poorest sanitation facilities and had suffered the heaviest outbreaks in the cholera epidemics of 1832 and 1849. But, beyond these practical considerations, hygiene also took on distinct ideological connotations. Haussmann frequently appealed to the Enlightenment tradition of Voltaire, Diderot, Rousseau and Saint-Simon to legitimate his reconstruction, characterizing Paris as a 'sick' body with defective organs and circulation routes, and casting himself in the role of surgeon. As Vidler (1978: 91) notes:

> After the prolonged pathology, the drawn out agony of the patient, the body of Paris, was to be delivered of its illnesses, its cancers, and its epidemics once and for all by a total act of surgery. 'Cutting' and 'piercing' were the adjectives used to describe the operation; where the terrain was particularly obstructed a 'disembowelling' had to be performed in order that arteries be reconstituted and flows reinstated. The metaphors were repeated again and again by the pathologists, the surgeons, and even by their critics, becoming so firmly embedded in the unconscious analogies of urban planning from that time the metaphor and scientific nature of the action were confused and fused.

The context of this radical urban surgery was a new stage in the development of capitalism. Harvey (2003: 107–16) notes that the transport and communication infrastructure necessary for the integration of the national economy was largely put in place between 1850 and 1870. The rapid expansion of rail and telegraph networks, and the improvement of roads, opened Parisian industry to inter-regional competition, but also lowered input costs for production. Both trajectories shifted conditions in favour of larger enterprises with their greater scope for benefiting from economies of scale, and disadvantaged the local workshop system. Above all, these changes intensified demands for the rationalization of the city itself. As Vidler (1978: 93) puts it:

> The city had to be opened to itself and to the world. No longer should it take fifteen minutes to walk from rue Saint Denis to the Hotel de la Ville. With

a population that had doubled in fifty years, expanding suburbs that demanded access to the center, businesses that required efficient services, the entire infrastructure of the old Paris was rendered hopelessly inadequate.

Improvement in transport meant the city's food supply was no longer dependent on local produce, leading to the demise of the orchards and vegetable gardens that had once flourished within the city's centre. In addition, Haussmann's tax and land concessions were designed to force 'dirty' industry to the periphery, while reconstruction along the new boulevards added to changing patterns of land use.[11] As a result, the centre of Paris came to be dominated by monumental representations of imperial power.

## Cannonball boulevards

If Haussmannization can be defined by the convergence between the strategic demands of class war and the new economy manifested in a shift to a monumental urbanism, Haussmann's declared ambition was nothing less than the *rationalization* of urban space: what Choay (1969: 15) aptly terms the urbanization of 'regularization'. To initiate the reconstruction, Haussmann commissioned the first accurate cadastral and topographic map of Paris, completed in 1853.[12] This general plan formed the basis for the realignment of Paris away from its older principal axis around the Seine to multiple axes based on the new railway stations. Haussmann's passion for the straight line, which became the subject of jokes during the 1860s, was consummated in the new boulevards, which cut the old neighbourhoods apart.[13] What was achieved, above all, was the materialization of an urban system of *perspective*. As much as he established a circulatory system vital for economic flows and political stabilization, Haussmann produced an urban space that showcased monuments:

> In effect I have never ordered the tracing of any way whatsoever [ ... ] without concerning myself with the point of view that one could give to it. (Quoted in Vidler 1978: 95, 96)

The primacy of the urban vista over the architectural coherence of specific structures was exemplified in the famous dispute over the Tribunal de Commerce, where Haussmann forced the architect Bailly to shift the dome so that it was aligned with the perspectival axis from the new Boulevard de Sebastopol rather than respecting the form of the building itself. Harvey (2003: 100) recounts: 'A local asymmetry was created to produce a symmetrical effect at a grander urban scale.' The idea of using the street as a *frame* for a view wasn't new, having been integral to classical architecture.[14] However, while Haussmannization may have followed the letter of classical aesthetics, it distorted its humanist scale. Some of the new boulevards, such as the Rue de Rivoli, were 3 miles long. While this distance can be readily accommodated as an abstract line on a topographical map, it proved far more difficult for residents accustomed to narrow, winding streets and more varied urban textures. What Siegfried Giedion (1967: 739) memorably dubbed 'the "cannonball boulevard," seemingly without end' challenged the spatial habitus of 19th-century Parisians. The scale and geometric rigour of the new streetscapes inspired experiences of disorientation which would later be defined as 'agoraphobia', dramatized by Zola in his 1876 novel *L'Assomoir* (The Dram Shop):

> The outer boulevards had long since been enlarged by the people who demolished the toll barrier, and given carriageways on each side and a promenade in the middle for pedestrians, set with four lines of little plane trees. It was a vast crossroads extending its endless roadways towards the distant horizon, with their bustling crowds merging into the chaos of building works [ ... ] Gervaise felt entirely alone and abandoned in the bustle of the broad pavement, beside the little plane trees. These vistas along the avenues into the far distance made her stomach feel even more empty [ ... ] Yes, it was all too big and too beautiful; her head was spinning and her legs gave way under her, beneath this exaggerated breadth of grey sky spread above such a vast expanse of land. (Zola 2000: 398–99)

This sense of disorientation was accentuated by the standardization of building facades imposed as a condition of redevelopment.[15] In the *Paris-Guide* of 1867, Charles Yriarte complained that Haussmann's straight lines had 'killed the picturesque':

> The Rue de Rivoli is a symbol; a new street, long, wide, cold, frequented by men as well dressed, affected and cold as the street itself [ ... ] The street existed only in Paris and the street is dying. (Quoted in Clark 1999: 44)

In Benjamin's (1999: 12) analysis, the general effect of Haussmannization was to 'estrange Parisians from their city'. However, while the street was disappearing as a form of life belonging to the *quartier*, it was emerging as a new form of life belonging to the modern spectacle. The new economic flows went hand in hand with new forms of cultural display. The boulevards, which facilitated the displacement of local workshop production centred around the *quartier* by a more nationally integrated system of factory production, also promoted a revolution in retailing and leisure. As Harvey (2003: 112–13) notes:

> The flows between the newly established railway stations, between centre and periphery, between Left and Right bank, into and out of central markets like Les Halles, to and from places of recreation (Bois de Bologne by day, the grand boulevards by night), between industry and commerce (to the new department stores) were all facilitated by the construction of some ninety miles of spacious boulevards that reduced the cost, time, and (usually) the aggravation of movement remarkably.

Symptomatic of the fundamental changes in patterns of consumption which characterized the new culture were the big department stores, exemplified by Bon Marché which opened in Paris in 1852.[16] Bon Marché was based on three novel principles. First, it offered goods at a small mark-up, compensating with large sales volume and rapid stock turnover. The success of this economic model depended on replacing local custom with a mass of customers drawn from all over the city, giving the department store a direct dependence on the new boulevards. Second, the goods were sold at plainly marked fixed prices. Third, customers were not separated from the goods, but could enter and browse without obligation to buy. As Sennett (1977: 143) notes, these shifts in selling practice were a direct consequence of the greater volume of goods generated by machine production. To cope with high volume sales, more employees were needed. However, this brought about a decline of the sorts of personal service traditionally provided by individual shop owners, which in turn necessitated the end of mutual bargaining. As C. Wright Mills argued in his classic *White Collar* (1951: 179): 'If the entrepreneur himself does not sell, he has to have one price; he cannot trust clerks to bargain successfully.' Sennett (1977: 142–43) argues the overall result was greater public passivity, since the seller no longer took time to extol the goods, nor the buyer to bargain. The space of bargaining was instead increasingly occupied by the rise of modern advertising. Given that the quality of the first industrially manufactured goods, such as cooking utensils and clothes, was often indifferent, there was a greater need to endow them with value by association in order to convince people to purchase them. Advertising techniques such as the juxtaposition of quotidian and exotic objects emerged in this period, pointing towards the use of large window displays and sophisticated lighting in later decades. *Entre libre* and consumer browsing helped to stimulate impulse sales, and also accentuated the role of visual pleasure in simply *looking* at goods. In this context, the 'use value' of objects ceded ground to 'exchange value', and commodity fetishism gained increasing social prominence. By the end of the 19th century, Sennett (1977: 145) argues that mass-produced consumer goods had increasingly taken on a paradoxical function: not so much expressing the buyer's social status but their 'personality':

> A dress in 1750 was not a matter of what you feel; it was an elaborate, arbitrary marking of where you stood in society [ . . . ]. By 1891, your clothes, even if mass-produced, 'express' you. (Sennett 1977: 147)

### *Flânerie* and spectacle

The newly constructed public spaces, from department stores to cafés, parks and the boulevards themselves drew a heterogeneous mix of people into the city. New classes of employee such as bank clerks and shop assistants mingled with tourists, foreigners and *flâneurs*. If this increased social circulation aroused anxieties over class and gender 'contamination', it also underpinned the transition to what Harvey (2003: 113) aptly calls a more 'extroverted form of urbanism'. For Kracauer (2002: 105), the boulevards constituted a 'home for the homeless'. But they were no ordinary home, insofar as they formed a world of movement lacking traditional anchorages:

> This was the period when the *flâneur* originated, the aimless saunterer who sought to conceal the gaping void around him and within him by imbibing a thousand casual impressions. Shop window displays, prints, new buildings, smart clothes, elegant equipages, newspaper sellers – he indiscriminately absorbed the spectacle of life that went on all around him. [ ... ] To the *flâneur* the sights of the city were like dreams to a hashish smoker. (Kracauer 2002: 121)

On the boulevards, the city assumed a distinct visual existence, experienced as somehow separate from the daily life of the inhabitants who constituted it. For Benjamin, (1999b), the *flâneur* was the most precise register of the ambivalence of this new social experience. However, while the *flâneur* carried a latent potential to disrupt older class relations, this radical edge was gradually blunted by the growing commodity culture.[17] The ambivalence of *flânerie* is eventually resolved by Haussmannization in favour of what Clark (1999: 36) argues is the prototypical modern spectacle. In Debord's terms, spectacle is the flip side of the developed money economy, manifested by growing political passivity in the face of the increasing abstraction of social relations. If this outcome cannot be seen as Haussmann's conscious purpose, 'Haussmannization' nevertheless enabled the city of Paris to be consumed in the increasingly abstract terms corresponding to a more fully fledged market economy. Clark (1999: 60, 63) contends that the spectacular nature of Haussmann's Paris proved salutary for future urbanism: 'it points to the ways in which the city (and social life in general) was presented as a unity in the later nineteenth century, as a separate something made to be looked at – an image, a pantomime, a panorama.'

The shift in the scale of the boulevards meant that the experience of traversing them became something of a paradox. Despite Haussmann's efforts to place visible monuments as the culmination of every vista, the elongation of the street effectively transferred the focus from the object at its end to the experience of movement itself. Shelley Rice (1997: 44–45) captures this change perceptively:

> The city had once been a physical structure based on units – people, buildings, neighbourhoods; it was now a place in which these units were subsumed into a broader relational context whose range far exceeded that of its inhabitants. And the street that had once served simply as a link between stable buildings and *quartiers* had suddenly burst into motion – had become not only the means of circulation but the end. In this context, the boulevards that provided enriched experience for the individual also called into question not only one's primacy but also the primacy and stability of all one's reference points. The streets that were the stomping ground of the flâneur simultaneously began to threaten him with negation, for in them the point of view of the promeneur was superseded by the larger, extra-human systemic overview.

This transition from 'object-oriented' perception to a mode of perception foregrounding the *relations between* objects is fundamental to the emergence of what I call relational space. If object-oriented perception barely had to broach the question of point of view, because the stability and centredness of vision could be largely taken for granted, relational perception poses the question of 'point of view' in a way which cannot easily be answered, nor yet dismissed. Modernity comes to be increasingly characterized by its inability to arrest the multiplication of possible points of view.[18] These tectonic shifts in the relationship between space and subjectivity were most acute in Haussmann's Paris. While the boulevards enshrined elements of a system of perspective dating from Rome, their primary addressee was no longer the human eye. Instead, they formed an urban space increasingly directed towards the camera.

### Photographing Paris

While Marville's photographs are today most often associated with the vanishing of 'old Paris', this nostalgia has more to do with contemporary sensibility than his own. As Hambourg (1981) points out, Marville was equally as concerned to document the process of destruction and the results of reconstruction, as to show what previously existed.[19] This stance was dictated by Haussmann's need to underline the contrast between the old and the new, in order to prove both the magnitude of his undertaking and the superiority of his design.

Marville's Parisian *oeuvre* includes sub-sections on monuments, open spaces and street furnishings such as street lamps, *vespasiennes*, kiosks and fountains. With regard to photographing the streets and boulevards themselves, Marville was notable in his adoption of a systematic method based on the Prefect's plan. He photographed each street slated for demolition twice from different angles – the direction the camera is pointing is usually specified – and subsequently returned to photograph the different stages of destruction and construction. Hambourg (1981: 10) notes that 'many of the pictures describe the place where the imaginary trajectory of a future street would encounter the material resistance of the city's structures.'

While Marville is not renowned as an innovative photographer, his street photographs employ a definite stance. Compared to his photographs of monuments, fountains or sculptures, which generally place their subject in the centre of the frame, the street images are shot from notably lower to the ground. The centre of the frame is often an expanse of the street surface itself. This choice of low perspective had distinct effects. On the one hand, it tended to accentuate the claustrophobic enclosure of the medieval streets. The image of the *Rue des Trois-Canettes* is typical of a formula repeated scores of times: a dog-leg street with a central gutter and no pavement, shot from ground level so that the buildings abut the edges of the frame, obscuring the sky and reducing it to a mere scrap. Marville

Figure 2.1    *Charles Marville (c1865–1868), Rue des Trois-Canettes. (Courtesy Bibliothèque Historique de la Ville de Paris.)*

deliberately presents the street as a 'closed' frame, emphasizing not only its narrowness, but the undulations of the cobblestone surface and the lack of natural light. The vantage point ensuring the twisting street seems to form a *cul-de-sac*. The viewer's eye is directed towards the confined space at the centre of the frame rather than towards what lies beyond.

Figure 2.2  *Charles Marville (1877), Rue de Rivoli. (Courtesy Bibliothèque Historique de la Ville de Paris.)*

The photographs of the new boulevards, such as the image of *Rue de Rivoli* shot in 1877, repeat the same formula to opposite ends. Here the effect of shooting at street level is to place a large expanse of evenly paved surface in the foreground, while the newly constructed uniform buildings lining both sides of the street frame a large expanse of sky above. Sighting the camera straight down the boulevard emphasizes the industrial scale of the development. Instead of using Corbusier's 'ruinous curve' to close the image, here the street stretches to the horizon and beyond. By breaking the frame, the 'cannonball boulevard' suggests the radical possibility of a street without closure, the metropolitan equivalent of the endless steel railway lines which marched across the 19th-century imagination.

The centrality of the street in Marville's photographs embodies their fundamental contradiction. The street's growing function as a conduit for the new economic flows and dynamic cultural forms contradicts the resolutely *static* nature of Marville's images. Of course, all photographs embody a tension between movement and stasis, but Marville heightened it in two ways. The first was through his choice of relatively slow exposure times. Even though faster processes capable of capturing moving street life had been available for some time when he began his project in 1856, Marville continued to photograph with exposure speeds varying from 3 to 12 seconds.[20] As a result, his images erase the bulk of pedestrians, effectively eliminating the contingency of street life in favour of its formal architectural composition. This privilege of urban 'structure' over 'agency' provides a striking contrast to the enthusiasm Kracauer and Benjamin would later display for the camera as the ideal device for recording the ephemeral encounters that Baudelaire placed at the heart of modern city life.

Marville's images are static in a further sense. Even though his subject is the massive transformation of Paris – an undertaking accomplished, as Benjamin reminds us, largely by pickaxe and manual labour – labour itself remains largely absent from his images. Demolition and reconstruction appear in Marville's photographs not so much as a process carried out by human beings but as a series of results. Even those relatively few images which depict workers on site show them posed with their gaze directed towards the camera, as if to be photographed in the act of working was somehow improper. This stance was in keeping with Marville's artistic contemporaries, such as the Impressionists who represented industrial structures such as factories and chimneys as minor notes in their landscape of pleasure.[21] But the deeper significance of his avoidance of the process of labour lies in the way Marville displaced movement onto multiplicity. Ultimately, this was less a question of individual style than of the demands levied by the new urban conditions. If Haussmannization subordinated locality to coordinated totality in a manner which, to Giedion (1967: 739) made Paris 'the metropolis of the industrial era', Marville adopted the logic of industrialized vision. Marville's principal innovation in mapping the reconstruction of Paris was to treat it systematically, as a unified project conducted over an extended time. This approach meant that individual images could no longer be treated as singular entities. Rather, each photograph belonged to a series or set – *and was conceived from that point of view.*[22]

From this standpoint, the most significant legacy of Marville's work is the way it registers the transition from individual views to the cumulative knowledge established by the series or set. In Marville's project – and those which soon followed it in other industrial cities – images coalesce into an information flow in which *relations between* images assume heightened importance. This point is worth emphasizing because this approach has now entered common sense. After more than a century of rapid urbanization paralleled by a pervasive culture of throw-away images, we are no longer surprised by either saturation photography, nor by the 'before and after' comparison of cityscapes which change far more rapidly than the human life span. However, in the 1850s, this condition was emergent rather than dominant. Paris, site of the most extensive reconstruction of urban space, became the site in which the transition to serial images of urban space was pioneered.

Over the course of his project, Marville shot thousands of images, employing fairly limited variations. Stock formulas are repeated time and again for the different genres. The salient point is not so much his attempt to be comprehensive, but that his work has the effect of foregrounding repetition itself. Repetition enhances the homogenizing effect of seriality; all the images start to feel similar, to substitute for one another. As Rice (1997: 98) notes: 'Seeing

Marville's Paris photographs as serial images allows one to perceive single prints [...] as variations on a theme that has a much larger conceptual context.' The larger context in which the serial image develops is, of course, the unified urban space of Haussmannization.

## Paris by postcard

If Marville's serial photography can be read as a logical response to the demand for innovative forms of mapping corresponding to the emergent space of modern urban spectacle, this approach soon entered the realm of popular culture. Invented around the time that Haussmann was deposed as Prefect, the postcard forms an important element of late-19th-century metropolitan discourse. In Naomi Schor's (1992) terms, the postcard offered a 'softer', pleasurable counter-part to the harder panoptic gaze which characterizes the official institutions and scientific forms of knowledge of 19th-century disciplinary society.

Both an image of modernity and a modern commodity in its own right, the postcard played a critical role in disseminating the modern city as a visual spectacle. The postcard feeds the emerging apprehension of the city as a collection of fragments, a terrain comprising multiple perspectives, a space which can no longer be contained by the single authoritative shot. Postcards quickly assumed a major role in the new Paris, corresponding perfectly to the 'age of the exposition'. Souvenir postcards from the Centennial Exhibition of 1889 established the Eiffel Tower as modernity's first great icon, while, the Universal Exhibition in 1900 marked a high point in postcard panopticism. Schor (1992: 217) emphasizes the immense scope of the undertaking, noting that the major postcard series comprised some 10 000 views of the city, and were complemented by many smaller, more specialized series. Collectively, the anonymous photographers of these series adopted Marville's approach – which is more properly regarded as the logic of 'technical reproducibility' – of multiplying perspectives and points of view. Schor (1992: 219) notes: 'In the most extensive series each number corresponds to a particular view, and major sites are photographed from every conceivable angle [...].' Technological images generate the conditions in which it is possible to not only imagine but to actually *construct* an urban inventory, district by district and street by street. This 'territory of images' (to borrow Allan Sekula's evocative phrase) grafts a virtual city over the grid of Haussmann's boulevards and *arrondissements*.[23]

The significance of postcards as a novel cultural form lies in the way they do not attempt to conceal their serial nature. Postcards are routinely displayed as identical copies belonging to sets. The sameness of their views and their standardized repertoires are not accidental signs of deficiency, but are essential to their social function. Postcards are emblematic of the process in which the modern image gradually and irretrievably loses the meaning pertaining to its uniqueness, and instead finds a new level of meaning precisely in its seriality. In this respect, they belong to the logic of the Saussurean theory of the sign that was proposed around the same time that postcards became popular. Lacking the intrinsic significance of unique images, postcards find meaning as differential elements belonging to a *set*. While meaning is no longer contained by the single unit, each image draws nourishment from the semantic flow generated by the larger series in which it is embedded.

What the popular success of the postcard confirmed was the gradual uncoupling of image and referent initiated by the development of technological images. In the mass circulation of postcards, and related visual media such as illustrated newspapers and picture magazines, images assumed a new sense of autonomy. Postcards speak to the sensibility of the collector – or rather the consumer. They enable the complex reality of the modern city to be reduced to a series of discrete visual units that can be easily manipulated and readily consumed. But even as they pander to a dream for panoptic mastery of the modern city, postcards sow the seeds of its confusion. When points of view multiply so excessively, it becomes increasingly difficult to believe in the authority of a master shot or to limit oneself to the stability of a centred perspective. Postcards feed the modern understanding of the city as a fragmented, discontinuous environment, essentially unrepresentable *except as a series*. It is this sense of the city – unmoored and in perpetual transformation – which, consciously or unconsciously, informs metropolitan discourse in the 20th century.

### Urban detectives

As Benjamin (1999b: 839) pointed out, if the modern city is a labyrinth, it is not formed according to the classic medieval pattern of wandering, meandering streets, but constitutes a new prototype generated by industrial regularization itself. The disruption of established social spaces and communication networks placed new pressures on personal and collective identity, demanding the development of new strategies for deciphering urban appearances. The full significance of serial photography is best appreciated in relation to a number of other practices which were born more or less contemporaneously, including 'urban physiologies' and the genre of detective fiction. All point to the emergence of new forms of knowledge corresponding to the transformation of city life.

Benjamin (1999b: 447) clearly positions the passion for 'vulgar physiognomy' as a response to the new social conditions of the city. The 'physiologies of Paris', which appeared in the 19th century were small paperbacks which described the types of people one might encounter on the city streets.[24] Like the postcard's systematic classification of urban space, they offered a way of regulating the circulation of strangers in the city crowd by providing a repertoire of categories to which individuals could be distributed. Benjamin (1997: 39) makes their adaptive role explicit:

> They assured people that everyone was, unencumbered by any factual knowledge, able to make out the profession, the character, the background and

the lifestyle of passers-by [ . . . ]. If that sort of thing could be done, then, to be sure, life in the big city was not nearly so disquieting as it probably seemed to people.

Physiognomy informs the practice of *flânerie*, and also underpins the rise of an important successor to the *flâneur*: the detective.[25] Like the physiologies, the detective story was a distinctive invention of 19th-century urban culture. Influential figures such as Poe's Auguste Dupin and Conan Doyle's Sherlock Holmes exemplify the mobilization of scientific reason as a technique for deciphering the secret life of the city. However, unlike the priest, or older scientific philosophies of determinism, the modern scientific detective deals less in truth than probability. In solving 'The Murders in the Rue Morgue' (often acclaimed as the 'first' detective story), it is noticeable that Dupin does not claim absolute knowledge – 'I do not *know* it,' said Dupin. 'I am not *sure* of it' (Poe 1938: 163) – but rather to have made 'legitimate deductions'. Similarly, in 'The Mystery of Marie Roget', when Dupin discusses his chain of reasoning which occupies the bulk of the narrative, he freely acknowledges that each factor may be individually inconclusive. However, the *sum* of all factors is a different matter: 'Each successive one is multiple evidence – proof not *added* to proof, but *multiplied* by hundreds or thousands' (Poe 1938: 187). Chains of reason are not simply means of solving crimes. Like serial photography, they constitute a new technique for securing the relation between cause and effect that the growth of the industrial city threatened to stretch beyond recognition.

By learning to read the city differently, the detective reconstructs individual traces in the manner of photographer.[26] Like Dupin, Sherlock Holmes combined the indolence of the *flâneur* with a keen observation capable of seeing what others miss. In 'A Scandal in Bohemia' (1891), Holmes reproves Watson:

(H)  You see but you not observe. The distinction is clear. For example, you have frequently seen the steps which lead up for the hall to this room.
(W)  Frequently. [ . . . ]
(H)  Then how many are there?
(W)  How many? I don't know.
(H)  Quite so. You have not observed. [ . . . ] Now, I know that there are seventeen steps, because I have both seen and observed. (Conan Doyle 1985: 209–10)

In *The Sign of Four* (1890), Holmes startles Watson by reading his elder brother's character solely from traces found on his pocket-watch:

(W)  [H]ow in the name of all that is wonderful did you get these facts? They are absolutely correct in every particular.
(H)  Ah, that is good luck. I could only say what was the balance of probability. [ . . . ]
(H)  But it was not mere guesswork?
(W)  No, no. I never guess. It is a shocking habit – destructive to the logical faculty. (Conan Doyle 1985: 76)

Mere guessing, like 'feminine intuition', is a world away from the rational calculus of the male detective. It is significant that the detective is a figure capable of moving through vastly different social strata. Holmes is at home with all levels of society from royalty to street urchins. He is an adept of physiognomy, able to read the signs of a rigidly class-based society so as to accurately pigeonhole strangers at a glance, and also able to manipulate these signs to his own advantage. Holmes is renowned for assuming disguises which not only fool his adversaries, but give his closest associates occasion to pause. In *A Scandal in Bohemia*, Watson recounts:

> It was close upon four before the door opened, and a drunken looking groom, ill-kempt and side-whiskered, with an inflamed face and disreputable clothes, walked into the room. Accustomed as I was to my friend's amazing powers in the use of disguises, I had to look three times before I was certain that it was indeed he. (Conan Doyle 1985: 219)[27]

The fetishization of visible class differences by physiognomy, like the fantastic disguises adopted by detectives and their opponents, betrays growing anxiety over the stability of class relations. The new forms of circulation which arose in the modern city were coextensive with developments which undermined the reliability of appearances as a guide to class position. Sennett (1977: 164) argues this produced a crisis in older forms of public life. While massive urban upheaval generated a desire for social conformity, manifested in the adoption of mass-produced clothes, this quest proved paradoxical in a context in which visible appearances were increasingly treated as 'signs of the personality of the wearer'. By the late 19th century reading such signs was no longer a general social skill, but instead fell to initiates such as the detective. Sennett (1977: 168) concludes that the new dynamics of public life demanded the assumption of new public roles: 'Detectives are what every man and every woman must be when they want to make sense of the street.'

The rise of the detective as a general mode of public subjectivity belonged to the displacement of the more local forms of life sustained in the older city. The inhabitants of the modern city were increasingly asked to comprehend a complex territory, a new totality paradoxically manifested in the simultaneity of heterogeneous and apparently disconnected occurrences. Like the distinctive spatial organization adopted by the newspaper, with its juxtaposition of varied events linked only by the time or place of their occurrence, the detective story functioned as a tool giving shape to this increasingly abstract and seemingly amorphous urban terrain. In this endeavour, the shadowy figures of Moriarty and Fantômas, counterposed to Holmes and Juve respectively, play a vital role. Hidden by the density of urban life in London and Paris, these master criminals function to instil a sense of order into the incipient chaos of the city. But it is a paradoxical order, based on a generalized conspiracy theory that posits a single controlling force behind the myriad crimes and random acts of violence which afflict urban life. Gino Starace's famous 1911 image of Fantômas as a masked figure straddling the city of Paris brilliantly illustrates this function: the apparent randomness of big city life is depicted as a unity, but only by dint of a force of malevolence.[28]

## Statistical society

Recourse to scientific logic to map urban space and identity, whether manifested in physiognomy, the detective story or serial photography, reveals the extent to which the older urban milieu of the *quartier* was becoming a nostalgic point of reference. In the place of the fixity of class-based 'character', new forms of knowledge were needed to comprehend the more fluid exigencies of urban life. As Joan Copjec (1993: 169) points out: 'The origins of detective fiction coincide [ ... ] with what Ian Hacking has termed "the avalanche of numbers".'[29] Statistical knowledge was fundamental to the expansion of the more abstract economics of industrial capitalism. In a practical sense, it underpinned the growth of financial mechanisms, such as insurance to deal with the increased shipping losses of expanded international trade. In this respect, statistics provided the means for assessing the 'calculable' risks that Beck (1992) positions as the first phase of the emerging 'risk society'. Statistics soon gained a wider purchase on social and cultural life in the context of the more abstract social relations experienced in industrial cities. With the erosion of classical determinism, statistics became fundamental to the invention of the modern concept of 'normalcy'. Statistical knowledge constituted a key threshold in the formation of Foucault's 'disciplinary society'. As Hacking (1990: 2–3) notes:

> The printing of numbers was a surface effect. Behind it lay new technologies for classifying and enumerating, and new bureaucracies with the authority and continuity to deploy the technology.

Statistical knowledge translates the undifferentiated mass of the 'crowd' into the new social categories which comprise modern cities and nations: a process Hacking (1990: 3) aptly describes as 'making up people'. These new modes of distributing citizenship and identity were pivotal to the transition to political modernism, as the power formerly invested in the king was gradually transferred to new institutions, discourses and practices.[30] Copjec (1993: 175) emphasizes the way that statistical society fundamentally transformed the nature of the social bond:

> The statistical accounting of citizens resulted in their normalization by assigning to each citizen a value that was merely the translation of its relation to the others. The modern social bond is, then, differential rather than affective; it is not based on some oceanic feeling of charity or resemblance, but on a system of formal differences.

Once the social bond is defined by a shifting play of formal differences rather than apparently intrinsic qualities, identity and place become disenchanted signs which have to be apprehended as *relational* terms. This is the terrain that Anderson (1983) describes in terms of the 'imagined community', in which formal social relationships are increasingly extended across spatially distributed media networks. Understanding the importance of statistical society to the transformation of the modern social bond situates the deeper relation between Marville's photographic project and the urban space created by Haussmannization. Statistical comparison demanded, above all, the submission of individual qualities to a more general order. In the words of the four mathematicians reporting to the *Academie des Sciences* in Paris in 1835:

> In statistical affairs [ ... ] the first care before all else is to lose sight of the man taken in isolation in order to consider him only as a fraction of the species. It is necessary to strip him of his individuality to arrive at the elimination of all accidental effects that individuality can introduce into the question. (Quoted in Hacking 1990: 81)

Haussmannization applies precisely such a 'stripping' of local qualities to urban space, liberating 'space' from 'place' to produce its radical conception of an urban unity. The process is mapped by the seriality of Marville's images in which various sites become more or less interchangeable, losing their unique identities in favour of the more abstract collective identity of the set.[31]

The generative force of the logic underlying the reconstruction of the city, and its apprehension as a territory of images, is made more apparent by Simmel (1997: 149) when he discusses the transition from named to numbered houses in 19th-century Paris:

> Only fifty years ago, the residents of the Faubourg St. Antoine in Paris were always said to have referred to their buildings by their names (*Au roi de Siam*, *'Etoile d'or*, and so on), despite street numbers already being in existence. Nevertheless, the difference between the individual name and the mere number of a house expresses the difference in the relationship of its owners and residents to it, and thus to their surroundings [ ... ] The house that is called by its own name must give its inhabitants a feeling of spatial individuality, of belonging to a *qualitatively* fixed point in space. Through the name associated with it, the house forms a much more autonomous, individually nuanced existence; to our sensibility, it has a higher type of uniqueness than when designated by numbers, which are repeated in the same way in every street, with only quantitative differences between them.

Simmel emphasizes that the transition from naming to numbering involved not simply the imposition of order but the shift from one system of ordering to another. Instead of the 'individualization of place' which characterized the qualitative spatial relations of the *quartier*, the modern city was to be defined quantitatively by numbering. Uniqueness of place was sacrificed to utility:

> The *named* house cannot be immediately located; its position cannot be construed objectively, as is the case with current geographical designation. For

all their indifference and abstractness, numbers do after all represent as ordering numbers a definite place in space, which the proper name of the locality does not.

Objective location was becoming more essential – and eventually more natural – as new forms of expanded circulation, such as the national postal service, made it necessary for strangers, such as postal officials, to be able to locate individual citizens. In Simmel's (1997: 150) terms, the two systems display the tension between the 'life contents' of the individual with 'their qualitative determinacy', and their incorporation into a calculable order 'valid for everyone'. Drawing on Simmel's distinction between qualitative and quantitative differences, Benjamin later related photographic seriality to the 'reality-testing' of statistics. Benjamin (1999a: 255–56) argued:

> Uniqueness and permanence are as closely entwined in the [artwork] as are transitoriness and repeatability in the [reproduction]. The stripping of the veil from the object, the destruction of the aura, is the signature of a perception whose 'sense of sameness in the world' has so increased that, by means of reproduction, it extracts sameness even from what is unique. Thus is manifested in the field of perception what in the theoretical field is noticeable in the increasing significance of statistics.[32]

The increasing subjection of everyday perception to the 'reality-testing' of technological images means that what was primarily a 'sociological distinction' for Simmel has taken on new overtones for Benjamin. While Benjamin suggests that 'testing' can still exert a progressive political function through the liquidation of aura, he acknowledges that the outcome is ambiguous. In the present, when information scarcity has been decisively displaced by overabundance, this ambiguity seems far more tenuous. Image analysis is increasingly the explicit function of statistical – or rather algorithmical – interpretation. In this context, meaning becomes a form of 'sampling'; a shift formalized in the probabilistic conception of information divorced from semantics proposed by cybernetics. In Hayles' (1999: 34) terms, the displacement of 'possessive individualism' by computation as the ground of being is the threshold of 'posthumanism'. In Beck's (2003) terms, it corresponds to the new 'individualization' of fully fledged risk society. In urbanism, it means the function of urban surveillance cameras and the territory of images they generate switches from the formation of an archive to the provision of real time data for predictive strategies of crowd control.

The emergence of serial photography constituted a key threshold in this trajectory. Paul Virilio (1994a: 48) has argued that industrialized warfare, with its intense demands for new modes of surveillance and time-based observation, was pivotal in this shift.[33] But the origins of such an approach are arguably found in the 'war' waged on the old metropolitan centres in the second half of the 19th century, as major cities outgrew their densely built narrow streets. The reconstruction of Paris under the rule of Haussmann's straight line, and its imaging through Marville's serial photography, both contribute to the reconstruction of urban space according to the more abstract principles of the expanded market system. Like the statistical sociology that attempted to map mass urban populations, Marville's serial photography constitutes a pioneering example of the data flow that eventually swells into the paradox of the 'information society'.

## Notes

1   Goncourt (1962: 53); Benjamin (1999b: 12).
2   Haussmann was appointed in June 1853, some seven months after the *coup d'etat* which established the Second Empire and installed Napoleon III as Emperor.
3   Frampton (1982: 23–24) links Haussmann's redevelopment of Paris not only to the redevelopment of other European centres, such as Vienna's 'Ringstrasse', but to Burnham's 1909 grid plan for Chicago. Ambitious modernizers such as Le Corbusier and Robert Moses would later claim Haussmann's mantle for themselves.
4   David Harvey (2003), for instance, reproduces many of Marville's images, but treats them purely as historical illustrations and does not question the forces underlying their production.
5   Benjamin (1999b: 439) noted the influence of James Fenimore Cooper on Dumas and his contemporaries, commenting: 'it becomes possible for the novelist in an urban setting to give scope to the experiences of the hunter.' He adds: 'This has a bearing on the rise of the detective story.' I will discuss the development of the detective story further below.
6   Harvey (2003: 86–88) later argues that, in contrast to Balzac, Flaubert no longer treats the city as a sentient being, a 'body politic', but as a backdrop, akin to a stage. Balzac's confidence in being able to 'possess' the city has been overtaken by speculators, finance, and developers – in short, by 'Haussmannization'.
7   Haussmann was often credited with – and blamed for – more than his due. The reconstruction of Paris under his reign certainly built on ideas, debates and actual developments that were initiated in the 1830s and 1840s. Harvey (2003: 80) locates the ideological 'prelude' to Haussmannization in the scientific socialism of Saint-Simon, and the utopic schemes of Fourier and others.
8   Engels (1970: 69) goes on to add:

> No matter how different the reasons [for urban reconstruction] may be, the result is everywhere the same: the most scandalous alleys and lanes disappear to the accompaniment of lavish self-glorification by the bourgeoisie on account of this tremendous success, but – they appear again at once somewhere else, and often in the immediate neighbourhood.

9   Fierro (2003: 14) notes: 'As Haussmann's Paris marked the first consideration of a city as a single organism, it also marked the birth of urbanism as a disciplinary study.' Vidler (1978: 95) concludes that following Haussmann: 'The sense of the city as an entity was never so strong; villages had congealed – districts had communicated with each other before, but the understanding of the city, from east to west, north to south, was now a part of the daily experience of every inhabitant of every quarter [ . . . ].'
10  After the 1832 cholera epidemic Victor Considerant was damning: 'How ugly Paris seems after an absence, as one suffocates in these dark, narrow and humid corridors that one would rather call the streets of Paris' (quoted in Vidler 1978: 68). Engels' (1971: 33) account of the conditions of 1840s London, Dublin, Glasgow, Leeds, Bradford, Edinburgh, and, above all, Manchester provide a similar picture: 'The streets are usually unpaved and full of holes. They are filthy and strewn with animal and vegetable refuse. Since they have

neither gutters nor drains the refuse accumulates in stagnant, stinking puddles.'

11 Harvey (2003: 131–32) notes that Haussmann depended on new finance capital to fund the reconstruction. This led to a clash with the older propertied bourgeoisie, and, after 1858 'betterment values' accrued to landlords rather than the State. The conflict culminated with Haussmann's eventual dismissal from office in 1870, but, by then, the cumulative effect of the reconstruction was irreversible.

12 Fierro (2003: 14) notes: 'Prior to this great scheme, Paris had never been surveyed comprehensively.'

13 Haussmann's use of the straight line struck an enthusiastic response in Le Corbusier (1971: 16), who proclaimed in 1924:

> But the modern city lives by the straight line, inevitably; for the construction of buildings, sewers and tunnels, highways and pavements. The circulation of traffic demands the straight line; it is the proper thing for the heart of a city. The curve is ruinous, difficult and dangerous; it is a paralysing thing.

By the end of the 20th century, the circle had turned once again. Under the influence of digital technology, Lars Spuybroek (2002: 70) could argue; 'A curve is a better-informed, intelligent straight line'. This shift will be discussed further in Chapter 4.

14 Vidler (1978: 30) has traced the history of the 'theatrical' street from Rome to the Renaissance:

> From the streets of Palladio and Serlio, to those of Vasari (Uffizi) and Fontana (Rome) the great perspective project of the Renaissance was logically realized. [ . . . ] The streets, reduced to corridors for public procession, became in a very real sense outdoor passages where the buildings that enclosed them were simply facades of an international city. The tragic street was thus the instrument for urban control and regulation, inserted at the will of the planner into a hitherto private realm. The streets of Fontana and the boulevards of Haussmann two and a half centuries later shared this common role.

15 While Haussmann dictated the appearance of exteriors in accordance with the overall aesthetic he wanted to create, Rice (1997: 41) notes: 'he ignored the fact that many buildings with fine exteriors had slum-like interiors.'

16 The department store emerged as a distinctive architectural and retail type between 1840 and 1870, with the opening of Harrods (London, 1843), Bon Marché (Paris, 1852), Macys (New York, 1857), Wanamaker's (Philadelphia, 1861) and Marshall Fields (Chicago, 1868). The extension of Bon Marché into a giant new building, which is the context of Zola's *Au Bonheur des Dames* (The Ladies Paradise, 1883), took place from 1869–87, coinciding with Haussmannization.

17 This issue is discussed further in Chapter 6.

18 Just over a decade after Haussmann's deposition as Prefect, Nietzsche made the epistemological manifestations of relational perception explicit. In *On the Genealogy of Morality* (1887), he proposed his radical model of *perspectival knowledge*, in which he rejected the concept of a transcendent 'God's eye' vision with the bold declaration: 'There is *only* a perspectival seeing, *only* a perspectival "knowing" [ . . . ]' (Nietzsche 1998: 85).

19 This concern for the whole process of reconstruction sets Marville's approach apart from projects seeking to garner support for 'slum clearance', such as Thomas Annan's work for the Glasgow City Improvement Trust (1868–81) – the first major urban redevelopment scheme undertaken in Britain. By contrast Marville's photographs were seen as a valuable complement to the work of the city archivists in Paris and ownership of the negatives was vested in the City Council's Permanent Sub-Committee on Historic Works (commonly known as *Travuax Historiques*).

20 The capacity of the new processes to capture pedestrian life had been successfully demonstrated in the street photographs of Adolph Braun as early as 1851. See Rice (1997).

21 On the Impressionist disinterest in industry and labour, see Clark (1999: 182, 189).

22 This logic was made explicit half a century later by Kracauer in his 1927 'Photography' essay, and more famously by Benjamin in his 'Artwork' essay (1935–39). See Chapter 3.

23 This is not to argue that the postcard actually produces a complete image of the city. Despite its sheer weight of numbers, the postcarding of Paris remained a selective representation focused around the emerging leisure economy and the construction of the modern tourist itinerary.

24 The physiologies offered popularized versions of the 18th-century physiognomies of scientists such as Johann Kaspar Lavater and Ferdinand von Gall which had inaugurated the 'science' of reading character from the external appearance of the face. Vidler (1978: 77) argues 'the science of physiognomy provided the most fashionable, and perhaps the most characteristic, mode of perception of the age.'

25 Benjamin (1999b: 429) first aligns the *flâneur* with physiognomy: 'The phantasmagoria of the flâneur: to read from faces the profession, the ancestry, the character'. He later adds that: 'Preformed in the figure of the flâneur is that of the detective' (Benjamin 1999b: 442).

26 Benjamin (2003: 23) posits an integral relation between the detective story and the existential crisis of modern urbanism: 'The original social content of the detective story focused on the obliteration of the individual's traces in the big city crowd.' He also directly relates the sensibility of the detective to the emergence of photography: 'Photography made it possible for the first time to preserve permanent and unmistakable traces of a human being. The detective story came into being when this most decisive of all conquests of a person's incognito had been accomplished' (Benjamin 2003: 27).

27 This facility is shared by other contemporaries, including the detective Juve from the popular *Fantômas* serial, which was first published in February 1911 and quickly became a favourite of the Parisian *avant-garde* through Louis Feuillade's films of 1913–14. Juve's capacity for disguise is exceeded only by Fantômas himself, a figure who shifts identity so constantly that any sense of authentic self is abandoned.

28 Starace's cover-image for the first novel was plastered on kiosks, columns and metro walls throughout Paris. Vertov later used a similar image of the cameraman straddling the city in *Man with the Movie Camera* (1929).

29 Hacking (1990: 3) argues: 'Statistical laws that look like brute irreducible facts were first found in human affairs [rather than natural science], but they could only be noticed after social phenomena had been enumerated, tabulated and made public. That role was well served by the avalanche of printed numbers at the start of the 19th century.'

30 The demise of monarchical power involved the decline of what Habermas (1989) has termed the *publicness of representation*, in which the sovereign displayed him or herself as the embodiment of higher power. Instead, modern political power would come to be legitimated through new forms of publicness and publicity (see also Chapter 7).

31 Hacking (1990: 5) dates the emergence of modern numeracy from around 1840, a date which coincides with the public release of the camera. He also points out the leading role played by Paris in the formulation and deployment of statistical knowledge, noting that 'Paris set the model for the publication of social data', unleashing an 'avalanche of printed enumerations of social conditions' beginning with Fourier's *Recherches statistiques of Paris and the*

*Seine*' in the 1820s and culminating with Durkheim's *Suicide* of 1897. See Hacking (1990: 46).

32 Benjamin is quoting Danish writer Johannes Jensen (1999a: 276).

33 Virilio (1994a: 48) cites Edward Steichen's role in the American Expeditionary Force's aerial surveillance in 1917 as exemplary:

> With a force of fifty-five officers and 1,111 enlisted men, Steichen was to organise aerial-intelligence image production 'like a factory', thanks to the division of labour (the Ford car assembly was already in operation in 1914). Aerial observation had in fact stopped being episodic from the beginning of the war; it was not a matter of images now, but of an uninterrupted stream of images, millions of negatives madly trying to embrace on a daily basis the statistical trends of the first great military – industrial conflict.

# 3

## The City in Fragments

The life of a village is narrative [ . . . ] In a city the visual impressions succeed each other, overlap, over-cross, they are 'cinematographic'.

(Ezra Pound 1921)

I sensed a new reality in the detail of a machine, in the common object. I tried to find the plastic value in these fragments of modern life. I rediscovered them on the screen in the close-ups of objects which impressed and influenced me.

(Fernand Léger 1923)[1]

### The shattered city

In Alberto Cavalcanti's remarkable but little seen film *Rien que les heures* (*Nothing but time*, France, 1926), the opening shot shows a picturesque Paris street, a remnant of the old city Marville might have photographed prior to Haussmann's onslaught. But the image is immediately torn up, revealed as a picture postcard of the sort that had become popular since the 1880s. Paris in the mid-1920s, the film suggests, can no longer be contained by the still image, especially one which has already been reduced to a cliché. The modern city demanded new forms of knowledge and representation.

In his magisterial *The Production of Space*, Henri Lefebvre (1991: 25) contended:

> The fact is around 1910 a certain space was shattered. It was the space of common sense, of knowledge (*savoir*), of social practice, of political power, a space hitherto enshrined in everyday discourse, just as in abstract thought, as the environment of and channel for communications; the space, too, of classical perspective and geometry, developed from the Renaissance onwards on the basis of the Greek tradition (Euclid, logic) and bodied forth in Western art and philosophy, as in the form of the city and the town.

Lefebvre's ascription of such a broad transformation to such a precise date is less a statement of historical fact than an attempt to conjure the impact of complex and interlocking changes in technology, forms of production and social life. By 1910, it could be argued, so many things were changing, so rapidly, and on so many fronts, that there was a pervasive sense that the old world had indeed been broken apart. From around the 1880s, an array of technological innovations, including electricity, telephony, steel construction and glass curtain walls, had progressively redefined the urban domain. Electric trams ran through the streets, while subways burrowed under them. Elevators forged vertical pathways in new high-rise buildings, while bicycles and automobiles vastly expanded mobility on the streets outside. Department stores raised window-shopping to a popular art. The lighting of streets, factories and public spaces fundamentally altered the rhythms of work and leisure, while the uncanny light of cinema transformed the social circulation of images. Large-scale factories were beginning to organize their work forces according to the production-line logic formalized by Fordism and the 'scientific' principles of labour efficiency enunciated by Taylor. These changes were paralleled by fundamental shifts in science, art and politics, as the stranglehold of Newtonian science was loosened, the 'realism' of geometric perspective was challenged by Cubism, and the spectre of communist revolution seemed to confront capitalism at every turn.[2]

In short, the urban-industrial life-world was transformed beyond recognition in little more than a generation – a time frame rapid enough to produce what Lefebvre described as the 'shattering' of the space of the classical city. In the process, the modern city became a lived experiment in special effects, one which promised, or threatened, to alter the parameters of human identity. Robert Musil's influential *The Man without Qualities* (1930–33), set in Vienna on the eve of World War I, explored the atmosphere of uncertainty produced by such changes. As one of the novel's protagonists, Ulrich, comments: 'no one seems to feel quite at home in his own skin' (Musil 1979: 275). This uncanny sense of *not being at home* where one should be most familiar indicates the extent to which what Benjamin called Haussmann's 'eviction' of Parisians from their own city in the mid-19th century had assumed a broader currency in the rapidly modernizing cities of the early 20th century.

In this chapter, I want to examine changes in metropolitan experience in the first decades of the 20th century through the prism of what was arguably the most influential means of apprehending them: film. My argument begins from the thesis articulated by Benjamin and Kracauer in the 1920s and 1930s: namely, that cinema was not simply one art form among others, but enjoyed a privileged relation to the emergent space-time of the modern city.[3] In other words, unlike a number of recent books on 'cinema and the city' or 'film and architecture', I want to treat the cinema–city relation as more complex than one in which cinema simply offers a *representation* of the city.[4] Rather, I will argue that cinema is an integral step in the formation of the media city, pointing towards an emergent condition in which an expanded matrix of media feedback loops increasingly shape the ambiance and intensities of urban space.

Both Benjamin and Kracauer posited an epochal and potentially revolutionary role for cinema in the context of modern urban life. But, as much as film was capable of revealing the new conditions of life, and thereby waking city-dwellers from their commodity-inspired slumber, it also comprised a crucial adaptive mechanism amounting to a form of sensory training for modern city living. I want to trace this ambivalence here by focusing on the cycle of 'city-symphony' films that were produced in the 1920s, particularly Walther Ruttmann's *Berlin, Die Symphonie Einer Grossstadt* (*Berlin, Symphony of a Great City*, Germany, 1927; hereafter *Berlin Symphony*) and Dziga Vertov's *Cheloveks kinoapparatom* (*Man with the Movie Camera*, USSR, 1929). These two films stand out in this context not only for the scope and rigour of their attempt to capture the distinctive experience of modern urban life, but because they explicitly sought to pioneer a new visual 'language' adequate to the new urban environment. As Ruttmann declared when he abandoned painting for experimental film in 1918: 'It makes no sense to paint any more. This painting must be set in motion' (quoted in Macrae 2003: 253). Vertov evinced even bolder ambitions. The only title sequence of *Man with the Movie Camera* proclaims:

> This film presents an experiment in the cinematic communication of visible events.
>
> - without the aid of intertitles (a film without intertitles)
> - without the aid of a scenario (a film without a scenario)
> - without the aid of a theatre ( a film without sets, actors, etc.)
>
> This experimental work is aimed at creating a truly international absolute language of cinema based on its total separation from the language of theatre and literature.

It is no accident that this 'truly international absolute language' is pioneered in the context of big city life.

### The city as symphony

There is a long-standing dispute as to who originated the idea for the 'city symphony' film. Cavalcanti's Paris film appeared in 1926, but work started earlier on Ruttmann's *Berlin Symphony* which took a year to shoot. Vertov's *Man with a Movie Camera*, the film to which *Berlin Symphony* is most frequently compared, was not released until 1929. But, by that stage, Vertov had already produced a large body of film work including the 23 issues of the *Kino-Pravda* newsreel (1922–25) and the 6-reel *Kinoglaz* (1924) which had firmly established his trademark approach of 'catching life unrehearsed'.[5] Vertov's brother and camera operator Mikhail Kaufman had completed his own city film *Moscow* in 1926, while René Clair's *Paris qui dort* (1923) and *Entr'acte* (1924) mined a similar urban terrain to comical ends.[6] If you scan back slightly further, you find a number of short avant-garde projects including Léger's *Ballet Mécanique* (1924), Moholy-Nagy's unrealized film-project *Dynamic of the Metropolis* of 1921 and Paul Strand and Charles Sheeler's *Manhatta*, replete with Whitmanesque flourishes, shot in New York the same year.[7] Tracking back even further, Clair's comedies owe much to the absurdist satires on the functions and dysfunctions of the modern city played out in films produced by Mack Sennett's Keystone studio from 1912, while Sennett himself admitted 'I stole my first ideas from the Pathés,' referring to the inventive comedies made by the French company in the early 1900s (quoted in Brownlow 1979: 142).

In fact, the city was a cinematic staple right from the first 'actualities'. Tom Gunning notes:

> The first film shows were primarily 'big city' affairs [ . . . ] Nearly all early film documents present a *mise en abîme* of audiences filling vaudeville halls from busy city streets in order to see projected on the screen – busy city streets. (Quoted in Weihsmann 1997: 8)

If isolating the origin of the 'city-symphony' is of limited value, more significant is the way cinema was immediately recognized for its ability to capture the distinctive qualities of the modern city. The fleeting and ephemeral social encounters extolled by Baudelaire and Poe in the mid-19th century reappear as the content of countless early films – an affiliation quickly recognized by one of the Lumières' principal camera operators, Mesguich, who asserted that the domain of cinema 'is the dynamism of life, of nature and its manifestations, of the crowd and its eddies' (quoted in Kracauer 1960: 31). Writing in 1926, Virginia Woolf (1950: 170–71) articulated the prevalent *avant-garde* view of cinema, arguing that film could become a new art adequate to modern urban experience, if only it stayed clear of the 'literary' scenarios dogging its steps:

> The most fantastic contrasts could be flashed before us with a speed which the writer can only toil after in vain [ . . . ] How all this can be attempted, much less achieved, no one at the moment can tell us. We get intimations only in the chaos of the streets, perhaps when some momentary assembly of colour, sound, movement, suggests that here is a scene waiting a new art to be transfixed.

Woolf's 'new art' intimated by the chaos of the streets found its most memorable expression in the blossoming of the city-symphony film. If the 'day in the life of the city' structure was a device borrowed from modern literature, film quickly made the terrain its own.[8] Beginning from the selection and juxtaposition of visible phenomena, the aim of the city-symphony was to reveal the underlying rhythms and patterns of modern urban life. In the mid-19th century Baudelaire had memorably portrayed the *flâneur* as 'a kaleidoscope endowed with consciousness'. By the first decades of the 20th century the task of apprehending the heterogeneous flows that created the distinctive environment of the modern city belonged less to the human eye than the technological apparatus of cinema.

### Montage city

While Kracauer is keen to underline the thematic continuity between the early actualities of the Lumiéres and the city-symphonies of the 1920s, there are dramatic differences in their presentation of the subject.[9] Early cinematic views of the city were essentially that: *views* comprising static shots taken from a single point. Movement remained the province of street life itself.

Even on those relatively rare occasions where the camera was set in motion, such as *Skyscrapers of New York City from North River* (1903) which shows Manhattan from the vantage of a ferry steaming up river, the coherence of the continuous visual field inherited from painting remained largely intact. However, in cinema's second decade the 'actualities' gradually gave way to the emergence of multi-shot narratives as films came to be composed by means of the fragmentation and re-assemblage of the visual field.

This transition constituted a major threshold in 20th-century culture. The dynamism of the cinematic image represented a clear challenge to the traditional image, and underwrites Benjamin's sense of the political possibilities of film in the context of modern industrial city. In the final version of his 'Artwork' essay (1939), Benjamin (2003: 267) famously contrasts painting and film:

> Let us compare the screen [*Leinwand*] on which a film unfolds with the canvas [*Leinwand*] of a painting. The painting invites the viewer to contemplation; before it, he can give himself up to his train of associations. Before a film image he cannot do so. No sooner has he seen it than it has already changed.

For Benjamin, the film image is a technological version of the dadaist 'missile'. Its inherently dynamic nature inscribes a fundamental difference between the spatiality characteristic of screen and painting. When Benjamin contrasted the painter with the camera operator, he compared the former to a magician and the latter to a surgeon:

> The painter maintains in his work a natural distance from reality, the cinematographer penetrates deeply into its tissue. The images obtained by each differ enormously. The painter's is a total image, whereas that of the cinematographer is piecemeal, its manifold parts being assembled according to a new law. (2002: 115–16; 2003: 263–64)

Benjamin's contrast between surgeon and magician belongs to a chain of oppositions in which secular rationality – a quality embodied for the 1920s *avant-garde* by the engineer – is privileged over the mystical practice of the shaman. While the auratic image of painting preserves the distance essential to the 'cult' value of pseudo-religious worship, the technological image obliterates distance in favour of 'exhibition value' and new forms of collective reception. The 'new law' for the assembly of cinematography is the law of montage, according to which the painter's 'total image' can be broken into fragments and then reassembled to form articulated sequences. For Benjamin (2003: 263):

> The illusionary nature of film is of the second degree; it is the result of editing. That is to say: In the film studio the apparatus has penetrated so deeply into reality that a pure view of that reality, free of the foreign body of equipment, is the result of a special procedure, namely, the shooting by the specially adjusted photographic device and the assembly of that shot with others of the same kind. The equipment-free aspect of reality has here become the height of artifice, and the vision of immediate reality the Blue Flower in the land of technology.

Benjamin's faith in the revolutionary potential of the technological image was a direct function of the extent to which the cinematic text no longer constituted a seemingly natural totality. The violence of cinema's disjunction from previous visual forms was first registered by the, perhaps apocryphal, stories of viewers who screamed at the sight of an oncoming train at early film screenings. The ambivalent nature of this assault generated by the unprecedented 'realism' of the film image was intensified by its extreme plasticity. If cinema initially struck observers such as Gorky as an apparition from the spirit world, the process of creating narratives by subjecting the photo-realism of individual shots to montage created what filmmaker Marcel L'Herbier evocatively described as the 'dialectical unity of the real and the unreal' (quoted in Virilio 1991b: 65).

The extent to which montage demanded that audiences *learn* a new mode of reception was underlined by Benjamin (1999a: 14) in his 1927 essay on Russian film:

> It has become clear, for example, that the rural audience is incapable of following *two simultaneous narrative strands* of the kind seen countless times in film. They can only follow a single series of images that must unfold chronologically, like the verses of a street ballad. [ . . . ] To expose such audiences to film and radio constitutes one of the most grandiose mass-psychological experiments ever undertaken in the gigantic laboratory that Russia has become.

For Benjamin (1999a: 14), the fact that peasants 'have seen neither towns nor modern means of transport' intensified cinema's shock effect. But even in the big cities, widespread exposure to new media such as film and radio amounted to a 'mass psychological experiment' with uncertain political effects. By the time Benjamin wrote his essay in 1927, a set of narrative conventions was already being institutionalized as the dominant form of film production, and this tendency would be consecrated over the next decade with the introduction of synchronized sound. As Miriam Hansen (1991: 16) puts it, the institutionalized mode of narration which came to dominate Hollywood, and eventually global cinema, made it possible 'to anticipate a viewer through particular textual strategies, and thus to standardize empirically diverse and to some extent unpredictable acts of reception'. The gradual development of recognizable narrative conventions enabled the construction of new forms of continuity from the formal discontinuity produced by montage.

A litmus test of this new narrative structure is the manner in which successive shots in films came to be read as referring to coherent and ostensibly continuous spaces. In the first multi-shot films, shot sequences were generally read as signifying linear temporal succession. Shots often overlapped on action as the means of conveying it to a new but proximate location. The development of parallel editing demanded that an alternate reading be entertained, in which two shots could signify spatially disjunctive sites of *simultaneous* action. Over time, the *narrative* organization of space and time through montage assumed a growing autonomy. Once the mere juxtaposition of two shots proved capable of creating 'causal' connections, the ambiguity as to whether the second shot should be read as successive or simultaneous came to be resolved in the text itself, measured as an effect of *narrative* coherence; a shift Jean-Louis Comolli (1980: 130) aptly describes in terms of the move from optical to psychological realism.

This shift situates the long-standing argument over the political effect of cinema: would it destabilize habitual forms of perception and subjectivity, or would it be harnessed into narrative forms that used its plasticity to augment the perceptual mastery of the autonomous subject?[10] Of course, this dualism is simplistic; in certain ways, film has always done both. Vertov's polemical disdain for Hollywood narratives led him to write in 1917: 'We go the movies/To blow up the movies/In order to see the movies' (quoted in Petric 1987: 30). Freedom to reconstruct the visible world through film was seized by *avant-garde* practitioners as the basis for a materialist investigation of the existing social order, including the emergent conventions of narrative film. As Vertov (1984: 88) asserted:

> Kino-eye uses every possible means in montage, comparing and linking all points of the universe in any temporal order, breaking, when necessary, all the laws and conventions of film construction.

While Vertov's self-reflexive cinema explicitly challenged Hollywood's attempts to yoke the radical effects of cinema's mobile gaze to a particular form of narrative coherence, it should not be assumed that mainstream narrative solved all the tensions raised by the introduction of the dynamic image. As Benjamin points out, even conservative films 'liquidated' cultural heritage insofar as they subjected culture to a new form of interrogation. Even as such texts heightened the experience of visual mastery, and thus bolstered the sense of autonomy underpinning the bourgeois conception of the modern individual, the fluid effects of cinematic perception under-mined the coherence of the spatial and temporal frameworks from which that mode of subjectivity had historically emerged.

The spatio-temporal malleability of film also conflicted at a fundamental level with existing urban form. Drawing on Benjamin's analysis, Virilio (1991a: 76) underlines the way in which cinematic space militates against traditional architecture:

> For the attentive observer, the slicing of physical space into different geometric dimensions, and the durable separation of geographic and constructed spaces, is replaced by the momentary break, due to the imperceptible interruption of different sequences of view-points and the perceptible interruption of broadcasting and reception. The new produced and projected space has less to do with lines, surfaces and volumes than with the minutiae of view-point, the dynamite of tenths-of-seconds.

In a world remade by machine technology, artificial light and rapid move-ment, embodied perception was increasingly susceptible to sudden switches and abrupt shifts. Walking down a busy city street was to experience an overlay of complex sensations tantamount to the alternation of separate 'shots'. In cities sliced apart by the insertion of railway lines, the incursion of large-scale industry or the sudden impact of 'modernization' projects inspired by Haussmannization, montage became a logical technique for new forms of cognitive mapping.

## Big city life

The similarity between big city life and the new mode of perception emerging in cinema is already apparent in Simmel's pioneering analysis of urban space.[11] For Simmel, the capacity to adapt to the spatial complexity of the big city stands as the mark of advanced consciousness. In 'The Sociology of Space', written in 1903, Simmel (1997: 152) argues: 'The more primitive is consciousness, the more incapable it is of conceiving the unity of what is spatially separated or the non-unity of that which is spatially proximate.' It is from this 'primitivist' standpoint, which reveals his total ignorance of the spatial complexity of indigenous cultures, that Simmel (1997: 153) can go on to speak confidently of the 'backwardness' of 'small town conditions' compared to the 'complexity and confusion of the city'. It is in the city that the inversions of distance and closeness that Benjamin associates with camera technology become commonplace, so that 'one grows accustomed to continual abstractions, to indifference towards that which is spatially closest and to an intimate relationship to that which is spatially very far removed' (Simmel 1997: 153).

While abstraction has its advantages – for example, the numbered house enables precise location among anonymous neighbours – it also carries new risks. Simmel's broad frame for understanding modernity in terms of the displacement of qualitative by quantitative values, first broached in his *Philosophy of Money* (1900), also underpins his famous 1903 essay 'The Metropolis and Mental Life'. Here Simmel develops what could best be called an *economy* of consciousness, paralleling the economic model of psychic functioning proposed by Freud and Breuer a few years earlier.[12] Simmel (1997: 175) contends:

> The psychological basis of the metropolitan type of individuality consists in the *intensification of nervous stimulation* which results from the swift and uninter- rupted change of outer and inner stimuli. [ . . . ] Lasting impressions, impressions which differ only slightly from one another, impressions which take a regular and habitual course and show regular and habitual contrasts – all these use up, so to speak, less consciousness than does the rapid crowding of changing images, the sharp discontinuity of a single glance, and the unexpectedness of onrushing impressions. These are the psychological conditions which the metropolis cre- ates. With each crossing of the street, with the tempo and multiplicity of economic, occupational and social life, the city sets up a deep contrast with small town and rural life with reference to the sensory foundations of psychic life.

Simmel's analysis of the sensory challenges of metropolitan life traces a familiar *fin-de-siecle* theme of crowding, acceleration and over-stimulation.

Asendorf (1993: 171) notes that experiments with electricity informed the theoretical models involving nerves and excitation shared by several of Simmel's Viennese contemporaries, including Freud. Simmel's description of metropolitan life also distinctly echoed Nietzsche's (1968: 47) warning about the 'tropical tempo' of the modern world, where the abundance of disparate sensory impressions leads to adaptive behaviour in which 'men unlearn spontaneous action, they merely react to stimuli from outside.' Nevertheless, reading Simmel through the retrospective lens of Benjamin is suggestive. The 'lasting impressions' which are characteristic of the small town can be aligned with the stable image of painting, while 'the rapid crowding of changing images' marked by 'discontinuity' and 'unexpected-ness' that Simmel finds typical of the modern metropolis, correspond to the dynamic film image.

Simmel (1997: 176) believed that the intensity of the new environment created an urban dweller who 'reacts with his head instead of his heart'. Intellectualism was a carapace grown by individuals faced with the incipient chaos of big city life. Impersonal social relations, exemplified by the timetable which coordinates the individual travel schedules of diverse commuters, become the key to the preservation of subjective life in face of urban over-stimulation. The darker side of intellectualism is what Simmel (1997: 178) calls the 'blasé attitude' arising from persistent over-stimulation:

> An incapacity thus emerges to react to new situations with the appropriate energy. This constitutes the blasé attitude which, in fact, every metropolitan child shows when compared with children of quieter and less changeable milieus.[13]

While Simmel locates the blasé attitude in the city, its root cause is the levelling effect of the mature money economy. In this respect, he directly follows Marx's (1977: 229) famous critique of commodity fetishism in *Capital* which described money as 'the most frightful leveller'. Simmel (1997: 178) adds:

> The essence of the blasé attitude consists in the blunting of discrimination. This does not mean that objects are not perceived, as is the case with the half-wit, but rather that the meaning and differing values of things, and thereby the things themselves, are experienced as insubstantial.[14]

For Simmel (1997: 179), the big city, where commodification dominates social relations, is where the blasé attitude becomes most evident: 'The large cities, the main seats of the money exchange, bring the purchasability of things to the fore much more impressively than do smaller localities. That is why cities are also the genuine locale of the blasé attitude [ . . . ].' In his later writings Simmel's concern with preserving a space for individuality in the face of the levelling effects of the mature money economy becomes increasingly evident. But his key concepts such as intellectualism and the blasé attitude remain limited. They form part of his predominantly *aesthetic* response to modernity, typified by a retreat into the inwardness characteristic of *jugendstil*. Frisby (1985: 82) astutely recognizes that the absence of a theory of historical change means that Simmel's attempt to recuperate individual experience in the face of economic 'levelling' lacks historical specificity and ultimately remains stuck in an 'eternal present'. Frisby (1985: 82–83) concludes that this impasse is the result of Simmel's own unreflected class situation: 'Reserve and indifference as defence mechanisms in the metropolis are most likely to be used by those social strata who, from a relatively secure social position, can afford to adopt this response.'

While Simmel's emphasis on urban space as a new matrix of social experience strongly influenced both Kracauer and Benjamin, the absence of a theory of historical change in his work was a lacuna they sought to redress. Under the influence of Marxism, they evince less interest in preserving bourgeois individuality than in making space for its creative destruction by the masses. And while they, like Simmel, posit a central role for 'aesthetics' in social analysis, it is not to painting but the new technological images that they turn for the 'redemption' of experience. Cinema becomes the force capable of breaking through the carapace of blasé indifference of big city life.

### Film as urban dynamite

Benjamin's conception of film as a form of *dynamite* with an historic role in unlocking the 'prison-world' of the modern industrial city was first articulated in his 1927 defence of Eisenstein's *Potemkin*, written shortly after his visit to the Soviet Union. In it he argued:

> To put it in a nutshell, film is the prism in which the spaces of the immediate environment – the spaces in which people live, pursue their avocations, and enjoy their leisure – are laid open before their eyes in a comprehensible, meaningful and passionate way. In themselves these offices, furnished rooms, salons, big-city streets, stations, and factories are ugly, incomprehensible, and hopelessly sad. Or rather, they were and seemed to be, until the advent of film. The cinema then exploded this entire prison-world with its dynamite of fractions of a second, so that now we can take the extended journeys of adventure between their widely scattered ruins. The vicinity of a house, a room, can include dozens of the most unexpected stations, and the most astonishing station names. It is not so much the constant stream of images as the sudden change of place that overcomes a milieu which has resisted every other attempt to unlock its secret, and succeeds in extracting from a petty-bourgeois dwelling the same beauty we admire in an Alfa Romeo. And so far, so good. (1999a: 17)

In this passage, Benjamin's description of the formal qualities of film, in which sudden and rapid changes of scene are paramount, echoes the proto-cinematic character of Simmel's account of urban experience. However, Benjamin's analysis is immediately more dialectical. While film dynamite has the *potential* to show the everyday world 'in a comprehensible, meaningful and passionate way', Benjamin's concluding 'so far, so good' signals his awareness of the limitations of a purely formal cinematic explosion. For Benjamin, the historical importance of cinema was not simply its dislocation and reassemblage of the visible world, but rather its capacity to engender collective political awareness by mirroring collective action back to the masses. Film dynamite should not only blow apart the prison-world of the bourgeois city, but convert the indifference of the masses into a 'collective in motion'.

> The proletariat, however, is a collective, just as these spaces are collective spaces. And only here, in the human collective, can the film complete the prismatic work that it began by acting on that milieu. The epoch-making impact of *Potemkin* can be explained by the fact that it made this clear for the first time. Here, for the first time, a mass movement acquires the wholly architectonic and by no means monumental (i.e. UFA) quality that justifies its inclusion in film. No other medium could reproduce this collective in motion. (1999a: 18)

Benjamin's 'film dynamite' metaphor is more famously reprised a decade later, appearing in both the 1936 and 1939 versions of his 'Artwork' essay. By this time, it has been ambitiously extended, via his reading of Freud's 'Beyond the Pleasure Principle' (1920), to include the concept of the 'optical unconscious':

> Our bars and city streets, our offices and furnished rooms, our railroad stations and factories seemed to close relentlessly around us. Then came film and exploded this prison-world with the dynamite of the split-second, so that we now can set off calmly on journeys of adventure among its far-flung debris. With the close-up, space expands; with slow motion, movement is extended. And just as enlargement not merely clarifies what we see indistinctly 'in any case', but brings to light entirely new structures of matter, slow motion not only reveals familiar aspects of movements, but discloses quite unknown aspects within them [ . . . ] Clearly, it is another nature which speaks to the camera as compared to the eye. 'Other' above all in the sense that a space informed by human consciousness gives way to a space formed by the unconscious. [ . . . ] 'It is through the camera that we first discover the optical unconscious, just as we discover the instinctual unconscious through psychoanalysis.' (2002: 117; 2003: 255–56)

The dynamite of film now goes beyond the 'fractions of a second' of montage to include camera techniques such as close-ups and slow motion, revealing the influence of Soviet filmmakers such as Vertov, who is explicitly mentioned in the final version of the essay. Importantly, film's capacity to defamiliarize the familiar has also been placed in a structural relation to the experience of 'shock', which, by the 1930s, Benjamin was positing as the quintessential experience of the modern city. Benjamin's concept of 'shock' derives not only from Freud and Simmel, but also from his reading of Baudelaire. In his 1939 essay 'Some Motifs in Baudelaire', Benjamin (2003: 328) connects developments in new technologies, such as telephony and photography, to the experience of big city life, particularly the movement of crowds through the city streets:

> In the mid-19th century, the invention of the match brought forth a number of innovations which have one thing in common: a single abrupt movement of the hand triggers a process of many steps. This development is taking place in many

areas. A case in point is the telephone, where the lifting of the receiver has taken the place of the steady movement that used to be required to crank the older models. With regard to countless movements of switching, inserting, pressing, and the like, the 'snapping' by the photographer had the greatest consequence. Henceforth a touch of the finger sufficed to fix an event for an unlimited period of time. The camera gave the moment a posthumous shock, as it were. Haptic experiences of this kind were joined by optic ones, such as supplied by the advertising pages of the newspaper or the traffic of the big city. Moving through this traffic involves the individual in a series of shocks and collisions. At dangerous intersections, nervous impulses flow through him in rapid succession, like the energy from a battery. Baudelaire speaks of a man who plunges into a crowd as into a reservoir of electric energy. Circumscribing the experience of the shock, he classes this man 'a kaleidoscope endowed with consciousness'.

This famous passage stresses the experiential impact of sudden 'switches' and 'shocks'. On the one hand, these disjunctions occur in relation to the space-time displacements generated by media and communication technologies, where the pressing of a single button is capable of unleashing a series of automated actions. On the other hand, these disjunctions also belong to the experience of the individual moving through urban space dominated by crowds and traffic. However, while the metaphor of the pedestrian subject to nervous impulses flowing like electrical energy from a battery clearly resembles Simmel's overburdened urban dweller, the ambition behind such a metaphor has shifted significantly. To appreciate this shift, we need to situate Benjamin's use of shock more firmly in the context of his theory of experience. Benjamin continually distinguishes between 'long experience over time' [*Erfahrung*] and the isolated 'experience of the moment' [*Erlebnis*]. Experience 'in the strict sense' is not the province of either the isolated individual or pure consciousness:

> Where there is experience [*Erfahrung*] in the strict sense of the word, certain contents of the individual past combine in the memory [*Gedächtnis*] with material from the collective past. (2003: 316)[15]

In 'Some Motifs in Baudelaire' Benjamin (2003: 336) criticizes the subjectivism of Bergson's *durée* for what he regards as its over-valorization of conscious choice: 'The *durée* [ . . . ] is the quintessence of an isolated experience [*Erlebnis*] that struts about in the borrowed garb of long experience [*Erfahrung*].' Benjamin (2003: 314) is more attracted to the Proustian formulation of *mémoire involontaire* as the basis for a theory of experience, because it depends less on 'facts firmly anchored in memory' than on a rich matrix of often unconscious associations. But he rejects Proust's suggestion that encountering involuntary memories, such as those triggered by the famous *madeleine*, is entirely a matter of chance. Instead he argues that the reduction of such encounters to quirks of personal fate is symptomatic of the transformation of experience in modernity:

> A person's inner concerns are not by nature of an inescapably private character. They attain this character only after the likelihood decreases that external concerns will be assimilated to one's experience. (2003: 314)

Echoing Engels' analysis of London crowds, Benjamin argues it is the 'private character' of the isolated individuals making up the urban crowd – in other words a social rather than a natural fact – which militates against the assimilation of experience.[16] This mingling of individual memory with material from the collective past once occurred in the context of rituals, ceremonies and festivals where 'voluntary and involuntary recollection ceased to be mutually exclusive' (2003: 316). However, the modern city is coextensive with the widespread disruption of these cultural forms, and the emergence of new forms of collective communication such as mass newspapers and museums in their place.

Benjamin then turns to Freud to deepen his understanding of the apparent poverty of voluntary memory in comparison to the richness of involuntary memory, taking up Freud's distinction between consciousness and 'memory traces'. The latter tend to be most powerful when they belong to an experience which *never entered consciousness*. In the stratified model of the psyche Freud outlines in 'Beyond the Pleasure Principle', consciousness functions as a 'protective shield' against stimulation:

> *Protection against stimuli* is an almost more important function for the living organism than *reception* of stimuli. The protective shield is supplied with its own store of energy and must above all endeavour to preserve the special modes of transformation of energy operating in it against the effects threatened by the enormous energies at work in the external world [ . . . ]. (Freud 1984: 299)

The proximity to Simmel's blasé attitude is strong. While Freud (1984: 295) never tried to historicize his theory, Benjamin (2003: 317) doesn't hesitate to address this lack, acknowledging that he seeks to 'apply' Freud to situations 'far removed from the ones he had in mind when he wrote'. For Benjamin, the central problem is the effect on experience of the new living environment dominated by the 'shocks' of big city life. Shock can be mastered retroactively by way of recollection or dreams, but as a rule, the reception of shock falls to consciousness. Borrowing Freud's model of consciousness as 'stimulus shield', Benjamin (2003: 319) contends:

> The greater the shock factor in particular impressions, the more vigilant consciousness has to be in screening stimuli; the more efficiently it does so, the less these impressions enter long experience (*Erfahrung*), and the more they correspond to the concept of isolated experience (*Erlebnis*). Perhaps the special achievement of shock defence is the way it assigns an incident a precise point in time in consciousness, at the cost of the integrity of the incident's contents. This would be a peak achievement of the intellect; it would turn the incident into isolated experience.

In other words, habituation to shock enables consciousness to 'screen' external stimulation more efficiently by locating it in a unilinear chain according to the historicist model of temporality. As a result, rather than entering 'long experience' in which individual memory and the collective past are intermingled, habituation allows stimulation to be reduced to the isolated individual experiences that Simmel described as intellectualism, or more ominously, the blasé attitude.

This understanding of shock as the symptomatic experience of the modern city underlies the importance Benjamin placed on the concept of 'distraction'.[17] Distracted perception was 'tactile' rather than 'optical', 'habitual' rather than 'conscious' (2003: 268). 'Distracted' perception was characteristic of architecture but also of cinema:

> Reception in distraction – the sort of reception which is increasingly noticeable in all areas of art and is a symptom of profound changes in apperception – finds in film its true training ground. Film, by virtue of its shock effects, is predisposed to this form of reception. It makes cult value recede into the background, not only because it encourages an evaluating attitude in the audience but also because, at the movies, the evaluating attitude requires no attention. The audience is an examiner but a distracted one. (Benjamin 2003: 269)

As Wollen (1993: 51) notes, Benjamin goes against the grain when he places distraction at the service of reason rather than its opposite. Benjamin's counter-intuitive move was to argue that, insofar as reception could be removed from conscious attention, the efficiency of the habitual 'stimulus shield' would be reduced. In this way, individual experience could potentially be reconnected to collective history. For Benjamin, any prospect of overcoming the contradiction between voluntary and involuntary memory depended first upon breaking with the positivistic understanding of history as a procession of neutral facts. Only when there was appreciation of both the content of history *and* the stake that the present has in the presentation of that past could there be reconciliation between individual and collective experience. It is from this perspective that he criticizes the reduction of the wisdom of the story to the informational mode of the newspaper, and argues instead for the pedagogical value of the dense associations embedded in 'dialectical images', particularly those sedimented in the material past of the city.[18]

Benjamin believed that film's capacity to bring these urban experiences before a mass audience gave it a unique potential to address contemporary life at a critical moment in history. It is from this perspective that the full weight of the concept of the 'optical unconscious' introduced in the 'Artwork' essay can be appreciated: the distracted perception characteristic of film was the key to unlocking the latent historical energy accrued in particular sites and modes of urban experience. With its capacity to address a collective audience, cinema could transform the lessons of the artistic *avant-garde* into a genuine political force. As Benjamin (2002: 116; 2003: 264) expresses it: *'The extremely backward attitude to a Picasso painting changes into a highly progressive reaction to a Chaplin film.'*

### Filming the city in fragments

The close alignment that Benjamin posits between film and urban experience reached a certain peak in the city-symphony films of Ruttmann and Vertov.

There are striking similarities between the two films. Both begin at dawn, show the gradual wakening of the city, the dynamism of street life, the transformation of labour by machine technology and conclude their 'day-in-the life' with demonstrations of sport and leisure. Neither film is concerned with private life, eschewing the interior of the home for the public spaces of the street. Each deployed innovative techniques for filming street life without being observed.[19] The two films also share strong formal similarities in terms of their preference for a *constructed* realism achieved via montage. While *Berlin Symphony* is notable for its rhythmic montage, *Man with the Movie Camera* exceeded it in almost every respect in its celebration of what Moholy-Nagy called 'vision in motion'. Vertov's city is built, according to the principle of Kuleshov's 'creative geography', from footage shot in Moscow, Odessa, Kiev and Kharkhov, and his film employs the full compendium of *avant-garde* techniques, utilizing unfamiliar angles, split-screen techniques, crescendos of ultra rapid montage, freeze-frame sequences, fast and slow motion, and 'subjective' point of view camera shots – in short, the entire cinematic arsenal that Benjamin conceptualized in terms of film dynamite.

Each film lavishes particular attention on the role of machines in production, transport and communication. Both have key sequences featuring the modern 'march of the machines', reflecting the dominance Fordism and Taylorism had achieved, coalescing into a worldview capable of bridging capitalism and communism.[20] In Ruttmann's film, the factory is depicted as a mechanical paradise in which workers are either absent or irrelevant. The workers that Ruttmann does show belong to the new class of white-collar employee who formed the subject of Kracauer's *die Angelstellten* (1930). Using montage to juxtapose a variety of different actions and reactions, Ruttmann underlines the extent to which the office, as much as the factory, has been subjected to the accelerated rhythms of the machine. Shots of typewriter keys being struck signal a crescendo of images alternating between manual and automated telephone exchanges. Vertov's film also features innumerable shots of cogs, flywheels, crankshafts and pistons shown with rapt attention to their 'mechanical ballet'. By 1929 this was already something of a cliché. But, unlike Ruttmann, Vertov also foregrounds the relation between worker and machine. While his ambition was no doubt to show unalienated labour, the sequences of women packing cigarettes, or working the telephone switchboard, seem far more ambivalent today. Despite their smiles, the workers' rapid repetition of unskilled tasks smacks of industrial *training* in Marx's pejorative sense.

As Gilbreth's chronophotography had demonstrated as early as the 1880s, the camera was an extremely useful tool for the Taylorist reconstruction of factory labour. Writing in 1914, Lenin (1964: 152–53), who was an enthusiastic advocate of Taylor, noted the way cinema was used in the West to improve production:

> The cinema is systematically employed for studying the work of the best operatives and increasing its intensity, i.e , 'speeding up' the workers [ . . . ]

> A newly engaged worker is taken to the factory cinema where he is shown a 'model' performance of his job; the worker is made to 'catch up' with that performance. A week later he is taken to the cinema again and shown pictures of his own performance, which is then compared with the 'model'.

Lenin argued that capitalism meant that these feedback mechanisms were introduced to the detriment of the workers, only intensifying their exploitation. Such contradictions were presumed to be dissolved by socialism.[21] Not everyone accepted this standpoint. For example, in Fritz Lang's blockbuster *Metropolis* (1927), released the same year as *Berlin Symphony*, the giant machines powering the city are portrayed as Moloch consuming human sacrifices. If this metaphor echoed Marx's (1863) description of the way capital appeared to classical economists, the comparison situates the political limits of the unconvincing mediation between head and hand at the climax of Lang's film. In the Soviet Union, Ilya Ehrenburg's 1976 novel *The Life of the Automobile*, published the same year *Man with a Movie Camera* was released, presented a far bleaker image of the Fordist production line:

> The worker doesn't know what an automobile is. He doesn't know what an engine is. He takes a bolt and tightens a nut [ . . . ] Upwards to the right, half a turn and then down. He does this hundreds, thousands of times. He does this eight hours in a row. He does it all his life. And that's all he ever does. (Ehrenburg 1976:19)[22]

But unlike these contemporaries, neither Ruttmann nor Vertov display a critical standpoint towards machine production. If the former focuses on machines to the exclusion of workers, the latter, working in a context where industrialization was still largely a dream, desires only further acceleration of machines to remake social life. The concluding sequence of *Man with the Movie Camera* shows 'life speeded up' in an image of the mechanically liberated future.

Outside the realm of labour, the emblematic element of both films is their observation of the ebb and flow of street life. Each film make extensive use of rapid montage to reveal the shifting contrasts and rhythmic patterns of transitory urban phenomena. Key sequences explore the movement of crowds. In order to successfully exploit economies of scale, Fordism demanded the spatial concentration of mass labour forces in factory and office complexes. This created the conditions for the emergence of urban commuting, and a new dependence on mass transit systems able to rapidly convey large numbers of workers to centralized workplaces. *Berlin Symphony* begins its film-day with the first trams setting out from their sheds. Occasional workers appear walking through the dawn streets. Gradually the number of pedestrians swells. Those on foot are joined by those on bicycles, trams and buses. Eventually large crowds congregate at train stations, the site at which women and men,

Figure 3.1 *Walther Ruttmann (1927)*, Berlin, Symphony of a Great City
(a) *Urban commuters, (b) Berlin street scene, (c) The modern office (d) Window displays. (Courtesy Film Preservation Associates and Eva Riehl.)*

blue- and white-collar workers, urban and country dwellers, all meet. While Vertov's film offers a looser chronicle of the day, its *leit-motif* is the complex interaction of pedestrians, trams and other vehicles in a crowded plaza. The scene is repeated numerous times with different techniques and emphases, much to Mikhail Kaufman's (1979: 69) chagrin: 'Do you remember that interminable number of trams?' Both films reveal the extent to which the movement of the crowd, which had inspired fear and fascination in the contemporaries of Baudelaire and Poe, had been partially controlled by new forms of collective coordination. In Simmel's (1997: 177) terms, the timetable becomes the impersonal means for mastering urban heterogeneity:

> The relationships and affairs of the typical metropolitan usually are so varied and complex that without the strictest punctuality in promises and services the whole structure would break down into an inextricable chaos. Above all, this necessity is brought about by the aggregation of so many people with such differentiated interests, who must integrate their relations and activities into a highly complex organism. [ . . . ] Thus the technique of metropolitan life is unimaginable without the most punctual integration of all activities and mutual relations into a stable and impersonal time schedule.

If the timetable provided one level of abstract organization to combat the contingency of the streets, montage offered another. In the famous 1923

Figure 3.2    *Dziga Vertov (1929)*, Man with the Movie Camera
*(a) The camera over the city, (b) The accelerated office,*
*(c) Trams (d) Reflexive cinema – the audience at work. (Courtesy*
*Film Preservation Associates.)*

manifesto 'Kinoks: A Revolution', Vertov (1984: 18–19) outlined the strategy which will be put to work in *Man with the Movie Camera*:

> A day of visual impressions has passed. How is one to construct the impressions of the day into an effective whole, a visual study? If one films everything the eye has seen, the result, of course, will be a jumble. If one skilfully edits what has been photographed, the result will be clearer. If one scraps bothersome waste, it will be better still. One obtains an organised memo of the ordinary eye's impressions.

This 'organized memo' based on the selection and juxtaposition of shots constitutes one of several levels of montage that Vertov practised.[23] The crucial point is the aim for the visual impressions to exceed the simple record of a human eye. The machine eye, with its capacity for accelerating and decelerating action and reaction, is able to penetrate the visible world in the manner of the experimental scientist:

> The mechanical eye, the camera, rejecting the human eye as crib sheet, gropes its way through the chaos of visual events, letting itself be drawn or repelled by movement, probing, as it goes, the path of its own movement. It experiments,

distending time, dissecting movement, or, in contrary fashion, absorbing time within itself, swallowing years, thus schematising processes of long duration inaccessible to the ordinary eye.

If Vertov's machine still relies on a human controller, their relationship is not ruled by the familiar master–slave relation. The controller needs to guide the machine, but also to trust it in order to learn from it.

Aiding the machine-eye is the kinok-pilot, who not only controls the camera's movements, but entrusts himself to it during experiments in space. And at a later time the kinok-engineer, with remote control of cameras.

In 'We' Vertov (1984: 7–8) claimed: 'The "psychological" prevents man from being as precise as a stopwatch; it interferes with his desire for kinship with the machine.' This Constructivist desire for fusion of 'man' and 'machine' was propounded with a similar ambition to Benjamin's film dynamite:

The result of this concerted action of the liberated and perfected camera and the strategic brain of the man directing, observing and gauging – the presentation of even the most ordinary things will take on an exceptionally fresh and interesting aspect.

### The limits of montage

Vertov's ambition was explicitly didactic: to draw contrasts between the old and the new, the past and the future, what exists in the present and what *should* exist. To this end, *Man with the Movie Camera* is structured around a series of contrasts between the 'new man' and the 'NEP man', the active and inactive body, the 'productive' woman worker and her 'unproductive' counterpart concerned with her make-up, the 'old' leisure of alcohol consumption – a scene in which the camera famously becomes 'drunk' – and the new workers' clubs featuring collective social spaces for rational recreational pursuits such as chess. By contrast, Ruttmann ostensibly avoided taking an explicit stance towards his subject matter. *Berlin Symphony* belonged to the *neue sachlichkeit* aesthetic which swept Germany in the mid-1920s in reaction to the magnified emotions of Expressionism and the overt hostility of Dada. Rather than using montage to underline political contrasts, Ruttmann aimed rather to provide a catalogue of urban diversity. When interviewed in 1939, cameraman Karl Freund outlined this expansive ambition:

I wanted to show everything. Men getting up to go to work, eating breakfast, boarding trams or walking. My characters were drawn from all walks of life. From the lowest labourer to the bank president. (Quoted in Kracauer 1974: 183)

In Kracauer's (1974: 181) terms, *Berlin Symphony* was the prototype of films which attempted to present a 'cross-section of some sphere of reality' in seemingly neutral terms. Yet, despite their apparent difference in political stance, the films share a deeper similarity which indexes a critical shifts in urban perception. As the linking of multiple shots through montage became an intelligible and emotionally satisfying way of organizing the shocks characteristic of modernity, film came to crystallize a heterogeneous array of fragmentary perceptions and intuitions about the city into affective experience. Cinema provided a means by which multiplicity and movement could be negotiated, offering the potential for mapping processes and patterns which resisted traditional forms of representation. In short, montage constituted cinema's formal equivalent to the shock effect of the big city. This equivalence situated its ambivalent effects.

While the convergence between form and content in Ruttmann's film might have been expected to appeal to him, Kracauer's (1974: 186) 1928 review was largely unfavourable. His principal criticism was not that the film fragments urban life but the fact that they remain unredeemed:

> Ruttmann, instead of penetrating his immense subject-matter with a true understanding of its social, economic and political structure [ . . . ] records thousands of details without connecting them, or at best connects them through fictitious transitions which are void of content. [ . . . ] The symphony fails to point out anything, because it does not uncover a single significant context.

The 'significant context' that Kracauer had in mind was the class society on which modern urban–industrial life was based. To be fair to Ruttmann, class divisions feature regularly in *Berlin Symphony*, which devoted much energy to contrasting similar acts performed by different groups, from people eating lunch or going out at night to children playing. The nub of Kracauer's criticism is that these juxtapositions serve no deeper purpose, merely demonstrating the manner in which different elements of urban life coexist side by side. He offered a far more sympathetic reading of *Man with the Movie Camera*, although the grounds for his preference seem less convincing today:

> [Vertov] is the son of a victorious revolution, and the life his camera surprises is Soviet life – a reality quivering with revolutionary energies that penetrate its every element. This reality has a significant shape of its own. Ruttmann, on his part, focuses upon a society which has managed to evade revolution [ . . . ] It is a shapeless reality, one that seems to be abandoned by all vital energies. (Kracauer 1974: 185–86)

Even as Kracauer wrote these words in 1928, the Soviet life 'quivering with revolutionary energy' was fast fading. Stalin was rapidly consolidating his control over the party. Mayakovsky shot himself in 1930, signalling the submission of radical experimentation in art and culture to the reactionary dogma of 'socialist realism'. Like many others of the 1920s avant-garde, Vertov soon found himself politically isolated and unable to work regularly.

Yet, even though Kracauer's declared reason for preferring Vertov over Ruttmann seems dubious, his suggestion that Ruttmann's film is a merely catalogue of details without context provides a useful starting point for assessing the political limits of montage. As Kracauer argued in his 1927 essay on 'Photography', when discussing the 'blizzard' of images which subsumed the modern world, as much as the technological image can blow everyday reality apart in order to reveal its hidden springs, it can also render the disconnected fragments seductive and inevitable. Kracauer (1995: 436) added:

> It is therefore incumbent on consciousness to establish the *provisional status* of all given configurations and perhaps even to awake an inkling of the right order of the inventory of nature.

While montage, with its capacity to fracture and reassemble the visible world, offers an invaluable lever for establishing the provisional status of 'all given configurations', the second step – establishing 'an inkling of the right order' – is more problematic. The same problem is restated time and again by the most perceptive analysts of technological images of the period, including Kracauer and Benjamin in Germany and Alexei Gan and Sergei Eisenstein in the Soviet Union. Fragmentation is both the alienated condition of modern urban-industrial life, but also a primary technique for its analysis and disputation. However, to be effective, fragmentation must be a way station rather than a final destination. In contrast to the postmodern suspicion that fragmentation might constitute an *irreducible* condition, these dialecticians insisted that the 'right order' remained to be established.

Eisenstein's (1963: 17–18) incisive observation about the 'trouble' with montage – 'no matter how unrelated [two shots] might be, and frequently despite themselves, they engendered a "third something" and became correlated when juxtaposed according to the will of an editor' – expresses the general condition that image and meaning enter in modernity. For Eisenstein, instability of meaning could only be countered by the discipline of the correct political ideology permeating every aspect of a film.[24] Gan's 'Constructivism in Cinema' (1922), which strongly influenced Vertov, proposes a similar solution:

> Film which demonstrates real life in a documentary manner – not theatrical film playing at life – this is what the new cinematic production should be. [ . . . ] But it is not enough to link individual moments of episodic phenomena of life through montage. The most unexpected accidents, occurrences, and events are always connected organically with the fundamental root of social reality [ . . . ] Only on this basis can one construct a vivid film of dynamic and concrete reality that substantially departs from the superficial newsreel. (Quoted in Petric 1987: 13)

Benjamin (1999a: 526) also reached a similar conclusion when he explicitly opposed the 'constructive' photography of Russian film to the 'creative' photography typified by Albert Renger-Patsch's popular book *The World is Beautiful* (1928):

> *The world is beautiful* – that is its watchword. Therein is unmasked the posture of a photography that can endow any soup can with significance but cannot grasp a single one of the human connections in which it exists [ . . . ].

If this echoes Kracauer's criticism of *Berlin Symphony*, Benjamin's advocacy of 'constructed' photography drew more heavily on Brecht:

> As Brecht says: 'The situation is complicated by the fact that less than ever does the mere reflection of reality reveal anything about reality. A photograph of the Krupp works or the AEG tells us next to nothing about these institutions. Actual reality has slipped into the functional. The reification of human relations – the factory, say – means that they are no longer explicit. So something must in fact be built up, something artificial, posed.' (Benjamin 1999a: 526)

Here Benjamin situates a critical shift in 'actual reality' which complicates the modern politics of 'realism'. Even if the aim is to reveal what Gan called 'concrete reality', the method cannot be direct. Accepting the necessity of 'building something up' through a montage of fragments assumes an understanding of the world as susceptible to fragmentation that was unimaginable prior to modernity. In an intellectual sense, the shift to montage constitutes an aesthetic analogue to the analytical disposition of modern science. But what Benjamin described as the 'second degree' illusion of film corresponded equally to profound changes in lived experience as the industrial city displaced 'nature' as the primary lived environment. The fundamental ambivalence of film's dynamite pivots not on its capacity to fragment the world, but on the uncertainty as to how the fragments might be reassembled into the 'right order'.

Adorno was highly critical of the reliance Benjamin and Kracauer placed on the radical potential of montage.[25] In *Dialectic of Enlightenment* (1973: 126–27), he and Horkheimer seriously questioned 'the viability of a procedure based on the principle of shock', equating lack of time for contemplation with spectatorial automatism. Later, in *Aesthetic Theory* (1984: 223) he argued that, even if montage was once a radical technique, it had been 'neutralized':

> The principle of montage was supposed to shock people into realizing just how dubious any organic unity was. Now that the shock has lost its punch, the products of montage revert to being indifferent stuff or substance. The method of montage no longer succeeds in triggering a communicative spark between the aesthetic and the extra-aesthetic; the interest in montage has therefore been neutralized [ . . . ].

While Adorno raises a pertinent issue about the way habituation can blunt a radical effect, he occludes the dialectical quality of the thesis that Benjamin and Kracauer were proposing. Both were far more attentive to the ambivalence of cinema than is often acknowledged. Each was acutely aware that failing to utilize the new cultural dynamic generated by technological images to achieve radical political change was potentially catastrophic. As Kracauer makes clear in the 'Mass Ornament' (1926), the formal process of fragmentation enacted in cinematic montage is neither inherently progressive nor reactionary. Failure in what he memorably dubbed the 'go-for-broke' gamble of history would be marked by capital sitting down 'at the table of consciousness', presaging an unprecedented integration of self with commodity in the 'Mass Ornament'.[26] Equally, for Benjamin, film is *both* a symptom of the hold of modern technology over consciousness, *and* a key to unlocking that hold. Failure to utilize this potential would be measured by the imposition of new forms of sensory training and the rise of the aestheticized politics of fascism.

A line deleted from the final version of the 'Artwork' essay rings with this ambivalence: 'The most important social function of film is to establish equilibrium between human beings and the apparatus' (Benjamin 2002: 117). The crucial question is the terms on which this 'equilibrium' will be established. In 'Some Motifs in Baudelaire', Benjamin (2003: 328) offered a rather more sanguine view of cinema than the 'Artwork' essay proposed:

> There came a day when a new and urgent need for stimuli was met by film. In a film, perception conditioned by shock [*chockförmige Wahrnehmung*] was established as a formal principle. What determines the rhythm of production on a conveyor belt is the same thing that underlies the rhythm of reception of film.

While the first part of this quote simply reiterates his position, established as early as 1927, that film is the historic reply to the conditions of modern life, the final comparison to the conveyor belt suggests a less heroic trajectory. Here film is aligned, not with the 'dynamiting' of the social world by laying bare the material conditions of everyday existence in 'a meaningful and passionate way', nor with revealing its 'optical unconscious', but has become part of the system of industrial 'training'. If such an alignment points towards new forms of evaluation of social life, it also risks the further destruction of 'long experience' [*Erfahrung*]. In the passage from the 'Baudelaire' essay describing the pedestrian as 'electrically charged', Benjamin (2003: 328) adds:

> Whereas Poe's passers-by cast glances in all directions, today's pedestrians are obliged to look about them so that they can be aware of traffic signals. Thus, technology has subjected the human sensorium to a complex kind of training.

While training is necessary for survival in modern conditions, the risk it creates is the wholesale submission of the human to the technological. This ambivalence is made clearer by Benjamin's comments on film as a form of mechanized aptitude test in the 'Artwork' essay. In the 1936 version, he argues that the film actor is in a unique position: in contrast to everyday working life, the technological apparatus is placed at his (or her) service.

> Meanwhile, the work process, especially since it has been standardized by the assembly line, daily generates countless mechanized tests. These tests are performed unawares, and those who fail are excluded from the work process. But they are also conducted openly, in agencies for testing professional aptitude. (2002: 111)

However, aptitude tests are unable to be displayed publicly and collectively. This is 'precisely where film comes into play'. For Benjamin (2002: 111): '*Film makes test performances capable of being exhibited, by turning that ability itself into a test.*' The 'ability' to which Benjamin refers is the actor's ability to maintain the appearance of humanity in the face of the camera-apparatus:

> To perform in the glare of the arc lamps while simultaneously meeting the demands of the microphone is a test performance of the highest order. To accomplish it is to preserve one's humanity in the face of the apparatus. Interest in this performance is widespread. For the majority of city dwellers, throughout the workday in offices and factories, have to relinquish their humanity in the face of the apparatus. In the evening these same masses fill the cinemas, to witness the film actor taking revenge on their behalf not only by asserting his humanity (or what appears to them as such) against the apparatus, but by placing the apparatus in the service of his triumph. (2002: 111)

By 1939 this section had been shortened significantly, with the remarks on the aptitude test being relegated to the footnotes. Nevertheless, Benjamin still posits the spatial displacement created by the camera as the key both to the destruction of aura through the abolition of distance, but also to the constitution of a new type of collective *participation*. The fact that the actor's performance takes place in the absence of the audience 'permits the audience to take the position of a critic'.

> The audience's empathy with the actor is really an empathy with the camera. Consequently, the audience takes the position of the camera; it's approach is that of testing. This is not an approach compatible with cult value. (2003:260)

However, while the liquidation of cult value is still seen as progressive, Benjamin's appraisal of the political tendency of cinema has become more hesitant. The 'shrivelling' of the actor's aura is reactively compensated by 'artificially building up the "personality" outside the studio' (Benjamin 2003: 261). The fact that the cult attitude of art lives on in the cult of movie stardom limits the 'revolutionary merit' of current cinema to its critique of traditional concepts of art, and occasional forays into criticism of social conditions and property relations.[27]

In some respects, Benjamin's ambivalence towards film mirrors the ambivalence of the Left towards the progressive role of 'Fordism' and 'Taylorism'. By the 1920s major figures such as Lenin and Gramsci were staunch advocates of the socialist transformation of industrial production along similar 'rational' lines to what was occurring in the United States, a tendency which would be institutionalized with the first Soviet 'Five Year Plan' of 1929. As Wollen (1993: 51) notes, Gramsci even treats Taylor's notorious quip about a 'trained gorilla' being able to perform the mechanical tasks of rationalized labour as a precondition for freeing the worker's mind for intellectual speculation. However, Benjamin's evocation of cinema as a training mechanism for modern society arguably owes more to Marx than to Left-Fordism. While Marx extolled the historically progressive role of capitalism in terms of the 'liquidation' of feudal society, and saw the system of factory production as instrumental in assembling the masses as a political force, he harboured few illusions as to the effect of the factory on workers' well-being.[28] When Benjamin uses the term training, he is clearly drawing on Marx's unfavourable contrast between 'training' and 'practice'.[29] Where practice depends on skills acquired over time from experience, training belongs to the strict division of labour and the fragmentation of work tasks. In Marx's (1977: 548) analysis of machine production: 'It is not the worker who employs the conditions of his work, but rather the reverse, the conditions of work employ the worker.' Benjamin (2003: 328) adds: 'The unskilled worker is the one most deeply degraded by machine training. His work has been sealed off from experience; practice counts for nothing in the factory.'

In the absence of fundamental political and economic change, the energies unleashed by the destruction of aura through the new technological apparatus could be directed towards radically different ends than the 'rationalization' of social life. Benjamin's (2003: 269) conclusion in the 'Artwork' essay pointing to the fascist *aestheticizing of political life* makes one possible trajectory clear:

> Imperialist war is an uprising on the part of technology, which demands repayment in 'human material' for the natural material society has denied it. Instead of draining rivers, society directs a human stream into a bed of trenches; instead of dropping seeds from airplanes, it drops incendiary bombs over cities; and in gas warfare it has found a new means of abolishing aura. (2003: 270)

While 'mass reproduction' created the democratic potential for ordinary people to 'come face to face with themselves' via the camera apparatus, the difference between the fascist 'aestheticization of politics' and Benjamin's riposte that 'Communism [ . . . ] politicizes art,' proved extremely difficult to stabilize. Where Benjamin's positive reference point in the 'Artwork' essay was the Soviet film-makers including Vertov, his footnote describing the 'great ceremonial processions, giant rallies, and mass sporting events' equally evokes the Nazis from whom he was already fleeing. Leni Riefenstahl's *Triumph of the Will*, released in 1935, effectively reinvented the scene of politics for the coming media age, submitting the political event to the camera's 'mechanical test'. It demonstrated the potential to unleash new forms of power by using the technological apparatus not for the destruction of 'aura', but for reinvesting the pseudo-religious energy of 'cult value' in the media spectacle of the Führer.

## Unfinished symphony

Built out of film dynamite at an historically potent moment, the city-symphonies of Ruttmann and Vertov register the profound tensions of the modern transformation of social life. If, for Benjamin, the political effects of fragmentation revolved around the extent to which the assembled shards of perception could generate collective meaning capable of entering individual experience, this was fundamentally a question of the extent to which the 'distracted' perception characteristic of cinema could become the *conscious* basis for recognition of the new conditions of existence.

Writing in 1938, Lewis Mumford was also moved to compare the 'modern city' to a symphony:

> Through its complex orchestration of time and space, no less than through the social division of labour, life in the city takes on the character of a symphony [ . . . ]. (Reprinted in Kasinitz 1994: 22)

On the one hand, Mumford is simply making an observation about the structural divisions of roles and processes that increasingly characterized modern cities. Yet the metaphor of the symphony deliberately evokes a higher unity. It points to the integration of complex differences and the transcendence of potential disorder through the coordination of diverse elements and functions. By 1938, this metaphor signalled less the 'bottom-up' contingency of ephemeral interactions of crowds on the street than the 'top-down' organizational role increasingly reserved for centralized urban planning. The logic of Haussmann's reconstruction of Paris, mixed with the production-line logic of specialization and 'training', had been formalized into the functional planning advocated by CIAM's Athens Charter of 1933, in which city space was to be rationally zoned according to centrally determined patterns of exclusive use.[30]

The city-symphony films of Ruttmann and Vertov stand on the cusp of this trajectory. They reveal the incipient contours of the new industrial order, including the extent to which it might be capable of penetrating aesthetics and cultural life. But they are by no means subsumed by that order. One of the saving graces of both films is that recording public inter-action is still enough of a novelty that people's responses to the camera remain largely spontaneous. The critical difference between the two films is, finally, not the ostensible political tendencies on which contemporary critics such as Kracauer focused, but the distinctive reflexivity of *Man with the Movie Camera*. With its predilection for organizing urban con-trasts into categories, *Berlin Symphony* demonstrated the way in which 'regularized' urban space could be aestheticized for popular consumption as the site of cosmopolitan diversity; an ensemble of places to be enjoyed, or rather *consumed*, as modern spectacle. In this respect, *Berlin Symphony* might be said to adapt the bourgeois subjectivity of the *flâneur* to the accelerated tempo of the industrial city. If mass production was fast transforming the city into a Corbusian 'machine for living in', *Berlin Symphony* gives that machine a compelling aesthetic form.[31] On the surface, *Man with the Movie Camera* constructs a similar vision of the city as machine-spectacle. But, because the material production of cinematic vision is integral to Vertov's analysis of modern life, even though Vertov shares Ruttmann's conception of the city as a machine, his method undermines the potential closure of the metaphor.

Constructing a reflexive filmic space is an integral part of Vertov's materialist conception of the modern social world. As the film demonstrates the process of its own construction, from shooting and editing to the conclusion in which audience collectively views the results in public, the centrality of the cameraman's vision is consistently put in question in favour of an analysis of the relationship between perception and representation. Such stylistic innovations were not well received, and notoriously led Eisenstein (1949: 43) to complain of the film's 'formalist jackstraws and unmotivated camera mischief'.[32]

Where *Berlin Symphony* points towards an orchestrated experience of the city as a kaleidoscope of visual contrasts, Vertov's film points in a different direction: towards his dream of a mobile army of *kinoks* armed with their own cameras who could film big city life in all its diversity. Vertov imagines a media city in which the crowd are not only bystanders and spectators, but producers and participants. If his celebration of machine aesthetics today seems rather overwrought and ominous, his ambition to use film to create reflexive social space remains important. Unlike Zamyatin or Orwell, Vertov is yet to imagine the reach of an omnipresent State which will render technological surveillance a nightmare. The city-symphony film of the 1920s is not yet the highly controlled and controllable image of the digital era, exemplified by the searchable database. Nor has Vertov imagined the transformation of surveillance into a popular spectacle, as the despised 'psychological drama' is grafted onto 'life caught unawares' to create the late-20th-century craze of 'reality TV'.

## Notes

1 Pound 1921: 110; Léger in Schaarf 1979: 314.
2 One of the best accounts of this changed world remains John Berger's 1969 essay 'The Moment of Cubism'.
3 While many of their contemporaries advanced this perspective to some degree, Benjamin and Kracauer both made it integral to their understanding of modernity.
4 For cultural studies approaches to 'cinema and the city' see, for example, Penz and Thomas 1997, Clarke 1997, Shiel and Fitzmaurice 2001, Barber 2002. For

'architecture and film' approaches, as it is usually dubbed in architectural circles see Albrecht 1986, Neumann 1996, Toy 1994, Fear 2000, Lamster 2000.

5   In his 1929 'Letter from Berlin', Vertov (1984: 101–02) described comparisons to Ruttmann's film as 'absurd', arguing that in the Kino-Eye films he had employed action which 'frequently developed from early morning to evening', adding: 'Ruttmann's recent experiment should therefore be regarded as the result of years of Kino-Eye's pressure through work and statements, on those working in abstract film.'

6   Vertov (1984: 163) recognized the proximity of Clair's comedies to his own concerns. In his *Diaries* on 12 April 1926, he wrote:

> Saw *Paris qui Dort* at the Ars movie theatre. It pained me. Two years ago I drew up a plan whose technical design coincides exactly with this picture. I tried continually to find a chance to implement it. I was never given the opportunity. And now – they've done it abroad. Kino-eye has lost one of its attack positions.

7   Other films in the cycle include Joris Iven's *De Brug* (*The Bridge*, Holland, 1928) and *Regan* (*Rain*, Holland, 1929) and Jean Vigo's *A propos de Nice* (France, 1930). The genre continues to reappear every now and then: for example Arne Sucksdorff's *Människor i stad* (Symphony of a city, USA/Sweden, 1948), Francis Thompson's *N.Y, N.Y* (USA, 1958), Godfrey Reggio's *Koyaanisqatsi* (1982) and Hubertus Siegert's *Berlin Babylon* (Germany, 1996–2001).

8   Berman (1982: 193) cites Gogol's 1835 story 'Nevsky Prospect' as an early prototype for the city-symphony, but a more pertinent point of reference is Joyce's *Ulysses* (1922), immediately acclaimed by Sergei Eisenstein as the 'bible' of the new cinema for its experimental montage structure.

9   Kracauer (1960: 31) wrote of the Lumières' early one-reelers: '[T]heir themes were public places with throngs of people moving in diverse directions. [ . . . ] It was life in its least controllable and most unconscious moments, a jumble of transient and forever dissolving patterns accessible only to the camera.'

10  This is the crux of arguments over 'narrative cinema' in journals such as *Cahiers de Cinema* and *Screen* in the 1970s.

11  David Frisby (1985: 3) perceptively describes Simmel as 'perhaps the first sociologist of modernity in the sense which Baudelaire had originally given it'. While Tönnies' distinction between *gemeinschaft* and *gesellschaft* can be clearly felt in Simmel's work, Simmel displayed less nostalgia than Tönnies for the pre-modern world. In contrast to Durkheim's more positivistic concerns, Simmel developed an urban phenomenology which explored modernity as a distinctive mode of *experience*. His approach strongly influenced the next generation including former pupils Benjamin and Kracauer in Berlin, and Park in Chicago. To Adorno's chagrin, Benjamin (2003: 209) still defended Simmel in a letter concerning his Baudelaire essay written in 1939: 'Regarding your sceptical view of Simmel: Isn't it time he got some respect as one of the ancestors of "cultural Bolshevism"?'

12  In their *Project for a Scientific Psychology* (1895), Freud and Breuer conceived the psyche as a relation of forces stratified by the differential excitation of mental particles, regulated by the presumption that consciousness will tend towards establishing equilibrium at the lowest levels of excitation.

13  There is some ambiguity in Simmel's account of the reach of the blasé attitude. On the one hand, it constitutes the most characteristic form of metropolitan life affecting 'every metropolitan child', yet he also suggests only 'certain personalities' adopt it in order to preserve themselves in the urban milieu 'at the price of devaluing the whole objective world' (1997: 179). Implied but not explicitly articulated is a point of psychic balance in which one must be blasé enough to survive urban life, but not so blasé as to lose contact with the objective world.

14   In *Capital* Marx writes: 'Just as in money each qualitative difference between commodities is extinguished, so too for its part, as a radical leveller, it extinguishes all distinctions.'

15   The contrast between *Erfahrung* and *Erlebnis* parallels that between *Gedächtnis* (the collection of often unconscious information) and *Erinnerung* (individual memories). See notes 7 and 11 in Benjamin 2003: 344–45.

16   In *The Condition of the Working Class in England*, Engels (1971: 30–31) noted:

> The vast majority of Londoners have had to let so many of their potential creative faculties lie dormant, stunted and unused in order that a small, closely-knit group of their fellow citizens could develop to the full the qualities with which nature has endowed them. The restless and noisy activity of the crowded streets is highly distasteful, and it is surely abhorrent to human nature itself. Hundreds of thousands of men and women drawn from all classes and ranks of society pack the streets of London. Are they not all human beings with the same innate characteristics and potentialities? Are they not all equally interested in the pursuit of happiness? And do they not all aim at happiness by following similar methods? Yet they rush past each other as if they had nothing in common.

Benjamin (1999b: 427–28) cites this passage in the Passagen-Werk.

17   See also Kracauer's 'Cult of Distraction' (1926), where Kracauer (1985: 326) argues for the *moral* significance of distraction: 'the audience encounters itself; its own reality is revealed in the fragmented sequence of splendid sense impressions.' However, 'this is only the case if distraction is not an end in itself.'

18   Benjamin's critique of news as a mode of information is articulated most cogently in his essay 'The Storyteller' (1936), while his critique of historicism and the concept of historical progress is most explicit in his 'On the Concept of History' (1940).

19   Kracauer (1974: 183) reported of Karl Freund, who was one of the principal camera operators for *Berlin*: 'He would drive in a half-enclosed truck with slots in the sides for the lens or he would walk about with the camera in a box that looked like an innocent suitcase.' Vertov's brother, Mikhail Kaufman (1979: 64), who, along with Vertov's wife Elizaveta Svilova, formed the so-called *Kinoki* 'Council of Three', recalled:

> I made myself up as a telephone repairman. There weren't any special lenses, so I went out and brought a regular camera and removed the deep focus lens. Standing off to the side, I could still get things very close up, and that's why you saw those wonderful faces of the children and of the Chinese magician in *Man with the Movie Camera*.

20   As Harvey (1990: 125–26) notes, the originality of Fordism, and its principal difference from Taylorism, was less its assembly line production or managerial organization than Ford's recognition that 'mass production meant mass consumption.' This was a key difference between the industrial models adopted in the United States and the Soviet Union. Harvey (1990: 127) notes that Fordism achieved relatively little penetration into European factory production prior to World War II where even the car industry remained largely craft-based production for an elite market. However, separation between the planning and control functions of management and the execution functions of labour was well underway in many industries, as was the transfer of skills from worker to machine and from work team to supervisor.

21   Lenin (1964: 156) concludes: 'The Taylor system – without its initiators knowing or wishing it – is preparing the time when the proletariat will take

over all social production and appoint its own workers' committees for the purpose of properly distributing and rationalizing all social labour.'

22 The dehumanizing consequences of the production line were also pointedly satirized in the United States in Chaplin's *Modern Times* (1936). In the opening sequence, Charlie's inability to complete his particular task in the time allotted by the pace of the conveyor belt causes chaos to his fellow workers. Since the machine takes no notice of his working pace, Charlie can never catch up; the phrase 'up to speed' to describe the acquisition of new labour skills becomes literal in the machine environment which constantly evaluates human performance. The deeper psychological cost of the production line to the worker is portrayed through rather anxious humour: Charlie internalizes the machine's routines and acts them out compulsively in inappropriate situations, tightening objects such as the buttons on women's clothes which resemble the bolts he once tightened on the production line.

23 'Montage means organizing film fragments (shots) into a film-object.' Vertov (1984: 89, 99–100) distinguished three stages in what he described as a 'continuous process of editing': inventory, observation and central editing.

24 Whether Einstein's rather Pavlovian desire to direct audiences towards 'final thematic effects' is actually born out in his films is a different matter. The montage in his early films such as *Strike, Potemkin* and *October* in particular points towards the displacement of the omniscient spectator in favour of a much more decentred and contingent mode of perception. While Vertov and Eisenstein saw themselves as fundamentally divided by their differences over the 'acted' film, Vertov's editing practice was in fact far closer to Eisenstein's concept of 'intellectual montage' than either could admit.

25 Adorno (1981–82: 202) strongly regretted Brecht's influence on Benjamin, and later argued that Benjamin's theory was conceived 'with the explicit purpose of outdoing the provocative Brecht and thereby – this may have been its secret purpose – gaining freedom from him'. While Adorno (1981–82: 202) called Kracauer's the 'most plausible theory of film technique', he criticized its 'sociological abstention'.

26 While Kracauer never totally abandons his sense of cinema's political potential, there is a marked difference between his 1920s essays and the post-war books such as *Theory of Film* (1954) for which he is still better known. In a perceptive reading of the genesis of *Theory of Film*, Miriam Hansen (1993: 445) describes Kracauer's transformation from 'a radical Weimar critic into a cold-war liberal humanist', adding: 'Whether this process was triggered by any specific pressures (a number of Kracauer's friends were either victims of McCarthyist persecution, like Jay Leyda, or feared they would be, like Adorno); whether Kracauer's back was broken by his enforced exile and renunciation of his native language, as Adorno asserts; or whether it was perhaps the reinforcement of a life-long tendency to collaborate with the status quo, as Adorno insinuates, is an open question'.

27 The inadequacy of arguing that Benjamin unambiguously favours 'new media', as for instance Poster (1994) does, is demonstrated in Benjamin's (2003: 110–11) 1938 letter to Adorno, where he compares Adorno's analysis of recorded music to his own writing on the revolutionary effects of photography and film:

> In my piece, I tried to articulate the positive moments of this upheaval as clearly as you have done for the negative ones. I thus see a strength in your work where there was a weakness in mine. [ . . . ] It is becoming clearer to me that the launching of the sound film must be seen as the industry's effort to rend the revolutionary hegemony of the silent film, which tended to evoke reactions that were difficult to control and therefore politically dangerous. An analysis of sound film would yield a

> critique of present-day art which would mediate in a dialectical way
> between your perspective and mine.

This passage underlines the need to situate Benjamin's analysis in the historical moment of its production. For a more detailed response to Poster, see
McQuire 1994.

28 This is not only the 'early Marx' of the 1844 Manuscripts where creative labour
is conceptualized as integral to being, but also the 'mature Marx' of *Capital*
which is riddled with descriptions of the dehumanizing impact of factory
production on workers. In these conditions Marx (1977: 481–42) argues that
'The absurd fable of Menenius Agrippa, which presents man as a mere
fragment of his own body' becomes realized.

29 For this reason, I don't entirely agree with Wollen that Benjamin accepts the
progressive character of Fordism with perfunctory argument.

30 The Congres Internationaux d'Architecture Moderne (CIAM) had been
formed in 1928 by twenty-four leading modern architects including
Le Corbusier. The theme of the 4th congress in Athens was 'The Functional
City'. While Mumford was scarcely an advocate of this sort of functionalism,
he nevertheless shared the ambition for centrally planned urban development
as a cure for the ills of the industrial city.

31 In the 'Mass Ornament' (1926), Kracauer had outlined a third trajectory to
Benjamin's polarity between fascism and communism, in which the revolutionary energy loosed by the destruction of aura was harnessed directly in the
service of the commodity. This tendency, pioneered in the mass consumer
society of the United States, produced new cultural forms, exemplified by the
Busby Berkeley musicals of the 1920s in which human motion was tightly
organized into machine patterns. Writing in 1931 about female dancing groups,
Kracauer (1994: 565) commented:

> The girls' poses recall the play of the pistons. They are not so much of
> military precision as they correspond in some other way to the ideal of
> the machine. [ . . . ] When they formed themselves into an undulating
> snake, they delivered a radiant illustration of the virtues of the conveyor
> belt; when they stepped to a rapid beat it sounded like 'business, business';
> when they raised their legs with mathematical precision above their
> heads, they joyfully affirmed the progress of rationalization [ . . . ].

32 Perhaps under the same political imperatives that led to Eisenstein's
uncharacteristically churlish appraisal, Vertov later recanted his approach. In
1958 he defensively described *Man with the Movie Camera* as a 'film about film
language', adding that if the 'means' stand out, it was because the goal was to
acquaint people with the means (Vertov 1984: 154–55). Elsewhere Vertov
(1984: 125) was even more damning: 'In my previous work I frequently
presented my shooting methods outright. I left the construction of those
methods open and visible, Meyerhold-style. And this was wrong.'

# 4

## Liquid Cities

And as the big cities grew, the means of razing them developed in tandem.
What visions of the future this evokes!

(Walter Benjamin 1938)

You will be able to build a building in light so you can walk around and
change it.

(Stephen Coons 1968)[1]

In Alex Proyas' film *Dark City* (1997) a man wakes up in a room with a dead
woman who has been brutally murdered. His memory is hazy, fragmented.
He can't remember what happened. He can't remember his own name. The
film conjures a compendium of *noir* elements – seedy hotels, shadowy streets,
hard-boiled cops, a string of dead women, a hero accused of murder, his torch-
singer wife – all set in what seems to be the *noir* heyday of the 1940s. The
plot, as with so many *noir* tales, revolves around a search for memory and
identity. Underneath the surface of everyday life lurks a massive conspiracy.
Someone – a group of strangers – is after him. They want to kill him, but no
one believes it. His quest to recover his personal identity becomes a journey
into the underbelly of the city, an exposure of its double life.

Filled with an influx of strangers, the modern city became an intoxicating
world of random encounters shadowed by the risk that a single step off main
street could plunge one into an unfathomable abyss. The modern detective
story maps this existential dilemma, stretched between the poles of identity and law. But, as Chandler's Marlowe ponders in 1930s Los Angeles, how
do you remain true to your self when the whole system is corrupt? In film
*noir*, urban alienation is inevitably shrouded with sexuality, and the
problematic spaces of the city are often figured as feminine: seductive,
sphinx-like and dangerous. A lonely man searches among the shifting crowds
for a moral compass. Is redemption to be found in love? Or in death? Who
will pay the price for his desire? In narrative terms, *Dark City* keeps faith
with the *noir* tradition in which the task of redeeming the night-world falls
to a solitary man. The possibility of a broader *social* justice, which animated
Benjamin and Kracauer in their analysis of the radical potential of cinema in
the 1920s, now exists only as repressed longings and symptoms.

The most interesting aspect of *Dark City* is the way that it explores the
logic of brute materialism – the belief that the milieu 'makes the man' – as
a narrative conceit. The 'dark city' of the film's title is revealed as a sociological experiment run by aliens engaged in a Faustian search for the human
soul. This science fiction story is augmented by the science fiction modes of

perception enabled by digital imaging. In a series of bravura sequences, the urban landscape warps and morphs before our eyes: buildings sprout from the ground, rooms stretch and contract, tenements become mansions and mansions shrink to hovels. All that is solid seems to literally melt right before our eyes. The liquid city is born.

In the *noir* tradition, the power relations underpinning the contradictions of the urban milieu are rarely named. Instead, they are routinely displaced, producing a series of dark tales which notoriously find their resolution in punishing the corrupting deeds of a seductive but false woman. On the surface, *Dark City* complies with this tradition. However, read symptomatically, its fable of strange beings who conjure a new city each night, changing it at will for their own ends, evokes the mutation of the older industrial cityscape which proceeded apace with urban redevelopment schemes at the end of the 20th century. The post-industrial wave which flattened the mixed economy of lower Manhattan and gave birth to the World Trade Centre Towers in the 1970s grew into a global tsunami in which the manufacturing facilities and port infrastructure of older industrial centres were swept away by 'loft-living', funky art galleries and urban gentrification.[2] In the process, lives were re-routed, identities altered, whole populations dispersed, subject to seemingly invisible forces which threaten to render the metropolis as malleable as the digital images swimming through it.

While 'creative destruction' has been endemic to the modern cityscape at least since the mid-19th century, the transformations of the late 20th century differed significantly from 'Haussmannization'. First, economic restructuring no longer operated on a primarily national scale, but was globally dispersed across numerous sites and cities. Second, the time-frame separating innovation from obsolescence had further contracted, honing the distinctive modern sensibility conditioned by cyclical loss to razor sharpness. The longevity of urban form which was once taken-for-granted has shifted into a register tinged by the uncanny.[3] How should we understand this new paradigm in which fluidity has emerged as a dominant metaphor, not only in architecture and urbanism, but to describe the condition of contemporary social life?[4]

Throughout the 20th century, *avant-garde* architects dreamt of cities on the move. This ambition was to be realized along a number of different pathways. One was to literally produce portable structures and mobile dwellings.[5] A second approach, originally articulated in the 1920s by Constructivism, de Stijl and the Bauhaus, was to utilize new materials and design strategies to produce multifunction objects and spaces. A third trajectory, prefigured in the light-based experiments conducted by Moholy-Nagy in the 1920s, was to use media to reconfigure spatial ambiance. By the 1960s, the production of flexible 'environments' was increasingly seen in terms of amalgamating the multifunction design principles of modernism with the new media of computers. This convergence of media and architecture introduced a new dialectic affecting urban space, pivoting on issues of technological control, access and agency. While networked computing has since made it increasingly possible to construct user-configured environments which respond directly to their inhabitants, it has also created sophisticated forms of centralized control over urban space and social interaction. If the gaseous dispersion of urban structures is one possibility entrained by digital networks, its other side is the enhanced capacity for tracking individual movements, choices and communications, and aggregating them into searchable databases.

Both the replacement of people by numbers that Kittler (1996: 723) posits as the primary effect of modern media, and the regularization of urban space into controllable forms which inaugurated 'Haussmannization', have been greatly extended through the computerization of culture. The transformation of 19th-century 'statistical society' into 20th-century cybernetics has profoundly altered the relation between information and matter. Where the 1920s 'city-symphony' registered the contingency of urban life, revealing the incompleteness of cinema as a technique for mastering modern urban space, the computer turns film's capacity to record contingent social interactions into an *operational* quality. Digitization transforms camera images into information streams which can be tightly controlled and are potentially tightly controlling. The 'liquid city' generated by the new primacy of mobility in contemporary social relations is not necessarily the expression of new social freedom, but may in fact reflect the generalization of control mechanisms. The feedback loops of digital media can all too easily be configured into a functional totality surpassing the urban unity at which 'Haussmannization' was aimed.

In this chapter, I want to explore the transformation of the cinema–city couplet which characterized *avant-garde* theories of the 1920s industrial metropolis into the new coupling of computer-city. Each coupling produces distinctive ways of conceptualizing and intervening in urban experience. The machine logic of fragmentation, which conditioned the 'shock' experience of the urban dweller, has been redefined in terms of the network logic of flows, feedback and resistances. The abrupt cut of montage has been displaced by the real time melt of morphing, and the sequential narrative ordering of images on a single screen by the simultaneous viewing of multiple 'windows'. Hard buildings have given way to soft cities, structural rigidity to organizational flexibility, stable walls to responsive surfaces, permanent dwelling to nomadism.

In what follows I want to trace the two main trajectories along which the computer has shaped architectural imagination and urban discourse. In the 1960s and 1970s those such as Archigram and Nicholas Negroponte emphasized the potential of computer networks to promote social participation and user-configuration. However, in the 1980s, as 'digital cinema' began to take off, this trajectory was overtaken and largely displaced by visions of the computer as a tool for image-making. Once the process of designing buildings using CAD systems became similar to the process of finishing films on digital workstations, the 1920s metaphor of the 'cinematic city' gained a new generation of adherents.[6] While neither trajectory is entirely separate from the other – and both are conditioned by the heightened instability of urban form following World War II – they manifest quite different understandings of the 'liquid city'. The first points towards a post-industrial society of 'flexible' regimes of production and mass customization. The second promotes an understanding of architecture and the material world in general as radically malleable – an alignment neatly summed up by the internet-driven hyperbole of 'A Magna Carter for the Knowledge Age' (Dyson et al. 1994) which declared: 'The central event of the 20th century is the overthrow of matter.' Both vectors have manifest contradictions. If the first asks us to re-imagine the social bond in terms of the hyper-individualization enabled by ubiquitous digital media, the second belongs to a crisis of urbanism which found a symptomatic outlet in the spate of urban disaster movies driven by digital special effects in the mid-1990s.

What both trajectories leave undeveloped is the possibility that the new nexus between media and architecture might be used to explore new *collective* interactions which are materially situated in urban space. This neglect is somewhat ironic. Even as the menu of special effects such as warping, twisting and morphing, which are deployed to such dramatic ends in *Dark City*, became synonymous with computer design, the rapid growth of digital networks was making computer-led urban democracy a more realistic, if yet unrealized, possibility. The rapid extension of digital networks and the emergence of social networking software over the last decade has not only extended the scale of 'virtual communities' beyond their initial confines, but has also altered their dynamic, as fixed access from home or workplace has given way to mobile forms of public access. What remains in contention is the extent to which this new potential for user-configuration will enable decentralized, collective interventions in urban space, or, conversely, be channelled towards narrower, user-pays models in which communication is further reduced to a commodity.

### Cities on the move

Antonio Sant'Elia's famous *Manifesto of Futurist Architecture* (1914) marked a signal shift in urban discourse. Even as the impact of industrialization became more apparent in terms of the mass and scale of urban infrastructure, Sant'Elia (1973: 170) was eulogizing 'the light, the practical, the ephemeral and the swift'. If, on the one hand, *la citta nuova* was to be fashioned in homage to the massive shipyards and railway stations Sant'Elia extols, the new city's fundamental characteristic would be 'impermanence and transience'. 'Things will endure less than us,' Sant'Elia (1973: 172) proclaimed. While this stance echoed the accelerated obsolescence enforced by capitalist production norms, as the lifespan of goods was reduced to a marketing calculation, it also signalled a fundamental rupture in the relation of architecture to time and movement.

Reyner Banham long ago argued that Sant'Elia was the first to introduce modern architecture to the habit 'of thinking in terms of circulation, not vistas'. Sanford Kwinter (1986: 111–12) sharpens this insight by pointing out that Sant'Elia's vision of a city composed of different intensities – a city *becoming liquid* – was heavily influenced by Umberto Boccioni's theories of physical space. In a series of essays written between 1910 and 1914, Boccioni drew on contemporary scientific developments to posit the modernist *avant-garde*'s most thoughtful aesthetic analogue to field theory. The most radical postulates of field theory were, first, its Riemannian conception of space as both partaking in physical events while also being contained by them, and, second, its conception of time as relative and variable rather than absolute and invariant. As a result, field theory no longer treated space and time as independent properties, but as inextricably merged. Boccioni translated this convergence into his sculptural notion of 'plastic dynamism' in which material objects and the spaces between them were reconceived in terms of their dynamic interpenetration. In his 1913 essay 'The Plastic Foundations of Futurist Sculpture and Painting', Boccioni (1973: 89) proposes:

> Areas between one object and another are not empty spaces but rather continuing materials of different intensity, which we reveal with visible lines which do not correspond to any photographic truth.

These lines do not belong to a traditional space composed of point, line and plane, but are 'force-lines' which map the ceaseless becoming of the world in motion. Sant'Elia's 'new city' is similarly composed of dynamic force-lines which supersede the organizing role of static elements, opening the city to time in a fundamentally different way. Once structures and movement can no longer be separated, it becomes increasingly possible – even necessary – to think the city as what Tschumi (1981) calls an 'event'.[7]

While both Boccioni and Sant'Elia were both killed in World War I, their insights into the dynamic nature of modern urban space were subsequently taken up by those such as Moholy-Nagy and Siegfried Giedion. Moholy's pioneering experiments with kinetic art, such as his Light-Space-Modulator (1922–30), which prefigured contemporary immersive environments, led him to argue for a conception of space similar to Boccioni's:

> The fact that kinetic sculpture exists leads to the recognition of a space condition which is not the result of the position of static volumes, but consists of visible and invisible forces, e.g. of the phenomena of motion and the forms that such motion creates [ . . . ]. The phrase 'material is energy' will have significance for architecture by *emphasizing relations instead of mass.* (1947: 41–63)

Giedion also drew on new forms of motion to propagate the field theory notion of 'space-time' to a much wider audience. In the first edition of his influential *Space, Time and Architecture* (1941), based on lectures he gave at Harvard in 1938–39, Giedion (1967: 826, 831) presented the new 'parkway' and cloverleaf interchanges created in New York by Robert Moses as the climax of modernism:

> As with many of the creations born out of the spirit of this age, the meaning and beauty of the parkway cannot be grasped from a single point of observation, as was possible from a window of the château at Versailles. It can be revealed only by movement, by going along in a steady flow, as the rules of traffic prescribe. The space-time feeling of our period can seldom be felt so keenly as when driving.

Giedion's archetypal modern image of flow emphasized the extent to which the culture of automobility necessitated a break with the stable point of view presumed by classical geometry. While the spatial effect of mechanical vehicles such as trains and automobiles seemed paramount to those such as Sant'Elia and Giedion, the mobility created by screens and networks has since assumed a new urgency in defining urban space. This involves less the supersession of mechanical motion than its re-inscription in the space-time of electronic media.

This trajectory becomes more explicit in the post-war period. Yona Friedman's 1958 *L'Architecture mobile* manifesto catalyzed a new generation of architects across the world, including Constant in Amsterdam and Archigram in London.[8] Like many younger architects, Friedman felt impelled by the explosive post-war growth of cities, and the perceived inability of modernist orthodoxy to deal with the increasingly urgent questions posed by the rapid growth of high-speed transport and instantaneous electronic communications. However, Friedman initiates an important shift of emphasis compared to the earlier *avant-garde*. The mobility he envisages belonged to neither machine nor building, but is rather the result of flexible spatial configurations directed by users. To achieve this outcome Friedman proposed the construction of a 'spatial city' consisting of several elevated tiers of mobile lightweight 'space-defining elements' superimposed over existing cities. In contrast to modern architecture constructed for the mythical 'average man', the spatial city was to be left deliberately unfinished. Friedman (1999: 22) argued: 'The structures that form the city must be skeletons, to be *filled* in as desired'. To this end GEAM's Programme proposed:

> Constructions should be variable and interchangeable.
> The spatial units produced by these constructions should likewise be alterable and interchangeable in their use.
> The inhabitants must be given the opportunity to adapt their dwellings themselves to the needs of the moment. (Reprinted in Conrads 1970: 168)[9]

Far from repudiating modernism, Friedman demanded (like Gropius and Corbusier before him) the full utilization of industrial techniques, including mass production and prefabrication. However, the end result he envisaged was significantly different to that imagined by his predecessors. Not only would the interior walls of Friedman's 'spatial city' be moveable, but also its exterior walls, floors and ceilings. In addition, services such as water and power supply, and garbage disposal, would be easily reconfigured in order to promote greater freedom of movement for residents. Instead of the omniscient architect determining the optimum living environment, this role was reallocated to the inhabitants themselves.

Friedman's themes of nomadism, mobility and user-configured environments were taken up and extended by Constant in his ambitious 'New Babylon' project.[10] Beginning from the presumption of economic plenty predicated on the technological elimination of labour, New Babylon envisages a creative society in which *homo ludens* displaces *homo faber*:

> For the first time in history mankind will be able to establish an affluent society in which nobody will have to waste his forces, and in which everybody will be able to use his entire energy for the development of his creative capacities. (Quoted in Sadler 1998: 136)

As proposed in his 1960 essay 'Unitary Urbanism', Constant's utopia is neither natural nor Arcadian but emphatically urban and technological. Given the huge size of the structures proposed for New Babylon, 'the levels are largely inaccessible to sunlight, so the interior of the city is artificially lit, ventilated and air-conditioned' (Constant 1960: 134). If this echoes Corbusier's faith in the capacity of technology to construct the modern home as a machine for living in, Constant (1960: 134) evinces no nostalgia for the sort of contact with nature which had animated Corbusier's window-walls:

> There is no attempt to effect a faithful imitation of nature, however; on the contrary, the technical facilities are deployed as powerful, ambience-creating resources in the psychogeographical game played in the social space.

Instead of nature, technology becomes the primary means of generating spatial ambiances of varying intensity. For *homo ludens*, space is 'a toy rather than a tool. And as such he wants it to be as mobile and variable as possible' (Constant 1973: 225). In stressing the ephemerality and variability of the environment, Constant sought to recreate the sociability of the old city street, but with a twist. Familiarity of place and stability of social identity would give way to an *avant-garde* existence in which chance encounters and unpredictability were elevated to social norms. If, like Friedman, Constant sought to remake the city as a labyrinth, it was no longer the 'classical labyrinth' which imperiously directed travellers to a hidden centre, but a 'dynamic labyrinth' bereft of fixed coordinates.

> New Babylon is one immeasurable labyrinth. Every space is temporary, nothing is recognisable, everything is discovery, everything changes, nothing can serve as a landmark. Thus psychologically a space is created which is many times larger than the actual space. (Quoted in van Haaren 1966: 12–13)

Where Benjamin saw industrial buildings as labyrinthine in their uniform seriality, Constant's 'dynamic labyrinth' was to be one of ceaseless transformation and perpetual decentring. Disruption of familiar habits and forms of perception would produce psychological disorientation. In the typically uncompromising view expressed by Guy Debord and Gil Wolman (1956, reprinted in Knabb 1981: 13): 'Life can never be too disorienting [ . . . ].' Constant shared this *avant-garde* view of disorientation as the gateway to a new society in which urban development would no longer be driven by capital and bureaucracy, but by widespread participation in shaping the urban environment. In keeping with Debord's (1957, reprinted in Knabb 1981: 25) precept that 'The situation is made to be lived by its constructors,' Constant's plans never developed the detail of contemporaries such as Team X and Archigram. Like Friedman's spatial city, the designs for New Babylon *could* not be prescriptive because the spaces were to be built and inhabited by New Babylonians themselves.

> New Babylonians play a game of their own devising, against a backdrop they have designed themselves, together with their fellow townspeople. That is their life, therein lies their artistry. (1960: 135)

This emphasis on user-participation suggests an analogy to the difference between the broadcast media model of consumer choice and the internet potential for increased user-production.[11] In place of rigid structures and static social forms, Constant (1960: 133) foresaw a technology-enabled nomadism in which private space gave way to social spaces consisting of 'gigantic halls' with moveable walls:

> They are used to construct veritable labyrinths of the most heterogeneous forms in which one finds special halls for radiophonic games, cinematographic games, psychoanalytical games, erotic games, games based on chance and on coincidence. (Constant 1960: 135)

If Constant envisaged people constantly on the move, this was not to accommodate the growing demand for labour market flexibility, but because they were travelling towards new experiences. However, despite the technological revolution of automation, the desired social and political transformation on which the utopia of New Babylon was to be built failed to emerge. After more than a decade of research, Constant was eventually forced to acknowledge the impossibility of building New Babylon in existing social conditions:

> I am very much aware of the fact that New Babylon cannot be realised now, that a way of life the New Babylon project is based on depends on new conditions in the field of economy. Automation now does not mean freedom from slavery and toiling, but poverty and boredom for the workers. (Quoted in Sadler 1998: 153)

This outcome highlights the limits to mobility and disorientation as radical political strategies. Taking these *avant-garde* values largely as articles of faith led to inevitable excesses. Certain pronouncements by Constant assume the chilling overtones of cold-war psychology and 'de-programming': 'A long sojourn in New Babylon would surely have the effect of brainwashing, erasing all custom and routine' (Constant 1960: 135). Any socially progressive role for custom and routine is dismissed without consideration. However, for many urban dwellers, the 'disorientation' resulting from the mobility impelled by post-war reconstruction would soon become a truism with a darker significance. For those who found their social milieu 'détourned' by the extension of commodity capitalism, disorientation was often experienced less as the relief of boredom than as the imposition of a state of unremitting anxiety. In this regard, it is not surprising that one of the characteristics of what Koolhaas (2004: 162) calls 'junk space' is that 'it promotes disorientation by any means possible'. Harnessing the progressive potential of the new forms of mobility which characterize the liquid city demands not only the dislocation of fixed spaces and social hierarchies but also their reconstruction along more inclusive lines.

## Electronic nomads

Where Constant was content to treat the automation of machine production as an established social fact against which the creative agency of the New Babylonian would emerge, Archigram explicitly foregrounded the role of computer technology in their vision of a new urbanism.[12] If Constant saw the liquidation of the static city as fundamental to his ambition for radical social change, Archigram's models of networked urbanism ('plug-in city', 'computer city', 'instant city', etc.) also deployed the rhetoric of nomadism to challenge the 'heroic modernism' of Mies, Gropius and Le Corbusier in the name of pleasure and choice. What distinguished Archigram from many of their contemporaries was the extent of their unswerving faith in new technology. As David Greene put it in a retrospective assessment:

> Behind all the work lies a persistent optimism in technology, pure faith in the future, and scorn poured upon the re-iterations of the modernist dogma [ . . . ]. This is a new terrain in which information becomes almost a substance, a new material with power to reshape social arrangements [ . . . ]. (Quoted in Crompton 1998: 2)

In Greene's words, Archigram sought to create:

> a new agenda where nomadism is the dominant social force; where time, exchange and metamorphosis replace stasis; where consumption, lifestyle and transience become the programme; and where the public realm is an electronic surface enclosing the globe. (Quoted in Crompton 1998: 3)[13]

Realization of this vision demanded more flexible technologies. Flexibility is at the heart of the various 'Plug-In City' projects of 1962–64. As Cook (1999: 38) notes: 'the central implication of the Plug-In city is its open-endedness [ . . . ].' In their approach, Archigram do not so much depart the modern design paradigm established by using interchangeable elements in standardized formats, but reorient it. By coupling the standardization inherent in mass production to the new possibilities for decentralized control enabled by ICTs, Archigram linked the modular design logic of an earlier modernism with a more consumer-oriented model:

> In a technological society more people will play an active part in determining their own individual environment. We cannot expect to take this fundamental right out of their hands and go on treating them as cultural and creative morons. The inherent qualities of mass production for a consumer-orientated society are those of repetition and standardization, but parts can be changeable or inter-changeable depending on individual needs and preferences, and, given a world market, could also be economically feasible. (Reprinted in Cook 1999: 44)

With an aesthetic strongly influenced by developments in aeronautics and rocketry, the 'plug-in city' was designed to enable users to select from a menu of networked services. Various capsules and pods could be connected to different components in order to satisfy different needs. In the editorial from *Archigram 3*, technical obsolescence is seized as a positive sign of a 'sophisticated consumer society':

> Perhaps it will not be until such things as housing, amenity-place, and workplace become recognised as consumer products, that can be 'bought off the peg' – with all that this implies in terms of expendability (foremost), industrialisation, up-to-date-ness, consumer choice, and basic product design – that we can begin to make an environment that is really part of a developing human culture. (Reprinted in Cook 1999: 16)[14]

By the second half of the 1960s, the prefab structures of 'Gasket Home' (1965) and 'Living Pod' (1966) gave way to more radically dematerialized 'piped environments'. These aimed to extend the instantaneity of communication technologies such as telephone, radio and television into networked 'instant cities'.[15] Drawing on Wiener's (1948) cybernetic paradigm, Archigram treated communication largely in terms of command and control, albeit with a 'democratic' flavour. In 'Control and Choice' (1968), the architect's role in building design was discarded in favour of user-directed feedback:

> The determination of your environment need no longer be left in the hands of the designer of the building: it can be turned over to you yourself. You turn the switches and choose the conditions to sustain you at that point in time. The 'building' is reduced to the role of carcass – or less. (Reprinted in Cook 1999: 68)

Computerization provided the missing link for optimizing the 'plug-in city'. It would also be the ultimate medium for the 'piped environment':

> The Plug-in City needed the Computer-City as its shadow, otherwise it could not function. The Control-and-Choice discussion revolved around the potential of the unseen micro-switches and sensors, but more than this: these devices would need the intelligence of a computed relay of information so that they came into your service at the moment when you needed them. (Reprinted in Cook 1999: 76)

In this vision the city is no longer controlled by experts from above, but has become the dynamic networked expression of individual desire which can be reconfigured at will. In spatial terms, older architectural structures ranging in scale from the room to the city would lose their stable contours. As Cook claimed in 1973: 'Our rooms expand indefinitely. Our walls dissolve into impermeable mists or into the imagery of stories and fables and dreams' (quoted in Crompton 1998: 72). The temporal effects of responsive architecture promised to be equally radical. Archigram's stated goal was the total elimination of any gap between the irruption of desire and its putative satisfaction: 'If only we could get to an architecture that really responded to human wish *as it occurred* then we would be getting somewhere' (quoted in Cook 1999: 80; emphasis added). The close resemblance between this dream of responsive architecture, and the investment in 'virtual reality' systems which emerged in the 1980s underlines the extent to which Archigram's dream soon morphed into cyberspace.

## Smart machines

While Archigram's designs remained speculative, a more pragmatic approach to computer design was being hatched at MIT. Nicholas Negroponte's 'architecture machine', first proposed in the mid-1960s, was predicated on the development of intelligent machines capable of entering into a dialogue with human partners. Noting that such machines 'do not exist at this time', Negroponte imagined a future machine becoming an associate rather than a slave. It was from this perspective that he rejected the use of computers to automate current design procedures in order to reduce costs. He equally rejected redesigning architecture to fit current computer technology, a move feared by contemporaries such as Lewis Mumford who decried the machine's 'denatured language'. In contrast to Ellul (1967), who influentially cast computerization as a technique of homogenization, Negroponte (1970: 3) argued that it was only through machine intelligence that the social problems caused by the generalist orientation of modern architecture and urbanism could be addressed:

> Ironically, though it is now difficult for a machine to have adaptable methods, machines can be employed in a manner that treats pieces of information individually and in detail. [A]n environmental humanism might only be possible in co-operation with machines [ . . . ] that can respond intelligently to the tiny, individual constantly changing bits of information that reflect on the identity of each urbanite as well as the coherence of the city.

Negroponte's intelligent machine was conceived as the ultimate agent of mass customization, an orientation which remained consistent in his columns for *Wired* in the 1990s later collected as *Being Digital* (1995).[16] Hence, while he recognized that the CAD systems pioneered by Sutherland's SketchPad (1963) had advantages in terms of their ability to produce unlimited sections and perspectives, he is more concerned with their lack of capacity for evolution and dialogue (1970: 21–22). Negroponte displayed little enthusiasm for the computer's ability to generate new visual forms. In *Soft Architecture Machine* (1975: 73), he declared:

> A myth of computer-aided design has been that computer graphics can liberate architects from the parallel rule and hence afford the opportunity to design and live in globular, glandular freeform habitats. I do not subscribe to this attitude.

History has since proved that many other architects did. As I noted earlier, it remains ironic that the network potential of computers was extolled in architecture at a time when it barely existed, only to be repressed once it became more possible. As computer chips became exponentially faster and cheaper, the function of the computer began to shift from large-scale applications such as payroll administration to other uses, including distributed computing and visualization.[17] But even as internet use was taking off, architectural emphasis on user-configured design and social networks was swept aside in favour of sophisticated computer graphics. As digital design grew from a marginal to a central architectural concern during the 1980s, virtual architecture became increasingly associated with 'globular, glandular, freeform' imagery. Frank Gehry's Bilbao Guggenheim Museum (which began construction in 1993 and opened to global acclaim in 1997) is symptomatic of this shift. Initiated and constructed as the dotcom boom gained momentum, Gehry's project utilized the computer not as a tool for communication but as a technique of architectural mastery. On the one hand, Gehry evinced a disdain for the computer:

> I never liked the computer. I always wondered when it would become obsolete. I don't like the images that come out of them. The architectural profession has been using the computer as a rendering tool and as a sales tool to represent the building to clients. (Quoted in Garfield 1996: 42)

But, on the other hand, Gehry goes on to advocate the computer as a solution to complex design problems such as drawing double-curved shapes:

> We connected with IBM and Desault, which makes the Mirage fighter. In struggling to figure out how to represent these shapes and to demystify them so that you could build them, we hit a gold mine. Because you could all of a sudden take these shapes and explain them to a builder in a way that didn't frighten them. [ . . . ] It puts the architect back as master builder.

While Gehry's casual reference to defence contractors is significant, underlining the longstanding dependence of advanced computing on military research and development, it is his conclusion which is most telling. Rather than decentring the architect by shifting power to either the user (Friedman) or the machine as a collaborator (Negroponte), Gehry celebrates computer technology precisely because it puts the architect back in control. The computer restores architectural mastery by enabling the translation of visionary ideas into visual forms which will not frighten the less visionary builders who must construct it. The unspoken agenda is that the ascendancy of the engineer signalled by Eiffel's tower will be redressed in the era of digital design.

Gehry's vision of digital architecture clearly resembles the stance of George Lucas, who has been one of the leading proponents of digital cinema. For Lucas, the principal attraction of digital technology is precisely the new level of control it offers:

> I think cinematographers would love to have ultimate control over the lighting; they'd like to be able to say, 'OK, I want the sun to stop there on the horizon and stay there for about six hours, and I want all of those clouds to go away. Everybody wants that kind of control over the image and the storytelling process. Digital technology is just the ultimate version of that.' (Quoted in Magid 1997: 52)

For Lucas, digital technology is merely the next logical step in the process begun by the introduction of studio-based film production – a step which was itself designed precisely to control pro-filmic events, and thereby alleviate risk in an environment where filmmaking was becoming more expensive.[18] Digital technology allows not only the replacement of physical sets with blue and green screen, or with 2D and 3D animation, but the extension of technological control to actors themselves who can now be replaced by 'synthespians'.

Clearly, Lucas' vision is not the only possible cinematic future. Nor is it the only trajectory supported by digital technology, which has significantly lowered the economic threshold for entry to film production through its impact on cameras, post-production and distribution.[19] Nevertheless, it is striking how little room Lucas' vision of cinema leaves for the sort of serendipitous and contingent urban encounters that were the principal fascination of the cinema–city coupling proposed by Benjamin and Kracauer in the 1920s. In place of the unexpected and the unanticipated is the highly controlled vision imposed by a master director who can dream of stopping the sun. This contrast highlights the tension which has shadowed the roll-out of digital technology from the beginning in all domains, as its capacity for decentralization is matched at every step by capacity for enhanced control. The fluidity of the digital image which allows new creativity in cinema also allows images to be manipulated down to the level of the individual pixel. The increasing speed and miniaturization of digital technology which render it ubiquitous, and the decreasing cost which lend it an egalitarian hue, are the very ingredients also heightening its potential for control 'from above'. The democratization of digital video cameras, which resembles Vertov's dream of a mobile army of *kinoks* moving through the city, is equally the condition for the increasing submission of urban space to networked surveillance.[20]

Gehry's Bilbao Guggenheim reveals the distance that 1990s digital design had moved from Archigram's 1960s proposals for a 'computer city'. Gehry's lack of interest in the computer as a tool for user-configuration of space led Archigram's Michael Webb (quoted in Cook 1999: 3) to suggest that the rhetoric of fluidity had subsided into merely formal concerns:

> [W]hereas Archigram tried to make what is essentially an inert object, a building, into something fluid, the formal evolution of a contemporary building such as the Guggenheim at Bilbao is the result of the fluid process arrested to create an inert object.

David Greene (1999: 9) was even more biting:

> Despite its contorted form, it does not engage time in the way that a rock spectacle does so effectively. The container yard beside the museum is a better example of late twentieth century architecture.

### Immaterial architecture

This displacement of concern for social relations onto the fluidity of architectural form is symptomatic of what Mosco (2004) aptly dubs the digital sublime. Transcending constraints, even and especially constraints of matter, became a common theme in the 1980s as the concepts of 'cyberspace' and 'virtual reality' flared like skyrockets.[21] Jaron Lanier, who coined the term 'virtual reality' saw it very much as a new 'reality' without constraints. Speaking at SIGGRAPH in 1989, Lanier argued:

> [H]owever real the physical world is [ . . . ] the virtual world is exactly as real and achieves the same status, but at the same time it also has this infinity of possibility. (Quoted in Whyte 2002: 16)

Similarly, architect Michael Benedikt (1991: 131) saw cyberspace as the realization of ancient dreams of overcoming the impediments of matter:

> The design of cyberspace is, after all, the design of another life-world, a parallel universe, offering the intoxicating prospect of actually fulfilling – with a technology very nearly achieved – a dream thousands of years old: the dream of transcending the physical world [ . . . ].

Marcus Novak shared a similar dream. Novak (1991: 228) argued the source of fascination with cyberspace 'is the promise of control over the world by the power of the will. In other words, it is the ancient dream of magic that finally nears awakening into some kind of reality'. For Novak (1991: 227), the sublime magic of cyberspace was characterized not so much by a loss of the body but 'an embodiment of the mind'. But this body would be radically transfigured; not only without organs, but seemingly without limits:

> Thus, while we reassert the body, we grant it the freedom to change at whim, to become liquid. [ . . . ] It is in this spirit that the term *liquid architecture* is offered. Liquid architecture of cyberspace; liquid architecture in cyberspace. (Novak 1991: 227)

While Novak's manifesto, with its emphasis on ephemerality, user-customization and disorientation, owes a clear debt to predecessors such as Sant'Elia, Friedman and Constant, what is most striking is the manner in which he grafts Archigram's fantasy of responsive architecture onto cyberspace. Sharing the cybernetic understanding of information as pure pattern, Novak (1991: 251) acknowledges: 'A liquid architecture in cyberspace is clearly a dematerialised architecture.' Mobilizing the dichotomy between the real and the virtual which characterized so much early writing about cyberspace, Novak (1991: 250–51) envisages an architecture of pure form capable of instantaneous transformation:

> [Liquid architecture] is an architecture that opens to welcome me and closes to defend me; it is an architecture without doors and hallways, *where the next room is always where I need it to be and what I need it to be*. (Emphasis added)

If the description initially evokes something as prosaic as an automated door, it concludes with a more radical agenda in which individual desire enters a realm of perpetual satisfaction. Heightened concern with 'what I need' points towards a future of individually customized worlds. The endlessly mutable cityscape of *Dark City* is not far away.

> Liquid architecture makes liquid cities, cities that change at the shift of a value, where visitors with different backgrounds see different landmarks, where neighbourhoods vary with ideas held in common, and evolve as the ideas mature or dissolve. (Novak 1991: 250–51)

This conception of the liquid city, which directly maps the fluidity of dataspace onto experience of the cityscape, raises fundamental questions concerning the public culture of cities. In cities where 'visitors with different backgrounds see different landmarks', what happens to the function of the street as the common space in which people from different classes or ethnic backgrounds intermingle? Will the unpredictable collisions which Sennett (1977) posited as essential to cosmopolitanism be smoothed away in favour of customized personal environments? If contingent encounters are minimized, will people lose their ability to interact productively and empathetically with strangers?[22]

### The city in ruins

The rise of cybernetics coincided with a fundamental shift in urban thinking. As Kittler (1996: 727) points out:

> The 'invisible city', with which Mumford concludes his world history as the history of the city, consists of more than mere information technologies operating seamlessly and at the speed of light. The computer commands for deletion are also ready to be called up.

By the 1950s, military strategists no longer conceived the city as a citadel to be occupied, but as a target to be destroyed. In 1938 Benjamin (2003: 52) had noted that the growth of the big cities was accompanied by the development of new means of razing them to the ground: 'What visions of the future are evoked by this!' Benjamin's exemplar was Haussmann's attack on Paris. While he wrote this passage under the shadow of the bombing of Guernica, he did not live to see the full consequences of war waged from the air. Kittler (1996: 727) argues:

> The total air war beginning in 1942 reconstituted the urban centres. The module for destruction, however, has ceased to be 'man'. Rather for phosphorous bombs it is a city; for uranium bombs, a major city; and, ultimately for hydrogen bombs, megalopolis.

The impact of Hiroshima and Nagasaki, as well as the fire-storm bombing of London and Dresden, lingered in the cold-war imagination, as military planners attempted to calculate the incalculable: how many cities could you afford to lose and still 'win' a nuclear war? As is well-known, the prospect of nuclear conflict was the major impetus behind the development of the decentred communications network which eventually became the 'internet'. The paradox of the military-led quest for post-apocalyptic order was that it demanded the development of feedback systems capable of providing reflexivity and autonomy. Martin (2003: 7) situates the emergence of what he calls the 'organizational complex', manifested by 'the dispersion of urban infrastructures into an increasingly horizontal network of communication and transportation lines', in relation to the anticipated nuclear disaster. The organizational complex was conceived as a tactical shield not only against external enemies but also the enemy within: 'the disorder that was anticipated with the demise of centralized government and civic authority in the immediate aftermath of a nuclear strike'.

The growth of new communication channels not only paralleled the post-war mutation in which the concentric circles of the modern industrial city gave way to 'junk space', but played an integral role in this dynamic. As Martin (2003: 7) notes, the new communication networks built around principles of self-regulation and self-organization 'in turn helped invent new kinds of cities, new kinds of architectures, and with them a new "self," none of which could be said to possess the traditional spatial properties that divided inside from outside in any meaningful sense'. While the growth of 'junk space' lent communication networks a new social utility, the 1990s saw the paradoxical retreat of architectural discourse from the social networking possibilities of the internet. Where internet enthusiasts such as Rheingold (1993) envisaged 'virtual communities' as the means for recapturing qualities that were being lost in the post-war evisceration of traditional public space, digital architecture was increasingly dominated by 'globular, glandular, freeform' construction. Emphasis on user-configuration gave way to interest in warping and morphing.

Sophisticated digital imaging tools were also increasingly available to filmmakers. James Cameron claimed in 1995: 'We're on the threshold of a moment in cinematic history that is unparalleled. Anything you imagine can be done. If you can draw it, if you can describe it, we can do it. It's just a matter of cost' (quoted in Parisi 1995). Here it is germane to recall exactly *what* filmmakers imagined. Alongside mutation of the human body, one of the most popular tropes to be explored in special effects-dominated cinema was the *city under attack*. If this can be partly seen in terms of a resurgence of the fearful anticipation of nuclear attack, it also registers the increasing sense that the city was dissolving under the combined forces of junk space and global media. While urban catastrophe films have a long history, block-buster films such as *Independence Day* (1996), *Godzilla* (1998) *Deep Impact* (1998) and *Armageddon* (1998) differed in a key respect. Instead of the destruction of a generic city, they showed the obliteration of recognizable buildings and urban landmarks. This shift belonged partly to rapid improvements in digital effects, which enabled them to grow from brief inserts that had to be carefully handled so that their limits did not become apparent, into more complex sequences that viewers were invited to contemplate at length. A second distinguishing feature of these films is that they foregrounded not the aftermath of destruction, but the actual moment of impact. Computer-generated shots showing catastrophic events such as the bombing of the White House, or the demolition of the New York sky-line, were repeated again and again. Film audiences around the world stared the unimaginable in the face, collectively partaking in what Bukatman (1994) aptly identified as a contemporary experience of the sublime.

In 1965, Sartre had scrutinized New York, not through the heroic lens of the 1920s *avant-garde*, but in terms of its inevitable decay:

> Already [the skyscrapers] are slightly neglected; tomorrow perhaps, they will be demolished. [ . . . ] it occurs to me that New York is about to acquire a history, that it already has its ruins.

If Sartre's image of New York's skyscrapers in ruins anticipated the financial crisis which soon led the world's self-styled capital to the brink of bank-ruptcy, the film cycle of the mid-1990s anticipated an event even more unimaginable: the attack on the World Trade Centre towers in 2001. The uncanny nature of this event – disbelief that it could happen combined with the sensation that we had already seen it so many times before – magnified its traumatic effect, producing a compulsion to repeat, or rather *replay*, the image of the moment of destruction. In the United States this compulsion was eventually mastered only by patriotic edicts concerning the impact on national morale.

How should we understand the fascination of these images of urban destruction? If one starting point is the modern conception of the city as a malleable terrain which began with Haussmann, it is the meeting between post-war junk space and the postmodern fear of nuclear attack which aids a more radical sense of the *loss* of the city. In this nexus, the city is rendered susceptible to dematerialization, reconceptualized as a virtual construct of information and images, a target susceptible to digital modulation and potential 'deletion'. Is it worth recalling that Charles Jencks, with tongue only partly in cheek, dated the birth of postmodern architecture from the moment at which the Pruitt-Igoe Towers in St Louis were dynamited? The technique of clearing urban space by using explosives had developed from a World War II necessity into an art form as the demolition of obsolete high-rise buildings became a popular urban spectacle. In Godfrey Reggio's *Koyaanisqatsi* (1982) a whole series of urban demolitions are shown in slow motion. Subjected to the 'testing' of the camera eye, the point at which each building loses its structural integrity and dissolves into liquid, becomes available to human perception. The collapse of the World Trade Centre towers on live television extends this perception of the city's fate into global trauma.

### Liquid societies

Contemporary fantasies of urban destruction proliferate alongside fantastic ambitions for ever-larger scale urban construction epitomized by giant projects such as Malaysia's Multi-Media Super Corridor or China's Pearl River Delta. The city in ruins is the dark side of CIAM's dream of the planned city, and its computerized successor, the dematerialized city of the organizational complex. Neither pole seems an attractive option for a viable urban future. The roll-out of digital networks over the last decade has created the conditions – at least for some of those living in wealthier cities – for the sort of electronic nomadism first proposed in the 1960s to become a social reality. However, the urban impact of heightened mobility in conjunction with the spread of digital networks has all too often resulted, not in the free invention of creative social space as those such as Friedman and Constant wanted, but in the dissolution of the modern city, and its paradoxical reconstruction as a 'liquid city': a city which is often experienced by its inhabitants as a disorienting 'junk space', but which is nevertheless a closely monitored territory under the aegis of the untrammelled market.

This social condition demands a re-evaluation of the *avant-garde* rhetoric of mobility. While Constant's utopic schema had an avowed political intent, it was fatally compromised by his over-commitment to the potential for disorientation to provide a basis for collective life, as well as by his highly deterministic understanding of the social effects of new technology. The problem for those such as Archigram and Negroponte was more their collapse of questions of power entirely into matters of individual choice. Defining urban agency in terms of individual choice not only ignores the need for the collective negotiation of social interactions in shared space, but privileges a consumer orientation which is all too easily incorporated by the culture of mass customization which is the dominant form of contemporary capitalism.

How might we begin to rethink these projects in the context of contemporary 'liquid societies'? As Baumann (2000: 3) notes, the first 'solids' to be liquefied by capitalism were 'traditional loyalties, customary rights and obligations which bound hands and feet, hindered moves and cramped the enterprise'. This phase of liquefaction cleared the way for a new order defined primarily in economic terms. However, over recent decades the process has increasingly moved into the 'micro' level of the social. Baumann (2000: 6) argues that what are now being melted are 'the patterns of communication and coordination between individually conducted life policies on the one hand and political actions of human collectivities on the other'. In Baumann's (2000: 7, 8) terms, this involves the shift from pre-allocated 'reference groups' to the epoch of 'universal comparison' in which 'pattern weaving' increasingly becomes an individual responsibility. If 'choice' is the *leitmotif* of contemporary culture, it is complicated by the fact that the reflexive individual has no choice but to choose. For Baumann (2000: 5–6), this means that the liquidity of contemporary society is, in fact, only a semblance. The 'melting of the fetters to individual freedom' manifested in various neo-liberal policies for 'releasing the brakes' through financial deregulation and 'flexible' production actually results in a new forms of rigidity and lack of *meaningful* choice.

Nevertheless, the social effects of heightened mobility created by the modern nexus between migration and media has also generated new modes of identity which are less defined by presumptions of social and geographical stability. As Paul Gilroy (1990) succinctly puts it: 'It ain't where you come from, it's where you're at.' Clearly, it is rash to simply dismiss the importance of 'place' in favour of nomadism in the manner of the most fervent modern advocates of mobility such as Constant and Archigram. As Marx recognized long ago, de-territorialization and acceleration are fundamental attributes of capitalist expansion. While increased mobility has undoubtedly disturbed traditional social and political arrangements, thus generating the potential for radical change, it guarantees neither the direction nor the outcome. Gilroy's embrace of mobility has a strategic political intent: to stress the migrant's claim to belong in the here and now rather than the past and the elsewhere. The limits of nomadism as a radical value become more apparent as what Virilio (1986) terms the modern 'obligation to move' is extended into a general condition. Questions about who can *choose* to move and who is *forced* to move remain fundamental to the emerging liquid society.[23]

A second point is that fluidity is frequently overstated. As those such as Castells and Sassen pointed out long ago, digital networks involve material instantiations. As much as digital networks generate new forms of flexibility and mobility, they impose new boundaries affecting access and ownership. This is not only about parallels between the ubiquity of passwords needed to gain access to networks, and the construction of border walls, such as those separating Israel from Gaza or the United States from Mexico. It is also about the extent to which agency in urban space is now exercised at the junction between electronic networks and material structures.

As Graham (2004: 155) argues, the hybrid spatial ensembles born of the fusion of media and other urban mobility systems 'become critical and strategic sites at which the very political organization of space and society becomes continually remade'. The free global flow of capital is counterpointed by new systems for intensively regulating social space based on capacity to pay. The growth of digitally monitored urban infrastructure such as tollways result in what Graham and Marvin (2001) have termed 'splintering urbanism' – urban infrastructure which does not serve to unify but to divide populations into segments.

This context suggests the importance of rethinking the relation between flow and structure in the contemporary city. Lars Spuybroek's concept of the 'wet grid' suggests one way this nexus might be reconceptualized productively. Spuybroek (2004: 4) clearly wants to demarcate his orientation from the dematerialized architecture dreamt of those such as Novak:

> The computer has reached a cultural stage, finally. The years that it was used for dreaming of perfect shape grammars and design automation [ . . . ], or worse, used for dreaming disembodied dreams of an architecture floating in cyberspace – those years are over.

While Spuybroek's designs share the 'globular' look of much earlier digital architecture, his work has more in common with the user-configured orientation of Friedman and Constant than the formalist approach of Gehry.[24] Spuybroek contrasts the 'wet grid' to the 'dry grid' of classical geometry, which was predicated on the fundamental separation of structure and movement. The exemplary expression of the 'dry grid' is the Miesian box or hall that uses mass production techniques to produce a generalist architecture 'that can absorb life, chance and change, while the structure itself must last and persist over time, to span the unforeseen with the foreseeable' (Spuybroek 2004: 356). While 'general openness' may work when all events are pre-programmed (e.g., a military barracks), it is fundamentally unsuited to the complex and contingent interactions characterizing big-city life. The aim of the 'wet grid', enabled in part by networked computing, is to displace the 'general openness' of modernism with an architecture of 'vagueness':

> We must replace the passive flexibility of neutrality with an active flexibility of vagueness. In opposition to neutrality, vagueness operates within a differentiated field of vectors, of tendencies, that allow for clearly defined goals and habits and for as-yet undetermined actions. [ . . . ] It is a structural situationism. It allows for derives and detournements as structural properties: the transparent intentionality of planning and habit is stretched by the sideways steps of opaque intentionality. (2004: 357)

A critical quality of what Spuybroek terms 'vagueness' is that it better allows for both formal and informal conduct. Vagueness enables the negotiation of difference.[25] This is the condition of social life in media cities where relational space becomes a social dominant. Social relations increasingly have to be actively made across heterogenous spatial regimes. Unmoored from the 'pre-ordained reference group', such relations are increasingly characterized by what Wellmann (2001) called 'personal networking', a form of social interaction which is highly dependent upon abstract technological systems. If the 'pre-ordained reference group' was already being displaced by informational techniques such as the timetable, which in Simmel's account of big-city life was the dominant form of 'generalized openness' for the coordination of mass society, personal media such as the mobile phone or internet now enable customized coordination. Personal media increasingly replace the general scheduling of broadcast platforms with 'do-it-yourself scheduling'.[26] However, this shift does not so much resolve the problem of the social bond in 'liquid society' as situate it on a new plane. As Sheller and Urry (2006: 7) note, the paradox of personal media is that personal freedom is achieved only through deeper dependence upon complex technological systems:

> As daily and weekly time-space patterns in the richer parts of the world are desynchronised from historical communities and place, so systems provide the means by which work and social life can get scheduled and rescheduled. [ . . . ] The greater the personalization of networks, the more important are systems to facilitate that personalization.

In this context, the loss of communication systems has become, for many, equivalent to the loss of their social networks. If the phone or internet goes down – or if you don't have access, or can't afford to use them, or if you are expelled from a game space for 'misbehaviour' or non-payment of fees – the social interaction can no longer be replaced by walking out on the street, or travelling to a common public place where you might expect to find members of your 'personal network'. No such place of collective assembly exists except via complex media systems. Growing reliance on technological systems to sustain basic social interactions, such as communication between family members, creates the potential for the further commodification of the social bond. As Kwinter (in Hookway 1999: 12) notes, we have already made 'communication' a fetish:

> If, as a culture, we have become morbidly obsessed with communication, it is because the communicational ethics compels, not so much our liberty as our participation in loops of social and psychic (i.e crypto-economic) production.

The fetishization of communication lies not so much in the mundane nature of the bulk of exchanges which take place via email or on mobile phones – these are in fact the grout of everyday life lived 'at-a-distance' – but rather in the extent to which such exchanges are now subject to metering, monitoring and time-based charges.

The long-term social effect of the sort of responsive environments that are increasingly being built in contemporary cities using interactive façades and wi-fi zones is uncertain. Anxiety due to loss of, or separation from, technological systems such as the mobile phone is merely the most visible symptom of the historical transition to what Mitchell (2003) calls 'Herzian' social space. But it is the underlying ambition for perpetual contact and instant response which seems most problematic. It represents the radical extension of the cybernetic goals of communicational transparency and immediacy across the entirety of social space. The emphasis on the present moment which dominates societies mediated by complex technological systems makes it increasingly 'rational' to pursue personal gratification while avoiding the consequences. What goes missing is the extensive temporal horizon needed to imagine collective responses to social problems such as ecological and environmental meltdown.[27] It is increasingly evident that a 'liquid city' with a digital infrastructure oriented towards transparency and immediacy will not produce a social space of 'vagueness' but one of perpetual customization and hyper-commodification. Realizing the promise of Spuybroek's 'wet grid' demands departure from the cybernetic logic of instrumental mastery over the city in favour of spaces and platforms for unplanned, contingent and unpredictable social alignments and interventions.

## Notes

1 Benjamin 2003: 52; Coons in Negroponte 1970: 35.
2 On the development of the WTC see Mosco (2004): 143–75. Of course industrial manufacturing does not simply disappear, but is relocated to low-wage territories with lower environmental standards. On the relation between urban redevelopment and the transformation of the place of art in the city, see McQuire and Papastergiadis (2005b).
3 Codrescu (in Siegal 2002: 11) argues that this sense of impermanence is most deeply entrenched in the United States: 'Grown-ups will rarely visit the places where they grew up because nothing remains of their first home, their grade school, or their tree-house.' Negroponte (1975: 105) points out that the spatial flexibility of the traditional village dwelling 'results from a permanency of home with which most Americans are unfamiliar. In an industrialized society, the pattern is to sell your house and buy a bigger one, then later, a smaller one'.
4 In social theory Castells' (1989) 'space of flows' has become an influential description of post-industrial society, while Baumann (2000) posits a new era of 'liquid modernity'. In architecture, Brodey's (1967) 'soft machines', Raban's (1974) 'soft city' and especially Negroponte's (1970, 1975) 'soft architecture machines' lead directly to Marcus Novak's (1991, 1996) 'liquid architecture'.
5 Portable cottages were constructed as early as the 1830s, while 'factory-made' houses designed for easy assembly became more common in the 1920s. Mobile campers and 'drive-in' architecture emerged in the United States around the same time. See Siegal (2002).
6 In this vein Eleftheriades (in Penz and Thomas 1997: 143) argued that as computers become standard 'the world of architecture will merge imperceptibly with the world of cinema.'
7 While neither Sant'Elia or Boccioni use the term, their work certainly implies a similar meshing of space, architecture and movement to that proposed by Tschumi in *The Manhattan Transcripts* (1981).
8 Friedman began working on *l'architecture mobile* in 1956, but published the manifesto in 1958.

9    Friedman's manifesto was adapted as the Programme for GEAM (Groupe d'Etude d'Architecture Mobile) which began meeting in late 1957 and lasted until 1962.

10   Constant Niewenhuys worked on the 'New Babylon' project for over a decade from around 1958 until 1970. He was associated with the Situationist International for a short time after its formation, but was expelled in 1960.

11   However, as Sadler (1998: 138) points out, Constant maintained a strict modernist separation of 'technical services' from the public spaces of New Babylon. The city's inhabitants would have been ignorant of its supporting mechanisms.

12   London-based Archigram consisted of Ron Herron, Dennis Crompton, David Greene, Michael Webb and Peter Cook. They officially formed as a group in 1963, although the first Archigram magazine was published in 1961. The five principals continued loose collaborations until the early 1970s.

13   This formulation echoed McLuhan's thesis that electronic media would dissolve intransigent urban structures – both material and institutional – in favour of a new nomadism. In *Understanding Media* (1964), McLuhan (1974: 366) argued: 'Before the huddle of the city, there was the food-gathering phase of man the hunter, even as men have now in the electric age returned psychically and socially to the nomad state. Now, however it is called information-gathering and data-processing. But it is global, and it ignores and replaces the form of the city which has, therefore, tended to become obsolete. With instant electric technology, the globe itself can never again be more than a village, and the very nature of the city as a form of major dimensions must inevitably dissolve like a fading shot in a movie.' While Archigram proselytized for electronic nomadism, Greene later acknowledged that: 'it would seem that the electronic nomads of the global financial system demand a permanence in their architecture that they do not require in their business' (in Crompton 1998: 3, 4).

14   While Archigrams extolled the choice available to car buyers in contrast to mass-produced housing, the narrowness of their approach is apparent when set against Debord's observation that such 'choices' do not amount to a choice over the social use of the car.

15   Instant City was presented at *Documenta* in 1972 utilizing holographs and large-screen projections: 'Eventually by the combination of physical and electronic, perceptual and programmatic events and the establishment of local display centres, a "City" of communication might exist, the metropolis of a national network' (Cook 1999: 87–89). Like many of Archigram's projects, Instant City drew heavily on the media-enhanced amusement park.

16   Negroponte's consistent preoccupation has been less architecture than machine intelligence. When he claimed in 1975 that the 'architecture machine' capable of handling 'qualities' rather than merely quantities had already been 'achieved and even superseded', it is in relation to his earlier discussions of machine intelligence that this claim seems most dubious (see Negroponte 1970: 62; 1975: 1).

17   Castells (1996) notes that by the 1990s the cost of processing information had fallen from around US$75 per million operations in 1960 to less than 0.01c. This occurred in several stages. The development of the silicon-based integrated circuit led to a massive 85 per cent fall in the price of semi-conductors between 1959 and 1962. A fall of similar magnitude in the price of cotton during the Industrial Revolution in Britain had taken 70 years (1780–1850). The average price of an integrated circuit fell from $50 in 1962 to $1 in 1971. At that point Intel engineer Ted Hoff invented the microprocessor. Whereas 2,300 transistors could be packed on a chip the size of a drawing pin in 1971, by 1993 there

were 35 million. These exponential increases in computing power radically changed the social uses of computing.

18    This issue was bound up with the need for cinema to transform itself from a fairground novelty to a mainstream entertainment capable of drawing middle-class audiences. The shift to narrative cinema involved the production of more complex films structured around a shifting point of view. This demanded much greater investment in individual films. Industrialization of film production in the studio system exemplified by Hollywood became the primary means for controlling the conditions of shooting, while the development of the star and genre systems as marketing tools became key ways of offsetting the higher investment risk.

19    See McQuire 1997, 2004.

20    See Chapter 6 for further discussion of urban surveillance.

21    The equally rapid disappearance of these terms suggests a lingering embarrassment as to the excesses prophesied in their name. As internet theorist Geert Lovink (2006) asserts, the dotcom crash of 2001–02 meant 'among other things, terms like "cyberspace" and "virtual space" have ended up being tossed into the dustbin forever'.

22    This issue is further discussed in Chapter 6.

23    As I will argue in Chapter 6, the celebration of digital nomadism by those such as Mitchell (2003) ignores such questions.

24    See, for example, the proposal for user-configured housing, OffTheRoad_5speed (1999–2000) in Spuybroek (2004: 115): 'All walls are removable and offer the client the opportunity to alter the house or change functions.'

25    Hence Spuybroek's (2004: 356) rejection of the straight lines that Haussmann carved through Paris and Corbusier celebrated as the epitome of modern reason: 'A curve is a better-informed, intelligent straight line. [ . . . ] It negotiates difference; it is differential precisely through connecting, through continuity. The dry grid is always segmented and Euclidean, while the wet grid is always a continuous network, topological and curved.'

26    This parallels what Beck and Beck-Gernsheim (2003: 3) call the reflexive or 'do-it-yourself' biography as a pre-eminent form of social identity.

27    See McQuire (1998) for a more detailed discussion of the paradoxical emphasis on the 'now' in media cultures.

## Part Two

Public Space: Streets, Lights and Screens

# 5

## Electropolis

Space no longer exists: the street pavement soaked by rain beneath the glare of electric lamps, becomes immensely deep and gapes to the very centre of the earth [ . . . ].

(Technical Manifesto of Futurist Painters 1910)

If you build buildings with lights outside, you can make them indefinite, and then when you're through with using them you shut the lights off and they disappear.

(Andy Warhol 1975)[1]

On the evening of 11 March 2002, two powerful searchlights shone vertically up into the night sky over Manhattan. Six months after the destruction of the World Trade Centre towers – the first major 'media event' of the 21st century – the void left by the absent buildings was filled by what were dubbed two 'pillars of light'. This commemorative event formed part of a long line of light-based architecture – most infamously Albert Speer's 'Dome of Light' created from 100 searchlights at Nuremberg in 1935 – in which electric light was used not only to illuminate urban space, but to effectively displace the solid volumes of built structures.

In this chapter I will argue that electrification forms a foundation of the media city. The roll-out of electricity not only established one of the prototypical urban networks, but the lighting of the city marked a critical threshold in the psychogeography of modern urban space. The impact of electricity, carrying new potential for both 'action-at-a-distance' and controlled illumination, was a major factor in urban space being increasingly experienced in terms of flows. Electric lighting created lived spaces in which the traditional function of architecture as a stable ground found itself subject to a growing mutability of appearances and fluidity of functions.

In the first chapter of *Understanding Media*, McLuhan made the affiliation between electric light and modern media clear when he seized the light bulb as his primary example of a medium *without* a message. In the context of proposing his famous argument that 'the "content" of any medium is always another medium,' McLuhan (1974: 16–17) added:

Whether the light is being used for brain-surgery or night baseball is a matter of indifference. It could be argued that these activities are in some way the 'content' of electric light, since they could not exist without the electric light. This fact merely underlines the point that the 'medium is the message', because it is the medium that shapes and controls the scale and form of human association and action.

The electrification of industry and transport, combined with the extension of electrical grids into public streets and private homes, has been one of the key technological vectors demarcating the modern industrial city from all previous social forms. Electrification underwrites the distinct patterns of dispersion and concentration which not only shape both production and social life, but also effectively transforms the modern industrial city into a perceptual laboratory, the site for the construction of new and often unexpected 'special effects'.

Strangely, while there are a plethora of biographical accounts of the discoveries and business strategies of inventor-engineers such as Edison and Tessler, and numerous economic histories of the ferocious patent wars and internecine political struggles to form some of industrial capitalism's most powerful corporations such as General Electric and Westinghouse, there are relatively few attempts to theorize the impact of electric lighting on the experience of urban space.[2] However, in the absence of systematic analysis, what can be found are snippets scattered through the writings of artists, architects, journalists, filmmakers and other observers of the modern city. One thing most of these reports make clear is that, from its inception, electrical illumination exceeded a purely functional role.[3]

This *excess* is central to understanding the divergence between the explicit rationale advanced for various schemes for lighting the cityscape, and the wider penumbra of social affects that lighting produced. On the one hand, lighting undoubtedly served a range of utilitarian functions from public security to the extension of potential working hours, all of which could be supported as rational measures proper to urban industrial societies (whether capitalist or communist). But, as Speer's dome showed with its intertwining of mass spectacle with the personality cult of the Führer, electric lighting could also be used to radically transform the spaces of social life and thereby redistribute political power. For this reason, electrification of the city needs to be evaluated on a double register. While the 'electropolis', as major light cities such as Chicago, New York and Berlin were dubbed in the 1920s, had a definite material existence, the experience of urban space that it housed indexed the ambivalent currents of the new social relations. As the city became a proto-cinematic environment, relational space assumed a new social purchase, and the image of the city illuminated at night became a potent metaphor for the forces of modernization. For Nye (1994: 197) the night city is the visual correlate of the abstract social processes of capitalist industrialization: 'It translated what Max Weber once termed capitalism's "romance of numbers" into a dynamic experience that redefined the historical subject.'

## The electrical sublime

From the moment of its discovery as an independent phenomenon, electricity was a source of profound wonder. Romantics rapidly identified it with a universal life force, dramatized in the archetypal modern creation scene of Mary Shelley's 1818 *Frankenstein* and distilled by no lesser authority than Goethe into 'the soul of the world' (quoted in Asendorf 1993: 153). A century later the prospect of widespread electrification literally dazzled the industrializing world, inspiring entrepreneurs, artists and revolutionaries alike with dynamic visions of an electrified future. When Lenin (1991–98) declared in 1920 that 'Communism is Soviet Power plus the Electrification of the Whole Country,' he was echoing an already familiar refrain.

As early as 1885, when Edison's incandescent lamp was less than a decade old and the illumination of public space a rarity, a scheme was mooted in the new journal *Electrical World* for lighting the entire city of Paris with what was grandly dubbed an 'artificial sun'.[4] The plan comprised one-hundred 200 000 candlepower lamps mounted on a single tower soaring 1100 feet in the Tuilleries Gardens. The fact that the scheme was both impossible, because lamps of such magnitude hadn't yet been invented, and impractical, because lighting the cityscape from a single point would cause enormous contrasts of light and shadow, merely underlines the extent to which the very idea of electrical illumination has long had a powerful symbolic pull. For Schivelbusch (1988: 4):

> Bourdais' Sun-Tower (Tour Soleil) is a monument to 19th century fantasies involving light. [ . . . ] The proposed tower marks the climax of a development in which earlier technical advances led people to believe that light could be produced in unlimited quantities.

By the 1880s, when electrical systems began to be more widely adapted to practical uses, electricity was seen as the key to achieving a new level of control over the lived environment. The ability to convert night into day at the flick of a switch offered the most striking proof of the superiority of the modern present over the past, the most compelling evidence of the ability of technological progress to subdue even the basic diurnal rhythms of nature. Equally telling is the rapture with which many people greeted their first sight of electric light. Only four months after Edison's famous demonstration outside his laboratories at Menlo Park in December 1879, the city fathers at Wabash hired the Brush Company to set up four 3000-candlepower arc lights on the courthouse. The event attracted 10 000 visitors to the small town. The local paper reported:

> People stood overwhelmed with awe, as if in the presence of the supernatural. The strange weird light exceeded in power only by the sun, rendered the square as light as midday [ . . . ]. Men fell on their knees, groans were uttered at the sight, and many were dumb with amazement. (Quoted in Nye 1990: 3)

While it is probably wise to take such a tale with a grain of salt – after all, boosterism is grist to the mills of small-town papers, which also reported that local farmers could expect giant pumpkins and corn stalks as a result of the new light – the report of the spectators' reaction shouldn't be discounted too quickly. Even read as an apocryphal tale in the genre of credulous cinema audiences fleeing the image of the Lumière Brother's onrushing celluloid train, it registers the extent to which electricity departed all previous protocols of illumination. Prior to the 1880s, artificial light came only from various forms of fire. Schivelbusch (1988: 5) notes that once the true chemical nature of fire was recognized, following Lavoisier's discovery that flames were fed by oxygen, it could be manipulated in a completely new way. This breakthrough led to the separation of the three original services provided by fire, as cooking, heating and lighting gradually split into specialized domestic forms. Nevertheless, lighting devices such as candles, kerosene lamps, and even gas, which spread from the 1820s, were all, at bottom, forms of fire. They were smoky, potentially dangerous, and their ability to illuminate was clearly linked to their consumption of fuel.

By contrast Edison's enclosed, vacuum-sealed, carbon filament light bulb, invented in 1879 and made public at the Paris Electricity Exposition in 1881, was a paradox.[5] While it produced a less intense light than arc lamps, it was far more powerful and also more controllable than either gas or kerosene lamps.[6] Moreover, it was a light which was smokeless, fireless and, given that it could be serviced by centralized supply, seemingly inexhaustible. If electric light seemed to be an anomaly contravening natural laws, it was one experienced by most 19th-century observers as miraculous rather than monstrous. The image of the Wabash public gazing at arc lights in silent awe indicates the extent to which electrical illumination belongs to what Leo Marx (1965) has aptly called the technological sublime. As David Nye (1994) has described, the electrical turbine not only generated electrical current, but a seemingly irresistible series of concepts and metaphors. As electricity entered everyday life in industrializing cultures during the 1880s, 'live wires', 'human dynamos' and 'electrifying performances' all became recognizable descriptors for a specific form of modern energy. To feel electricity in the air became synonymous with excitement, arousal and even love.

The ambivalence surrounding these developments underlines the close affinity of electrification with what I earlier called the technological uncanny. If the instantaneous 'action-at-a-distance' of electrical switches, exemplified by modern media such as telegraphy, telephony and radio, offered a new sense of control over the environment, including the promise of mastery over time and space themselves, they also posed profound challenges to the coherence of the modern subject. These challenges converged in the electropolis, above all in the new relation between material and immaterial space generated by electrical lighting.

### Bright lights, big city[7]

Electricity spread through the modern cityscape in several waves. Electric lighting was initially confined to isolated sites, such as the mansions of the wealthy and a few city centre department stores seeking a novel means of attracting shoppers.[8] A second wave was the gradual extension of public street lighting schemes along major transport routes, while a third was the expansion into large numbers of private homes.[9] To some extent, this pattern of dissemination reflects the different investments attached to electrification. Public lighting had been recognized as an important technique in policing public space since its origins in the 16th century.[10] While the spread of street lighting continued this trajectory, the manner in which electric lights were deployed vastly exceeded any rational desire for maintaining public order. As the Wabash city fathers found, demonstrations of electric light not only attested to the progressive orientation of a city or region, but proved capable of attracting large crowds of fascinated onlookers. This realization quickly inspired innovative entrepreneurs to install electric lighting as a novel form of advertising, particularly around city centre businesses such as theatres and department stores. Other businesses learnt to organize block street lighting, often via deals with electricity supply companies, as a way of attracting shoppers to their precinct at night. Electricity suppliers were happy to offer cheap power to increase the intensity of street lighting, recognizing its potential as a load-builder, since a brightly lit street demanded corresponding increases in the lighting of shop windows and signage. Adjoining areas were often forced to sign up too, as a defensive action. As Nye (1994: 177, 175) notes, this dynamic was a key to the extension of electric light in US cities prior to World War I:

> Shopkeepers understood lighting as a weapon in the struggle to define the business centre of the city, dramatizing one sector at the expense of others. [ . . . ] In the marketplace, the electric sign, the spotlight and even the streetlight become economic weapons.

While these changes had a significant impact on parts of the city, they were *ad hoc* and unevenly distributed. The first systematic explorations of using electric light to alter the ambiance of space occurred in the controlled urban environments of the World's Fairs from the 1880s to World War I. It was at these events that governments and corporations combined to produce coherent visions of a fully electrified society for public display.[11] The 1876 Philadelphia Exhibition is notable in being the last major exhibition based on steam power; it was also one of the last which closed at night. After the 1879 London Exposition featured Edison's new incandescent bulb as a chief attraction, subsequent fairs became key sites for lighting innovation. Electric signs, flashing signs, the searchlight, the spotlight and the floodlight were all first publicly displayed at World's Fairs.

Electrical lighting of the fairgrounds undoubtedly had a degree of utilitarian appeal, extending the hours available for leisurely consumption in the same manner that factory lighting had already extended the productive hours demanded of the working class. However, far more striking was the manner in which each city sought to outdo its rivals in the number of lights and the power of their illumination. The Chicago World's Fair of 1893 not only had more lights on its Electrical Building alone than were used by the entire Paris Exhibition of 1889 for which the Eiffel Tower had been built; the Chicago fairgrounds also contained more light than any contemporary city in the United States. As Nye (1990: 37) points out, millions of visitors to these fairs saw more artificial light than they had ever seen in their lives. With the transition from arc lighting to incandescent globes, they also saw it used in dramatic new ways; to delineate the outlines of buildings and pathways, to illuminate fountains and water jets, to probe the depths of the night sky. *Cosmopolitan's* reporter described the scene at Chicago in what can only be called glowing terms:

> Look from a distance at night, upon the broad space it fills, and the majestic sweep of the searching lights, and it as if the earth and sky were transformed by the immeasurable wands of colossal magicians and the superb dome of the structure that is the central jewel of the display is glowing as if bound with wreaths of stars. It is electricity! When the whole casket is illuminated, the cornices of the palaces of the White City are defined with celestial fire. (Quoted in Nye 1990: 38)

By the early 20th century the emphasis began to move away from the sheer quantity of lights to the use of hidden flood lighting which enabled buildings to be displayed as striking forms in integrated artificial landscapes. Electric lighting granted a far greater level of control over appearances than had the softer light of gas lamps which required manual

Figure 5.1 *Night view at the Pan-American exposition, Buffalo, New York, 1901 (Photograph by Oscar A. Simon & Bro. [1901], courtesy the Library of Congress.)*

lighting and extinguishment. With its capacity for automation and coordinating 'action-at-a-distance', electrification accentuated the possibilities of orchestrating rapid changes in lighting across large surfaces. Lighting effects enabled buildings to be variously represented as a collection of independent architectural details, or, alternatively, abstracted into a sculptural whole carved out of the surrounding darkness. Moreover, this process could be enacted as a time-based spectacle for a mass audience, who could experience a succession of effects previously reserved for the specialized interior spaces of the theatre, panorama and diorama. The World's Fairs showcased the potential for electric lighting to establish a new rhetoric of urban space, opening the way for the city to be transformed into a performative space in which fixity of appearances would give way to increasing flux, and the hierarchy of classical geometry would give way to relational space.

The new lighting techniques migrated rapidly from the idealized urban spaces of the World's Fairs into more prosaic but no less fantastic environments such as the amusement parks on Coney Island outside Manhattan. Maxim Gorky's visit to Luna Park in 1907 found him entering a fabulous terrain composed of 1.3 million lights:

> With the advent of night a fantastic city all of fire suddenly rises from the ocean into the sky. Thousands of ruddy sparks glimmer in the darkness, limning in fine, sensitive outline on the black background of the sky shapely towers of miraculous castles, palaces and temples. [ . . . ] Fabulous beyond conceiving, ineffably beautiful, is this fiery scintillation. (Quoted in Koolhaas 1994: 29)

Figure 5.2 *Luna park at night, 1904 (Photograph by Samuel H. Gottscho, silver gelatin print, courtesy the Library of Congress.)*

Similar developments soon affected the urban core, especially in the United States, where the installation of street and interior lighting for major businesses was followed by the widespread adoption of electrical signs as a novel form of public lighting. Illuminated signage soon became one of the most distinctive attributes of a modern city. The first blinking sign, spelling E-D-I-S-O-N, was displayed at the London Exhibition of 1882. By 1900, the use of commutators made it possible to organize visual sequences capable of producing the illusion of motion, exploiting the same effect of persistence of vision used by cinema. By 1910, more than twenty blocks on Manhattan's Broadway were covered in electrical advertising. The intensity of illumination lent the thoroughfare its famous sobriquet, and the 'Great White Way' would soon be imitated by countless cities laying their own claim to being 'modern'.

Such dramatic shifts in urban appearances did not go uncontested. As early as 1896, the proliferation of advertising signs in New York led William Dean Howells to observe:

> If by any chance there is any architectural beauty in a business edifice, it is spoiled, insulted, outraged by these huckstering appeals. [ . . . ] It seems as if the signs might eventually hide the city. That would not be so bad if something could be done to hide the signs. (Quoted in Nye 1994: 187)

Electric lighting significantly extended the commodification of urban space.[12] The transformation of the cityscape by advertising led to the formation of associations in major cities such as New York and London with the aim of having objectionable signs removed or their construction blocked. Undaunted, large corporations in the United States took brand promotion to a new level by floodlighting their skyscrapers. Icons of the age, beginning with the Singer Building in 1907, were baptized in light; the expense was justified by their conversion into blazing symbols visible to millions. The Woolworth Building, which took over the mantle of world's tallest in 1913, had exterior surfaces designed with electrical illumination in mind. If the electric landscape promoted a Whitmanesque merging of the self with the city's shimmering forms, Nye (1994: 198) notes that these forms assumed an indelible capitalist hue:

> The resulting landscape can quite literally be called the landscape of corporate America. It embodied the dominant values of individualism, competition, advertising and commodification, and at the same time it transformed these values into a disembodied spectacle with an alluring promise of personal transformation.

Yet the spatial impact of electricity cannot be entirely reduced to a corporate agenda. If the messy commercial reality of the electrified environment offended the *beaux-arts* aesthetic, with its preference for the orderly neo-classical lighting and idealized urban spaces on display at the World's Fairs, it proved ready-made for the European *avant-garde*. In his 1926 essay 'One Way Street', Benjamin (1996: 476) located a radical potential in the electric sign's form rather than its content:

> What, in the end, makes advertisements so superior to criticism? Not what the moving red neon sign says – but the fiery pool reflecting it in the asphalt.

Exceeding the sign's manifest message is electricity's dramatic spatial effects. The disturbance of customary spatial relations noted by the Futurists was matched by the novel capacity to address big city dwellers in a new way: as part of a *crowd* moving along the street. Electric signs enter the crowd's optical unconscious as an ephemeral environment consumed in distraction and producing a range of unexpected effects. As Nye (1997: 88) notes:

> For the millions of tourists who came to stare at them in Times Square, the signs only incidentally advertised an array of products. They came to see the sheer size and magnificence of the flashing signs; they were engulfed in a restless crowd, and the roar of the city. This electric landscape, even more than the new electrified factories, was the cultural ground from which modernism sprang.

The influence of New York's lights was attested by numerous visitors. On his arrival in New York in 1917, Marcel Duchamp famously declared the entire city to be a work of art. In 1924, Fritz Lang (quoted in Thomsen 1994: 97) was equally enthralled:

> And the sight of New York at night should be sufficient to make this signal of beauty the center of a film. The city flashes, revolves in Red, Blue and shining White, yells in Green and sinks into Black nothingness, only to experience that game of colours again, newly born a moment later. Streets, whose shafts are full of light, full of circulating, whirling, revolving light which is like a declaration of vitality. And above them, sky-high above the cars and metro-trains, towers emerge in Blue and Gold, in White and Purple, torn by searchlights from the darkness of the night. Advertisements reach even higher, up to the stars, beating them with light and glamour, living in endless new variations.

When the great revolutionary poet Vladimir Mayakovsky visited New York the following year in 1925, he, too, was impressed, above all, by the lights of Broadway:

> The street lamps, the dazzling lights of advertisements, the glow of shop windows and windows of never-closing stores, the lights illuminating huge posters, lights from the open doors of cinemas and theatres, the speeding lights of automobiles and trolley cars, the lights of the subway trains glittering under one's feet through the glass pavements, the lights of inscriptions in the sky. Brightness, brightness, brightness [ . . . ]. (Quoted in Woroszylski 1971)

Filmmaker Sergei Eisenstein's first impressions of New York in the late 1920s register its vertiginous impact in strikingly cinematic terms:

> All sense of perspective and of realistic depth is washed away by a nocturnal sea of electric advertising. Far and near, small (in the *foreground*) and large (in the *background*), soaring aloft and dying away, racing and circling, bursting and vanishing – these lights tend to abolish all sense of real space, finally melting into a single plane of coloured light points and neon lines moving over a surface of black velvet sky. It was thus that people used to picture stars – as glittering nails hammered into the sky. (Eisenstein 1963: 83)

While Eisenstein was prone to conceptualizing a wide range of phenomena, from literary images to Marxist dialectics, in terms of montage, his comparison alerts us to the extent to which the electrification of the modern city created a new perceptual matrix which strikingly paralleled the experience of cinema. The coincidence is worth remarking again. At the same moment in history that electric light charged the cityscape with spectacular effects previously reserved for specialized showplaces, the spread of new modes of rapid transit and the proliferation of glass architecture functioned to set every urban traveller's eye on a collision course with this shimmering, phantom city. This fusion of light, transparent and highly reflective surfaces, and mechanized movement rapidly became a hallmark of the modern city, introducing a new dimension into urban design. What emerges in the electropolis is a hybrid environment belonging to neither architecture nor sculpture as traditionally understood. Instead, the electric city is characterized by the interpenetration of material and immaterial spatial regimes, establishing the conditions in which relational space becomes a dominant social experience. When the lights come on, they reveal an *other* city; an oneiric city that proved both exhilarating and disorienting to its inhabitants; a city which exists only at night and whose dream forms have only tenuous connections to the prosaic spaces of the waking day.

### The oneiric city

The experience of the modern city seen under electric lights conferred a novel sense of mutability on the previously immutable and monumental. The skyscrapers of Chicago and New York, pierced by ever-greater windowed areas, or skinned entirely with glass curtain walls, proved most susceptible to the growing sense of architectural ephemerality. To some observers, light seemed capable of dissolving their mass entirely. After visiting New York in 1910, Ezra Pound was moved to describe the city, seen in the evening, as the most beautiful in the world:

> It is then that the great buildings lose reality and take on their magical powers. They are immaterial; that is to say one sees but the lighted windows. Squares after squares of flame, set and cut into the aether. Here is our poetry, for we have pulled down the stars to our will. (Quoted in Kenner 1975: 5)

In France, where electric lighting operated on a more restricted scale than in the United States, Le Corbusier's characteristic enthusiasm for new technology emphasized the possibilities for transforming architecture:

> One Armistice Day in the evening, M. Citroën offered us that undreamed of revelation: a floodlit Place de la Concorde. Not just lit up by its street lamps, or the Republic's standardized little gas flames, but illuminated with all the floods of light made possible by electricity. The idea had come from America, the projectors from the war. It was (and continued to be every evening) one of the most astounding lectures on architecture that it would be possible to attend 'in this wide world'. Sublime straight lines, and oh, sublime French rigor! On that Armistice night a dumbfounded crowd standing in the square, held in the grip of a grace unshadowed by a single jest – on the contrary, of a grace imperious in its command – that crowd was able to listen *to architecture itself*. (Corbusier 1964: 178)

Corbusier's vision of electric light converting mute architecture into a living, speaking entity situates the uncanny resonance of the new cityscape which was the forerunner of contemporary schemes for 'responsive architecture'. The alteration of customary relations of dimension, distance and materiality created a strange environment, as architecture 'came to life' under the influence of lights. The apparent loss of physical solidity, the rapid alteration of scale and proportion, the blurring of edges and the intermingling and overlapping of previously discrete spaces intensified the ambiguous relations between reality and fantasy. But such fantasy was rapidly becoming part of daily life. What Corbusier describes as a command performance in the *son et lumiere* tradition, in which controlled light was used to unlock the tongues of buildings, was increasingly part of everyday experience in the United States where nightly 'floods of light' converted the city into a dynamic field of shifting intensities.

Scrutinizing these shifts through the optic of the uncanny is useful in focusing attention on the ambivalence which dogs the electropolis, undermining every attempt to split the rational precept of Corbusier's 'radiant city' from its irrational double – the overcrowded Manhattan which gave birth to what Koolhaas (1994: 10) dubbed the 'culture of congestion'. While Corbusier applauded certain aspects of Manhattan (the skyscraper, the grid), he never stopped dreaming of a properly *ordered* Manhattan. Integral to his ambition for urban organization proper to *la ville radieuse* was control of light, both natural and artificial. Yet, in practice, the orderly use of light as an integrated element of rational design was inevitably outshone by the excessive use of light for spectacular forms of urban display. In this regard, it is important to recognize that the city flooded with light is in fact irreducibly joined to its double, the shadowy night city at the heart of Expressionism and film *noir*. But, if the light city and the dark city are recto and verso, both emerging from the same matrix of developmental forces, the dream of their bifurcation has structured many of the key theoretical treatises of modern architecture, as well as a host of popular narratives. Exemplary of the latter is Thea von Harbou's novel *Metropolis* (which formed the basis for husband Fritz Lang's epic film in 1926):

> The workman No. 11811, the man who lived in a prison-like house, under the underground railway of Metropolis, who knew no other way than that from the hole in which he slept to the machine and from the machine back to the hole – this man saw, for the first time in his life, the wonder of the world, which was Metropolis: the city, by night shining under millions and millions of lights. He saw the ocean of light which filled the endless trails of streets with a silver, flashing luster. He saw the will-o'-the-wisp sparkle of the electric advertisements, lavishing themselves inexhaustibly in an ecstasy of brightness. He saw towers projecting, built up of blocks of light, feeling himself seized, over-powered to a state of complete impotence by this intoxication of light, feeling this sparkling ocean with its hundreds and thousands of spraying waves, to reach out for him, to take the breath from his mouth, to pierce him, suffocate him [ . . . ]. (von Harbou, n.d.: 50–51)[13]

More noteworthy than von Harbou's florid prose is her recognition of the role of light in the vertically stratified metropolis, where the absence of light in the worker's underworld is counterpointed by the excess of light in the pleasure zones above. Unlike God's own light, which served to clarify truth for Descartes in his moment of radical doubt, electric light not only illuminates but intoxicates, doubling and redoubling the city, recreating its buildings, streetscapes and squares as floating, de-materialized zones. These ambient spaces were often transient, susceptible to sudden transformation or equally sudden disappearance. Writing about the new nightclubs which emerged in Berlin around the same time as *Metropolis* was released, Kracauer (quoted in Elsaesser 2003: 39) commented: 'Lighting is such an integral part that one cannot but think these places have no existence in the day.'

In the 'ecstasy of brightness' that von Harbou describes, the modern subject experiences the apotheosis of the technological uncanny. Facing a sea of lights, the self is magnified to the point of impotence, its oceanic aspirations annihilated by a spectacular, 'piercing', 'suffocating' space. Wholesale alteration of familiar spatial relationships promoted a new sense of fantasy, or rather, transformed the night city into a new fantasy space. The oneiric space of the night city became the symbolic screen on which the contradictory desires of the 20th century's 'new man' could be projected and played out, split between restless ambition for the endless conquest of new frontiers and a nostalgic longing for the security of a stable home. The heightened sense of control over space offered by electrical illumination is counterpointed at every step by heightened existential uncertainty. If electric light helped to turn the modern city into a promise – 'bright lights, big city' – capable of drawing millions out of the countryside and across the oceans, the spatial experience of the electropolis presented profound challenges to those who lived in it. If appearances could shift rapidly, so too could meanings. In this respect, the electropolis crystallized one of the defining dilemmas of modernity: enhanced possibilities for individual freedom and self-expression were counterpointed by a growing sense of displacement and disorientation. The quintessential modern fantasy of freedom to re-invent the self available to the more privileged was off-set for others by its price tag of increased alienation and chronic identity crisis.

The ambivalence of electric lighting is exemplified by the way it created a new 'map' of the city. Not only did the lighting of cities illuminate key urban landmarks, it effectively deleted others, casting unlit areas into impenetrable darkness. This novel capacity for architectural erasure was highlighted by Andy Warhol, who shot his most notorious film, the eight-hour *Empire*, following the floodlighting of the Empire State Building in 1964. 'The Empire State Building is a star,' Warhol declared in his characteristic deadpan fashion, and for most of the film, the building literally is the star, continuously visible for over seven hours in an unmoving frame. Around 2.00 am the floodlights were switched off, and the last 45 minutes of the film are almost totally black. Through this gesture Warhol demonstrates the close relation between city lighting and the technique of montage.[14] In an interview in 1975, Warhol commented:

> The best, most temporal way of making a building that I ever heard of is by making it with light. The Fascists did a lot of this 'light architecture'. If you build buildings with lights outside, you can make them indefinite, and then

when you're through with using them you shut the lights off and they disappear. (Quoted in Angel 1994: 15)

Lights enable modern skyscrapers, clad with glass curtain walls, to assume dazzling, indefinite forms, and then, finally, to disappear, as if their monumental forms are no more than a conjuror's trick. The extension of electrical illumination from individual structures and selected blocks to the entire cityscape created a perceptual whole whose impact vastly exceeded the sum of its individual parts. Massed electrical lighting provided a means through which the complexity of the modern city could be pared down to a few essential sites illuminated by floodlights, or grasped from above as a simplified pattern interspersed with unimportant blanks. Drawing on the 'pattern' theory proposed by Gyorgy Kepes in the 1950s, McLuhan (1974: 140) compared the oneiric spaces of the night city to the electronic images of television:

> From the air at night, the seeming chaos of the urban area manifests itself as a delicate embroidery on a dark velvet ground. Gyorgy Kepes has developed these aerial effects of the city as a new art form of 'landscape by light through' rather than 'light on'. His new electric landscapes have complete congruity with the TV image, which also exist by light through rather than by light on.

In McLuhan's account, the emergence of pattern from the chaos of urban form depends upon changing perspective (seen *from the air*) as well as changing media (light *through* rather than light *on*). But if the electropolis is gradually domesticated as pattern when seen from above, the experience of moving through its streets retains an uncanny excess which resists integration. This contrast is strikingly illustrated by the 'Grid' sequence in *Koyaanisqatsi* (1982). Where majestic shots of the city seen from the air reveal glowing force-lines traced by lines of moving vehicles, collectively generating dynamic urban patterns one can dream of deciphering, the perceptual effect of the same phenomena seen from inside one of the moving vehicles is quite different. Seen from street level, the city seems to decompose into an ever more violent flux, distilled by speed into the pure cinematic elements of light and motion.

### Virtual light

This immaterial city of pure flux found a new home in the 1980s as the uncanny urban spaces generated by electric light morphed into the informational flows of dataspace. It remains striking that the invention of 'cyberspace' owed a substantial debt to the visual experience of the night city. William Gibson's famous 'definition' of cyberspace in his 1983 novel *Neuromancer* – coded in the novel as fragments from an imaginary database – evokes a sublime excess of information exceeding any possible form of representation:

> Cyberspace. A consensual hallucination experienced daily by billions of legitimate operators, in every nation, by children being taught mathematical

> concepts . . . A graphic representation of data abstracted from every computer in the human system. Unthinkable complexity. Lines of light ranged in the nonspace of the mind, clusters and constellations of data. Like city lights, receding . . . . (Gibson 1995: 67 ellipsis in original)

Of all the metaphors Gibson uses to depict the 'unthinkable complexity' of the matrix, it is the final image of the modern city seen at night as an abstract grid of lights arrayed over a dark and indeterminate void which provides the most potent frame of reference for the 'non-space' of cyberspace. 'Like city lights, receding': the definition of cyberspace ends with a marked lack of definition, a gesture towards what Baudrillard had situated as a new technological trope of the infinite.[15] While cyberspace resembles the city seen from a distance at night, Gibson's cities are themselves a collection of post-industrial wastelands punctuated by blazing neon signs and giant holograms, and woven together by invisible networks and abstract linkages. In short, the urban condition is bloated by the same excess as information itself. This affects the boundaries of the city, as well as the means to represent urban space:

> Home. Home was BAMA, the Sprawl, the Boston-Atlanta Metropolitan axis. Program a map to display frequency of data exchange, every thousand megabytes a single pixel on a very large screen. Manhattan and Atlanta burn solid white. Then they start to pulse, the rate of traffic threatening to overload your simulation. Your map is about to go nova. Up your scale. Each pixel a million megabytes. At a hundred million megabytes per second, you begin to make out certain blocks in mid-town Manhattan, outlines of hundred year old industrial parks ringing the old core of Atlanta [ . . . ]. (Gibson 1995: 57)

Here Gibsonian cyberspace is offered as a new means of mapping an urban environment in which information flows have assumed priority. For adepts, cyberspace holds the promise of deciphering the complex order of a social and architectural milieu where order is felt to be lacking. But equally, the city – or at least a nostalgic modernist image of it – is offered as the means of navigating dataspace. This investment is made most explicit in Gibson's *Mona Lisa Overdrive* (1988: 19), where the matrix is described as 'all the data in the world stacked up like one big neon city, so you could cruise around and have a kind of grip on it, visually anyway, because if you didn't, it was too complicated, trying to find your way to a particular piece of data you needed'.[16]

If Gibson's recognition that positioning oneself in the contemporary city necessarily means positioning oneself in the data flows which increasingly shape urban experience is a necessary first step to mapping the contemporary media city, the way he mobilizes this nexus indexes some deeper problems in his conception of cyberspace. As Erik Davis (1994: 601) argues: 'The sense that there is a "true structure" of information is one of the most pervasive metaphysical myths of cyberspace.' This myth involves the simultaneous dislocation and re-grounding of experience, according to the double investment frequently made in modern technology. As Don Ihde (quoted in Haraway 1991: 22) puts it: 'I want the transformation that the technology allows, but I want it in such a way that I am basically unaware of its presence.' The experiential intensity of Gibsonian cyberspace depends on a transparent interface (direct neural stimulation) which shifts it from 'medium' to 'real' experience.

But, instead of using this paradox to open up the question of human habitation in the uncertain dimensions of the media city, Gibson avoids the issue in a very traditional way, by converting the contradictions of cyberspace into the transcendental experience of the initiate's quest.[17]

## Light architecture

By the first decades of the 20th century, the absolute values of space and time which defined the Newtonian universe had already been dethroned in science. The electrification of the city, in conjunction with the deployment of new vehicles such as trains and automobiles and new media such as cinema, telephony and radio, was perhaps the most spectacular manifestation of a parallel dislocation of the *social* relations of space and time. In the modern city, light no longer corresponded to the point-to-point configuration of optical phenomena described in Newtonian mechanics. As electric lights rapidly multiplied in both number and power, urban dwellers found themselves enveloped in an immersive environment lacking the fixed co-ordinates of the classical model. Ubiquitous lighting instead formed complex patterns of visual interference, producing a sensory and psychological impact that Crary (1999: 35) dubs 'non-localizable saturation'.[18] This experience challenged the dominance of the perspectival systems reinvented in the Renaissance to such dramatic effect, as well as the logic of such systems theorized in Cartesian philosophy. The night city was the perceptual milieu in which millions of people first experienced something as abstract as 'relativity' as an incipient social reality. Immersed in electric light, the stable spatial order of the modern subject able to imagine him or herself at the centre of the visible world, lost its tight grip.[19] As much as the railway carriage or the cinema, the electropolis was a key site in which 'relational space' first takes on a collective social reality.

Long ago Gaston Bachelard reminded us that: 'Everything which casts a light sees' (quoted in Schivelbusch 1988: 96). Electric lighting, with its unprecedented intensity, precision and control, set in motion a complex psychogeography of seeing and being seen which has become integral to the contemporary cityscape of promiscuous display and everyday voyeurism. The extension of electric lighting created the foundations for the camera-laden city of postmodernity, with its ubiquitous circuits of surveillance and counter-surveillance. Underneath the fantasies of individual transcendence supported by electricity's technological sublime lurks the potential for a 'control society' in which illumination merges with information, producing not so much the visibility of a rational civil society, but the overexposure of the searchable database. However, the contemporary electropolis also establishes the potential for experimental zones of space creation of the sort once imagined by Constant and Archigram. Since the 1990s, interactions between light, new media, architecture and public space have become the subject of increasing attention. Contemporary applications of what Riley (1995) calls 'light architecture' increasingly involve the use of computer-controlled illumination in conjunction with new types of electronic screens and active glass surfaces capable of differential reflection. This merging of lighting, computer and screen technologies has resulted in a further accentuation of surface effects, as the surface becomes an active membrane capable of rapid changes in appearance. Such a change signals a new threshold for both architecture and urban space: what Virilio calls the 'media building' does not simply create a new form of urban spectacle but a new mode of urban performance which alters the dynamics of public space. It is to these possibilities that I now turn.

## Notes

1  'Technical Manifesto' reprinted in Appollonio 1973: 28; Warhol quoted in Angel (1994: 15).
2  The notable exceptions are historians Wolfgang Schivelbusch (1988) and David Nye (1990, 1994), although Schivelbusch's main focus is gas rather than electric lighting.
3  As Morus (1998) argues, this excess was already apparent in the earliest public experiments with electricity conducted in London in the 1830s, where Sturgeon and Saxon used dramatic visual phenomena such as giant sparks to attract public attention.
4  Nye (1990: 29) discusses this plan. Schivelbusch (1988: 3–5) discusses a similar proposal by architect Jules Bourdais to erect a 360-meter tower near the Point-Neuf with arc-lights strong enough to illuminate the entire centre of Paris, noting that it was one of the final two projects considered for the celebration of the centenary of the French Revolution. It eventually lost out to another engineering triumph, Gustave Eiffel's tower.
5  Edison's popular status as the inventor of the light bulb is as much a result of clever marketing and patent skills as technical innovation. Bazerman (1999) provides a detailed account of Edison's machinations in relation to the major World's Fairs of the 1880s, which included payments to key members of the technical juries, as well as more conventional public relations. Schivelbusch (1988: 58) argues: 'Edison was important not because of an isolated invention but because he perfected existing elements and combined them in an operational technical unit.'
6  Arc-lighting, produced by the discharge of electric current between two carbon electrodes, was still a form of combustion since the electrodes gradually 'burned' down. Although observed as early as 1800, it took a long time to find practical uses. It wasn't until the development of Siemmens' dynamos (1867) that arc-lighting became more widely used in industrial production. Even then its intensity restricted it to large spaces, such as wharves, factories, railway stations and building sites. See Schivelbusch (1988: 54–56).
7  Salute to the great Jimmy Reed who wrote the song of this title in 1956.
8  In Zola's (1992: 28) The Ladies' Paradise (1883), the department store with its 'furnace like brilliancy' conquered the heroine Denise: 'In the great metropolis, black and silent, beneath the rain – in this Paris, to which she was a stranger it shone out like a lighthouse, and seemed to be of itself the light and the life of the city.'
9  A good account of this common pattern is found in Platt's (1991) economic history of the electrification of Chicago. However, it is important to recognize that the spread of electricity has been very uneven, both within specific countries as well as between them. While electrification of the world's major industrial cities began in the 1880s and was an established fact by World War I, electrification of regional cities, like the extension of power to rural areas or non-industrialized countries, has been a much slower process.
10  Schivelbusch (1988: 83–99) discusses the linkage between public lighting schemes in 16th-century Europe and the extension of the Absolutist State to

control over people's daily routines. Lantern-smashing was a popular act of rebellion against State authority in 19th-century Paris.

11 The World's Fairs also played a critical role in securing venture capital to finance the development of electrical technology and the roll-out of electrical infrastructure. While they were not profitable for electricity companies in themselves, the National Electric Light Association in the United States noted their value as 'load builders' instrumental in increasing demand for street lighting and other uses of power.

12 Nye (1994: 187) notes that in 1926, one company paid the startling sum of US$600 000 to rent advertising space on Broadway.

13 According to Lang (in Bogdanovich 1967: 15), his film was itself originally inspired by a visit to New York:

> I first came to America briefly in 1924 and it made a great impression on me. The first evening, when we arrived, we were still enemy aliens so we couldn't leave the ship. It was docked somewhere on the West Side of New York. I looked into the streets – the glaring lights and the tall buildings – and there I conceived *Metropolis*.

14 This process of 'editing' the city was something the camera had been doing for more than a century. Submission of urban space to what Benjamin dubbed the camera's 'mechanical testing' was integral to the selective appropriation of the modern cityscape in countless postcards, photographs and films.

15 In *America*, Baudrillard (1988: 51–52) positions the sight of Los Angeles seen from the air at night as a new *technological* sublime:

> There is nothing to match flying over Los Angeles by night. A sort of luminous, geometric, incandescent immensity, stretching as far as the eye can see, bursting out from the cracks in the clouds. Only Hieronymus Bosch's hell can match this inferno effect. The muted fluorescence of all the diagonals: Wiltshire, Lincoln, Sunset, Santa Monica. Already, flying over San Fernando Valley, you come upon the horizontal infinite in every direction. But, once you are beyond the mountain, a city ten times larger hits you. You will never have encountered anything that stretches as far as this before. Even the sea cannot match it, since it is not divided up geometrically. The irregular, scattered flickering of European cities does not produce the same parallel lines, the same vanishing points, the same aerial perspectives either. They are medieval cities. This one condenses by night the entire full geometry of the networks of human relations, gleaming in their abstraction, luminous in their extension, astral in their reproduction to infinity.

16 The ambition to navigate dataspace perhaps explains why Gibsonian cyberspace is not visualized in terms of the complex fractals that one might expect, but instead recalls the simple geometric forms of the early Suprematist art of Malevich and Lissitsky.

17 See McQuire 2002. This is made clearest in the final cyberspace 'attack' when the protagonist Case undergoes an extreme loss of self prior to attaining his goal, an experience resembling the classical narrative in which the (male) hero experiences dissolution of ego as the pre-condition for spiritual rebirth.

18 Crary is referring to the work of Dan Flavin, but his comment can equally apply to the general condition of electrically lit urban space.

19 On the link between Renaissance perspective and Cartesian philosophy, see 'The Geometric Universe' in McQuire 1998.

# 6

## Performing Public Space

The piazza, in fact, is 'un-American'. Americans feel uncomfortable sitting in a square: they should be working at the office or home with the family looking at television.

(Robert Venturi 1966)

I think we are still stuck with this idea of the street and the plaza as a public domain, but the public domain is radically changing. I don't want to respond in clichés, but with television and the media and a whole series of other inventions, you could say that the public domain is lost. But you could also say that it's now so pervasive it does not need physical articulation any more. I think the truth is somewhere in between.

(Rem Koolhaas 1991)[1]

During the 1980s television screens began appearing in a variety of public spaces. At one end of the scale, standard size monitors were utilized as electronic information surfaces in locations such as railway stations, while from the other end the Sony Jumbo Tron was exhibited at *Expo 85* near Tokyo. Video artist Peter Callas (1999: 71) recalls monitors massed into formations: 'The Sony consumer headquarters in Ginza, built in the early 80s, sported an entire wall of monitors that was seven or eight stories high.' From the initial experiments in cities such as Tokyo and New York, the migration of electronic screens into the cityscape has become one of the most visible and influential tendencies of contemporary urbanism. The old television *set* has morphed from a small-scale appliance – a material object primarily associated with domestic space – to become a large-scale *screen*; less a piece of furniture than an architectural surface resident not in the home but in the street outside. This transformation has intersected the other major transformations of media technology and culture over the last two decades: the formation of distributed global networks using satellite, cable and fibre optic transmission which multiply channels and erode regional and national boundaries, and the emergence of mobile media devices which displace the social architecture which accreted around fixed media forms. The cumulative impact of these developments on the relation between media space and public space has been profound.

While public screens were initially startling, their novelty soon waned as large screens with better colour resolution became cheaper to install and operate. Reminiscent of the rush in the 1920s to create 'Great White Ways' to rival Manhattan's Broadway, cities across the world turned *en masse* to large-scale screens as a popular strategy for 'reinvigorating' public space in the 1990s. By New Year's Eve 2000, people gathered in public squares in different cities around the world to celebrate the event – and to watch people in squares elsewhere celebrating via a global satellite link-up.[2] This distinctive manifestation of globalization, in which the idea of 'one world' can be *performed* by technology, proved a harbinger of things to come.[3]

How should we understand these new forms of *public* spectating? What impact will they have on public space? The decline of public culture, and the related demise of public space became a familiar tale in the late 20th century. Influential analysts such as Habermas (1989), Jacobs (1961), Sennett (1977), Berman (1982), Davis (1990) Sorkin (1992) and Harvey (2003) all argued that the public culture which had characterized an earlier modernism had been displaced by a pervasive withdrawal into domesticity and the private sphere. The rise of the suburbs was positioned as the nemesis to the public space of an older city. The integration of suburban life with national broadcast systems after World War II not only meant that electronic media such as radio and television colonized the public sphere, but media space subsumed more and more of the roles once reserved for public space. In this vein, Dayan and Katz (1992) defined the 'media event' largely in terms of the privatization of the public sphere, as events once experienced collectively in public space were increasingly consumed by spectators who watched from the privacy of their homes. Paul Virilio's (1994: 64) account of the displacement of traditional public spaces by the 'vision machine' sketches a similar trajectory:

> This public image has today replaced the former public spaces in which social communication took place. Avenues and public venues are from now on eclipsed by the screen, by electronic displays, in preview of the 'vision machines' just around the corner. [ . . . ] Really once *public space* yields to *public image*, surveillance and street lighting can be expected to shift too, from the street to the *domestic display terminal*.

In *Complexity and Contradiction in Architecture* (published in 1966 and recognized as one of the key texts of architectural postmodernism), Robert Venturi (1966: 33) put a more positive spin on the same transformation, famously polemicizing against older forms of public space: 'The piazza, in fact, is "un-American." Americans feel uncomfortable sitting in a square: they should be working at the office or home with the family looking at television. Chores around the house or the weekend drive have replaced the *passeggiata*.'

Whether the spatial paradigm established by electronic broadcast media led as inexorably from public to private as these accounts suggest, the emergence of new media platforms clearly demands that we re-examine this trajectory in the present. Large public screens and mobile media devices mean that media consumption is increasingly occurring in public space. What impact will the electronic screen have on the street, the self-proclaimed birthplace of modernism? How will pervasive media alter the dynamics of public space? New forms of public interaction clearly have the potential to transform existing configurations of power defining the uses and ambiance of public space. If urban space has historically been defined by the relation between static structures and mobile subjects, this dichotomy is fast giving way to hybrid spatialities characterized by dynamic flows which not only dissolve the fixity of traditional modes of spatial enclosure, but problematize the unified presence of the subject traversing their contours.

To better understand the contemporary interplay between media and public space, I will begin this chapter by tracing the trajectory which took modern culture from the street to the screen and then back again. Arguments for and against 'the street' as the site of cosmopolitan public culture not only register tensions in competing visions of the modern city, but serve as an important framework for understanding the contemporary function of electronic media as the *hinge* between public and private life. These older arguments also index the crucial political dimension to contemporary debates over the relation between media and public space. Part of the ambivalence surrounding digital media in the present is precisely its implication in contemporary developments to 'secure' public space through what Lyon (2001) calls 'surveillant sorting'. Yet new media technologies also offer tantalizing glimpses of more participatory and inclusive forms of mediated public space. While modern media technologies have historically been integrated into the spatial dynamics of the city along the two dominant axes of spectacle and surveillance, the extent to which contemporary media can be used to promote other forms of spatial agency remains a critical issue. At the conclusion of this chapter, I will suggest that the experimental practices of contemporary media art can offer a useful test-bed for exploring the critical potential of relational space – the demand to actively construct social relations to others across heterogeneous spatio-temporal regimes – by promoting new forms of public agency.

### Down in the street

In *All that is Solid Melts into Air*, Marshall Berman (1982) subtitled his chapter on Baudelaire 'modernism in the streets'. For Berman (1982: 148), Baudelaire's prose poems collected as *Paris Spleen* (1869) offer access to 'primal modern scenes', notably through their celebration of the street as the condenser of social heterogeneity.[4] In Berman's (1982: 196) terms, the street formed the 'common meeting ground and communications line' of the 19th-century city; in more contemporary terms, it was the *interface* at which different classes met and intermingled. While Haussmann's urban zoning meant that working-class housing in Paris actually became more segregated than previously, as many workers were relegated to outlying suburbs, Fierro (2003: 24) notes that the new boulevards nevertheless produced new patterns of social contact:

> As boulevards cut across the city in unrelentingly straight lines, they provided a sectional slice through *quartiers* that had been closed to view. Immediately

behind the regulated facades of the boulevard, neighbourhoods of the lower classes could be seen, and their constituents had full access to the city's major thoroughfares. Consequently, the boulevards provided an arena for the display of the bourgeoisie not only to each other, but to a wide demographic mix of economic classes and nationalities.

In grafting new forms of public visibility onto new modes of social mobility, previously unfamiliar conjunctions and contrasts became evident. In 'The Eyes of the Poor', Baudelaire describes the experience of sitting with a lover in a luxurious, brightly-lit café situated on one of the new boulevards, surrounded by piles of rubble – the debris of the old Paris which is being cleared to make way for the new. The poet becomes aware of a poor family watching them through the large glass window which was a distinctive feature of the new building. However, where the poet feels guilt and pity as a consequence of this scrutiny, his lover merely expresses her desire for the poor to be removed from her sight. Ultimately, this creates an emotional distance between the pair that leaves the poet disconsolate and angry. The poet's response indexes the ambivalence of Baudelaire's work – and the ambivalence of the practice of *flânerie* of which Benjamin regarded him as emblematic – to the social transformation conditioned by the extension of market capitalism. While Baudelaire clearly recognizes the novel interplay between architectural and class divisions underpinning the formation of modern culture, he evaluates the disjunction as a personal rather than a political relation.

On the boulevards of modern cities, the *crowd* emerged as specific social actor. As Simmel (1997) summarized it, the characteristic experience of the modern city is living among strangers *who remain strangers*. In other words, these strangers do not move on, as they would from a village, but neither do they necessarily become familiar in staying. Instead, mutual anonymity takes its place alongside various degrees of familiarity as the most common social condition in the modern city.[5] Building on Simmel's concept of the 'blasé attitude', Giddens (1991: 152) argues that modern public life is characterized by 'civil indifference', as personal knowledge of others is replaced by more abstract administrative forms of control and increased reliance on expert technical systems:

> The public only becomes fully distinguished from the private when a society of strangers is established in the full sense, that is when the notion of 'stranger' loses its meaning. From that time on, the civil indifference, which is the gearing mechanism of generalised public trust, becomes more or less wholly distinct from the private domain, and particularly from the sphere of intimate relationships.

It is this gathering of strangers, with its tendency to produce unexpected conjunctions, that underlies Richard Sennett's optimistic rationale for modern urban life. In Sennett's (1977: 296) terms, living among strangers means that experience is inevitably subjected to multiple collisions or jolts:

> These jolts are necessary to a human being to give him that sense of tentativeness about his own beliefs which every civilized person must have.

In other words, the *structural* conditions of modern urban life militate against absolutism and in favour of cosmopolitanism – the cosmopolitan being Sennett's (1977: 17) 'perfect public man'.

While Sennett's (1977) influential account of the 'fall' of public man shares common ground with Berman – both extol the cosmopolitan virtues of modern urban life, advocating the expansion of parochial experience through the 'shock' of difference, and both castigate the late-20th-century city for its loss of vibrant public spaces capable of sustaining such interactions – his more ambitious analysis departs Berman's in a number of key respects. If both writers see 19th-century Paris as a crucible for the formation of a new public life, Sennett (1977: 160) locates the demise of public culture significantly earlier than does Berman. For Sennett (1977: 125), the increased dynamism of the Parisian boulevards following Haussmannization was a sign that Paris was in fact 'ceasing to be a public culture', and was instead becoming a spectacle.[6]

Sennett argues that the flowering of public life in the 18th century was associated with the emergence of new public spaces in which strangers might meet, such as theatres and parks. However, the balance between private and public behaviour was progressively altered during the 19th century, obviating the 'distance' previously granted by social rules and conventions.[7] The importance of the loss of distance is a function of the pivotal role Sennett (1977: 29) gives to social role-playing in sustaining public culture among strangers: 'Playacting in the form of manners, conventions, and ritual gestures is the very stuff out of which public relations are formed [ . . . ].' Playacting among strangers is vital because it involves testing out boundaries, thereby moving social rules from the background of the taken-for-granted to the foreground of public consciousness. Playacting in public can therefore take on political connotations. It can become the basis for a collective reassessment of habit and custom.

While playacting demands the maintenance of social distance, Sennett argues that the capacity for public expression declined during the 19th century as 'playacting' gave way to 'intimacy'.[8] Sennett relates the rise of intimacy to the new conditions of commodity capitalism. As depersonalization became the increasingly routine consequence of economic transformation, it was reactively counterpointed by a heightened demand for 'authentic' personal interaction. The interplay of these two forces militated against the very forms of social interaction that had been vital to sustaining cosmopolitan public culture. Instead, they created the modern conditions in which people came to believe 'that community is a mutual act of self-disclosure', while at the same time undervaluing 'the community relations of strangers, particularly those which occur in cities' (Sennett 1977: 4). Once 'intimate relations determine what shall be believable', conventions, artifices and rules appear only as blockages to social interaction: they are 'obstructions of intimate expression' (Sennett 1977: 37). Sennett (1977: 37) argued that this severely diminished the social capacity for public expression:

> With an emphasis on psychological authenticity, people become inartistic in daily life because they are unable to tap the fundamental creative strength of the actor, the ability to play with and invest feeling in external images of the self.

As a consequence, public expression was reduced to a special quality, one thought to inhere only in certain individuals, such as actors, musicians, artists, and, importantly, politicians. However, for the majority of people, who did not believe themselves to possess these special expressive capacities, expression was relegated to the private sphere of family life. Silence and uniform behaviour emerged as defensive mechanisms for appearing in public.[9] The result was a public culture privileging looking over talking, detachment over engagement:

> There grew up the idea that strangers had no right to speak to each other, that each man possessed as a public right an invisible shield, a right to be left alone. [ . . . ] Public behaviour was a matter of observation, of passive participation, of a certain kind of voyeurism [ . . . ]. (Sennett 1977: 27)

In this context, the kind of ritualized interaction among strangers in public, which might lead to collective political action, was doubly displaced: first, by the retreat of authentic personal expression into the sanctuary of the family; and, second, by placing heightened reliance on charismatic secular leaders for vicarious public expression. This marks the historical point at which politics begins to become a media phenomenon in a modern sense.

Sennett's analysis accords in many respects with Benjamin's reading of Baudelaire, but sacrifices something of Benjamin's sensitivity to the *emergent*, and therefore uncertain, nature of the new social conditions. For Benjamin (1999b: 10), Baudelaire is a seminal figure precisely because, as the epitome of the *flâneur*, he registers the ambivalence of modern life so acutely: 'The *flâneur* still stands on the threshold – of the metropolis as of the middle class. Neither has him in its power yet. In neither is he at home. He seeks refuge in the crowd.' Where most 19th-century writers treated the crowd predominantly as a figure of menace or despair, Benjamin (2003: 324) argues that Baudelaire's initial attitude to the crowd is characterized by *fascination*. Like much else, it will not survive Haussmannization unchanged:

> If he succumbed to the force that attracted him to [the crowd] and that made him, as a *flâneur*, one of them, he was nevertheless unable to rid himself of a sense of their essentially inhuman character. (Benjamin 2003: 326)

As a result of this tension, Benjamin (2003: 343) argues that Baudelaire's work offers the first *aesthetic* recognition of the historic contradiction of modern life: 'He named the price for which the sensation of modernity could be had: the disintegration of the aura in immediate shock experience [*Chockerlebnis*]'. It is from this perspective that Benjamin locates a significant shift in Baudelaire's work as the commodity character of social relationships becomes more pronounced. As the rhythms of both economic exchange and social life accelerate, the prospects for *flânerie* diminish. What Benjamin (1997: 53) called the *flâneur*'s 'art of strolling' depended on the maintenance of barriers to urban circulation: he contrasts the Paris which still relies on ferries rather than bridges to cross the Seine to the London of Poe's 'Man of the Crowd' (1840) where rapidly moving urban dwellers have already been reduced to 'masses'. Impediments to circulation are the architectural counterparts to the mannered 'distance' that Sennett posits as social supports for interaction among strangers. A feature of the Parisian arcades was the way that pedestrians could linger without competing with vehicular traffic. Benjamin (1999b: 31) notes:

> Around 1840 it was briefly fashionable to take turtles for a walk in the arcades. The *flâneurs* would have liked the turtles to set the pace for them. If they had had their way, progress would have been obliged to accommodate itself to this pace. But this attitude did not prevail; Taylor, who popularized the catchphrase 'Down with Dawdling!' carried the day.

'Down with dawdling' could equally have been Haussmann's *motif*. By the time *Paris Spleen* was written at the close of the 1860s, Benjamin (2003: 343) suggests that the *flâneur*'s radical lustre had faded. In a letter written to Adorno in 1939, Benjamin (2003: 208) argued that the *flâneur* gradually becomes 'attuned to the commodity'. The liminal quality of the new public spaces ebbed away as the 'unproductive' practice of *flânerie* was gradually integrated into the economically 'productive' practice of shopping. For Benjamin (1999b: 10) 'The department store is the last promenade for the *flâneur*.' In the department store shopping was raised to the level of an aesthetic practice capable of generating pleasure through the new forms of commodity display born on the back of mass production.

The corollary of the spectacular society of which the department store is a symptom is the profound levelling of social experience. As those such as Marx and Simmel pointed out, the extension of the market economy into more areas of social life, meant that everyday experience was increasingly subjected to quantitative measurement. The growth of the money economy meant there was a growing sense that everything had a price and could be compared on that basis.

While there are significant differences between the analyses of public space proposed by Sennett, Berman and Benjamin, all three writers share a sense of the importance of a public culture in which people interact, not as voyeurs, consumers or commodities, but as active agents able to understand, and thereby alter, their own social situation. In their analyses the street constitutes a vital theatre for the formation of a specifically modern consciousness. The advantage of Benjamin's analysis is not only that he is more attentive to the political ambivalence of mid-19th-century public culture, but that he situates this ambivalence in relation to the emergence of technological media. Benjamin emphasizes that the isolated individuals observed by Engels in 19th-century London are not a 'natural' part of urban life, but the historically specific outcome of developments in industrial capitalism. While Benjamin evaluates the *flâneur* positively in contrast to the undifferentiated crowd, he also draws a negative contrast between the individualism underpinning *flânerie* and the imagined solidarity of a working class becoming conscious of its own life circumstances. It is this understanding that underpinned Benjamin's insistence that the technological image was the key to developing new forms of political collectivity, once the dynamite of film had blown apart the prison cell of the industrial city.[10]

## Repudiating the street

Benjamin (2003: 327) notes that: 'Fear, revulsion and horror were the emotions which the big-city crowd aroused in those who first observed it.' This statement also seems an apt description of the attitude taken by key figures of the *avant-garde* of modernist architecture. Fear of revolution merged with antipathy to the growing squalor and chaos caused by capitalist industrialization, creating the conditions for over-investment in the dream of the *planned* metropolis. Corbusier's 'architecture or revolution' coda added to *Towards a New Architecture* (1923) was symptomatic of a widely shared view that rational building was the key to rational social form.[11]

While there were many good reasons – and at least some good intentions – behind the numerous schemes for 'modernizing' the city that emerged in the wake of World War II, the general polemic against the street was marked. In place of the disorganized street, functional zoning and integrated infrastructure were distilled from Haussmann's example into a general programme of urban planning. The formation of the Congres Internationaux d'Architecture Moderne (CIAM) in 1928, and particularly the principles of its charter enunciated at its fourth Congress on 'The Functional City' held at Athens in 1933, established urban planning parameters which held sway until at least the 1970s.[12] While urban planning produced some undoubted gains with respect to the inefficient flows, miserable living spaces, and endemic health crises of the industrial city, amongst the many problems later identified is the problem of public space: at what point do attempts to rationally plan increasingly complex urban spaces and circulatory systems collapse into prescriptive attempts to control public behaviour? In retrospect, it is difficult to avoid the suspicion that, following Haussmann to the letter, many plans for 'rationalizing' the street were premised on the desire to eliminate any site which might enable 'the people' to constitute a collective revolutionary subject.[13]

The desire to tame the street became a staple of modernist architectural thought. Hugh Ferriss, one of the key figures behind what Corbusier dubbed the 'pitiful paradox' of Manhattan, opened his influential *The Metropolis of Tomorrow* (1929) with a memorable description of the view from his office tower into a stygian Manhattan fog. The subsequent descent into the street is figured as a traumatic encounter with the 'real':

> Going down into the streets of a modern city must seem – to the newcomer, at least – a little like Dante's descent into Hades. Certainly, so unacclimated

visitor would find, in the dense atmosphere, in the kaleidoscopic sights, the confused noise and the complex physical contacts, something very reminiscent of the lower realms. (Ferriss 1986: 18)

The need to systematize the street's benefits and pacify its dangers was stated most forcefully by Le Corbusier, and can be traced through all his early writings. The key urban problem, as Corbusier formulated it in the inter-war period, was congestion. On the one hand, the design and lay-out of city streets was set at the wrong scale. On the other hand, the speed of new vehicles, particularly the automobile, necessitated radical change. In *Towards a New Architecture* (1923), Corbusier (1946: 54–56) establishes what will be a recurring position:

> We should repudiate the existing lay-out of our towns, in which the congestion of buildings grows greater, interlaced by narrow streets full of noise, petrol fumes and dust; and where on each storey the windows open wide on to this foul confusion. The great towns have become too dense for the security of their inhabitants and yet they are not sufficiently dense to meet the new needs of 'modern business'.

Corbusier's solution to the needs of modern business is not the dispersion of the city into the suburban gardens of Howard or Wright, but the creation of even larger towers. By concentrating habitation, such towers 'will leave enormous open spaces in which would run, well away from them, the noisy arterial roads, full of traffic which becomes increasingly rapid. At the foot of the towers would stretch the parks: trees covering the whole town' (1946: 56). A similar vision animates *The City of Tomorrow* (1924) which proclaims: 'The "corridor-street" between its two pavements, stifled between tall houses, must disappear' (1971: 77). In its place, Corbusier (1971: 122) proposes: 'We must create another type of street'. Drawing on his favoured metaphor of machine production, Corbusier (1971: 131–32) asserts: 'The street is a traffic machine; it is in reality a factory for producing speed', later adding his famous assertion: 'A city made for speed is made for success' (1971: 179). In streets designed primarily for circulation, the *flâneur*'s 'art of strolling' can find no place.

Despite his advocacy of planned communities housed in high-rise buildings, Corbusier (1971: 165) did not support mass transit systems as a solution to urban congestion. After declaring: '*The tramway has no right to exist in the heart of the modern city*' (1971: 165), Corbusier's 'Voisin Plan' – so named for the car company who sponsored it – gave the private motor vehicle a striking dual role. Corbusier (1971: 275) proclaims: 'The motor has killed the great city. The motor must save the great city.' This is the basis of his plans for a multi-level circulation system, which included arterial roads bearing a striking resemblance to contemporary urban freeway systems (1971: 164–65). In *The Radiant City* (1935), the same theme is repeated: 'Streets are an obsolete notion. There ought not to be such a thing as "streets"' (1964: 121). What has changed by the mid-1930s is that the street's function is to be internalized: 'Most of the city's streets will now be *inside the buildings*' (1964: 113). Drawing, as he frequently did, on the model of the ship, Corbusier's building of the future was designed with internal circulation systems. The corridors of Corbusier's Unité d'Habitation (1947–52) not only looked back to Fourier's 19th-century *phalanstèry*, but forward to the future in which large-scale shopping malls replaced strip shopping centres located on public streets.

The modern separation of the social and circulatory functions of the street was eventually canonized by influential educators such as Lewis Mumford and Siegfried Giedion.[14] However, despite constant advocacy, the conflict between the automobile and human habitation of urban space has never been resolved, merely displaced. Indeed, even as Corbusier dreamed of new streets which submitted the ecology of public life to the rationalization of Fordist-Taylorist logic, the car found itself being increasingly overtaken by the higher speed of a new vector: that of electronic media. If the private car is the harbinger of the dominance of suburbs over city, it is electronic media which consolidates this new political settlement in which the political function of public space cedes ground to media space. While the spectacular space of the 1920s electropolis still radiated a level of political ambivalence – a sense that the destabilization of tradition could promote radical political change as a corollary to rapid technological and economic change – by the end of World War II this conception of public culture and public space was declining. Instead, the liminal space produced by the expansion of capitalism was welded into new social and political formations in which technological media played a key role. On the one hand, this gave rise to the destructive, false unities of racially based fascism and national communism, where media such as radio and cinema were used to engineer ecstatic fusion of the masses with a charismatic leader.[15] On the other hand, it found expression in the Fordist mass consumption lifestyle pioneered in the United States, where a radical image politics emerged from the fusion of the star culture of Hollywood with lifestyle marketing and expanded commodity circulation. After World War II, it was *this* political settlement which proved victorious, and spread across large swathes of the world. Fetishizing the individual in terms of private rights and consumer choice has proved to be incompatible with the values of public culture. As a result, the role of urban public space in animating an earlier modernity began to recede significantly, especially in the United States.

## Post-urbanism

If the 1920s can be seen as the zenith of the modern industrial city, the decline becomes far more evident after World War II. In the United States, official policies supported suburbanization. Subsidized Federal loans for returned soldier housing fuelled the flight from inner city areas which were themselves starved of funds. The scale of transformation was unprecedented: between 1940 and 1947, 60 million Americans – nearly half the population – moved to new homes (Dimendberg 1997: 70). Older city centres were increasingly becoming 'black' ghettos contrasted to the new 'white' suburban developments such as Levittown. This growing fear of the city looms large in *film noir* of the mid-1930s and 1940s.[16]

Suburbs significantly altered the balance between public and private space. As Kasinitz (1994: 275) argues:

> Suburbs [ . . . ] are notably rich in private spaces and poor in public ones. By the postwar era even the layout of American homes – spacious backyards and 'decks' replacing front porches and stoops – had come to express a turning away from the street and towards controllable domesticity.

In this 'turning away from the street' the public encounters that had characterized the social life of an older urban form were increasingly displaced onto the electronic media. As Virilio (1991: 25) sums it up: 'The screen abruptly became the city square.' The spread of the suburbs corresponds to the historical rise of broadcast media. Radio and television outflank traditional forms of interactions in public space by constructing alternative means for virtual participation in collective social life. As the home becomes a media centre, a *node* within radio and television networks, social life is increasingly characterized by a retreat to the private. This is the context for the emergence of a fully fledged image politics which depends, above all, on television becoming the dominant political medium. By the 1950s, television was bringing politicians 'close' to the audience in a double sense. While the use of close-ups gave access to facial expressions and previously unseen personal attributes, television delivered these into the living room, exemplifying the transfiguration of 'nearness' that Benjamin posited as the key effect of technological images. As late as the end of the 1950s, Tourraine still felt able to argue for the radical edge of this new mediated polity:

> Those who are 'home-centred', and who own a radio, a television, a record player, magazines, are by-passing the social hierarchy of their community, in order to make direct contact with broader social realities and values. (Cited in Sadler 1998: 38–40)

Half a century later, the democratizing credentials of 'direct contact' media seem far less certain. This is not only because the rhetoric of 'directness' is now routinely employed by contemporary politicians to justify their preference for media such as talkback radio or the internet which allow them to communicate with 'the people' while bypassing the scrutiny of professional journalists. It is also because the same forces which brought television viewers 'close' to politicians enabled intimacy to re-emerge from the bosom of family life and become the dominant model for political life. In Sennett's (1977: 220) terms contemporary public life is increasingly characterized by 'destructive *gemeinschaft*' in which social relationships are treated as 'disclosures of personality'. Since the Clinton presidency this is often called the 'character' issue: the tendency to judge politicians and other public figures according to what we think they are 'really like as a person'. On the surface, this marks some kind of return to what Habermas (1989: 5–7) called the 'publicness of representation' in which the feudal lord displayed himself publicly as the literal embodiment of higher power. However, a key difference in the present is that those subjected to such close examination are no longer chosen by birth or guaranteed by social hierarchy. Instead their status has increasingly become a function of the celebrity conferred by the circulation of technological images. This transition underpins the deepening of the convergence between the role of actor and politician, as power is increasingly meshed with media-defined circuits of celebrity. The effective politician, like the good actor or celebrity, is likely to be one who is able to 'be themself' on camera.[17]

Sennett's analysis of late-20th-century public culture undoubtedly has its limits. His critique of public intimacy can certainly be read in terms of his unspoken fear of the 'feminization' of public culture. However, it shouldn't be reduced to this. Sennett's key insight is that a critical public culture in a large-scale society needs to develop forms of public interaction independent of the putative 'authenticity' of the character of its participants. The problem with evaluating strangers in terms of 'character' is that modern social encounters, especially those orchestrated through the media, grant limited ability to make such judgements. Yet the nature of contemporary political debate means that such judgements are routinely demanded. The result is a raging trade in manufactured tokens of public intimacy extending well beyond official politics, spanning a cultural spectrum from the unofficial politics of advertising to the rise of 'confessional' media forms such as webcams, blogs and reality television.

## Control space

The flight of inner city urban populations was partially arrested during the 1980s, as defunct industrial sites in city centres around the world began to undergo widespread redevelopment. However, what emerged was strikingly different to older city centres. By the end of the 1980s Mike Davis (1992: 155) argued:

> The American city is being systematically turned inward. The 'public' spaces of the new megastructures and supermalls have supplanted traditional streets and disciplined their spontaneity.

Jane Jacobs' (1961) famous advocacy of New York's village model of mutual community supervision of the street stands as the last hurrah of an older urban public space. In its place emerged a new emphasis on techniques of *control*, from gated communities and 'business improvement districts' to the ubiquity of technological surveillance. In the shift from what Beck (1992) terms 'partial modernity' to the 'full modernity' of risk society, public encounters with strangers are treated as increasingly problematic, and control of the street has become part of a wider agenda to render urban space not only safe but *predictable*. The 'war on terror' announced in the wake of 9/11 has accentuated the burden placed on media technologies to police public space.

Building on Giddens' (1991) insight that the modern city comprised of strangers elevates questions of 'trust' to a pivotal position, David Lyon (2001) argues that the urban society of strangers created the conditions for the emergence of 'surveillance society'. While the mutual anonymity which is the gift of big city life opens space for self re-invention, it also generates the need for abstract systems of identification to facilitate social interactions among strangers. Lyon (2003: 104–05) notes:

> The modern world may be a society of strangers, but no one was able to maintain their anonymity for long. Bodies may well have 'disappeared' as it became possible to do things at a distance, without direct involvement or intervention, but they were made to re-appear courtesy of surveillance.

Lyon stresses that modern surveillance is not always, or even primarily, undertaken with the explicit intention of instituting police functions. Surveillance society emerges in the nexus of growing demands for economic and administrative 'flexibility'. Like Haussmann's boulevards, it is an outgrowth of the modern quest for efficient circulation. As technological tokens of trust, such as passwords, PINs and credit cards, assume a greater role in social life, social interaction becomes increasingly dependent upon the collection and checking of large volumes of information about individuals. Speed of comparison via the computer is the practical key to the viability of such routines. The searchable database which is the heart of 'information society' is equally the lifeblood of 'surveillance society'.

Contemporary surveillance deploying digital networks differs significantly from its modern predecessors. Not only has surveillance been increasingly displaced from personal observation to technological systems, creating what Virilio (1994) terms the 'vision machine' of automated recording, but individual cameras and sensors are now interconnected, and linked to face and pattern recognition software. Urban CCTV systems are no longer 'islands' located at specific sites such as banks or casinos, but merge into networks permeating wide swathes of urban space. Anyone travelling through a contemporary city is likely to leave a traceable record. This was strikingly illustrated in the wake of the 9/11 attacks, as the movements of Mohammed Atta were retraced from various financial transactions, and could even be watched on video. Lyon (2003: 88) notes: 'He could be seen on grainy CCTV footage entering a motel, paying for fuel at a gas station, picking up supplies in a convenience store, and so on.'

Two factors are worth emphasizing about such a record. First, it was not part of any official police or security operation, but merely the electronic 'footprint' which is a routine part of everyday commercial transactions. Second, digital convergence of older, more fragmented systems meant that authorities were able to assemble various streams of consumer and visual data with great speed. Lyon (2003: 97) concludes: 'Data-gathering is routine, generalized, and distributed across almost every sphere of daily life.' Routine data gathering is the condition for the emergence of what Deleuze (1992) dubbed 'control society' in which the stable separation of spaces that characterized Foucault's 'disciplinary society' is displaced by spatial flexibility and continual monitoring. In control society, Deleuze argues there are no longer 'masses' and 'individuals', but merely *'dividuals'*: the condition of the masses become digital samples, or *databanks*.

The speed and flexibility of digital data fundamentally alters the functions of surveillance. Lyon (2001: 57) argues persuasively that the retrospectivity of electronic 'record' has become the prospective orientation of risk management:

> When speed has become so central, not only knowing what is happening in the present, but also anticipating what is about to happen also becomes crucial. Surveillance overtakes itself, as it were, to produce data on events and processes that have yet to occur in real time.

While the rationale supporting the deployment of surveillance technologies in individual cases is often 'reasonable', the problem is the extent to which 'risk management' based on technological surveillance becomes the dominant philosophy for managing public space. As the pioneering studies by Westin (1967) and especially Rule (1973) demonstrated long ago, surveillance inevitably demands the differentiation of normal and deviant groups since 'total surveillance' is prohibitively expensive. As Rule (1973: 279–80) puts it: 'mass surveillance requires constant efforts of *discrimination*'. Without discrimination between those who belong and those who don't, surveillance loses any practical function. This logic assumes increasing importance in the context of the 'war on terror' with its demand for mass screening on the basis of gross profiling.

While such surveillance is invidious, it should not blind us to the fact that security policing remains merely the visible tip of a larger commercial iceberg. The bulk of contemporary surveillance, such as the data-mining of electronic transactions, is undertaken with the ambition of rendering desire more profitable via the formation of detailed personal consumption profiles. The integration of electronic surveillance into contemporary marketing epitomizes Crary's (1999: 73) notion of the 'attentive subject' who internalizes disciplinary imperatives, as individuals become 'more directly responsible for their own efficient or profitable utilization within various social arrangements'. Indeed, the internalization of technological scrutiny has now proceeded to the point that social responses to surveillance have altered significantly. No longer the nightmare scenario imagined by Orwell, surveillance sometimes becomes a mirror for experimental constructions of the self.[18]

## The dream of ludic space

If the heterogeneity of urban crowds which generated unexpected encounters on city streets has been central to the cultural dynamism of modernity, the crowd has also inspired fear, loathing and strategies of containment. As Vincente Rafael (2003: 415) notes: 'Centralized urban planning and technologies of policing seek to routinize the sense of contingency generated in crowding.' To these forms of scrutiny and control we could also add the extensive channelling of desire towards commodity consumption. The success of such strategies for organizing and harnessing the crowd's unruly energies has led to recurrent speculation as to whether there is still space for unplanned social interactions outside the dictates of the commodity spectacle and the increasing routinization of daily urban life. This question was the basis of the Surrealists' group pilgrimages to particular sites in and around Paris in the late 1920s. It was also central to the urban analysis proposed by the Situationists a generation later, and it remains a key issue in contemporary debates about public life in the media city of 'real time' interaction.

The Situationists famously rejected any possibility of reforming the existing city. Change had to be total, predicated on radical changes in the organization of social life. In this vein, Debord's 1959 'Theses on Traffic' (quoted in Knabb 1981: 57) refused to debate the merits of various schemes to promote efficient vehicular circulation, but stressed the need to change the *function* of vehicles in the city, arguing: 'we must replace travel as an adjunct to work with travel as a pleasure.' Situationist theory consistently stressed the street's role as a site of social encounter rather than vehicular circulation.[19] The street was the primary arena for psychogeographical investigations and techniques such as the *dérive* were designed to probe its varied ambiances. The purpose of such urban interventions was to alert people to their imprisonment by urban routine. In contrast to the functional divisions espoused in the name of centrally planned cities, the aim of 'unitary urbanism' was to reassemble the separated strands of life, including art and architecture, technology and poetry, ecology and machine production. In this new social space, the 'battle of leisure' created by modern technology was to be resolved in favour of endless adventure rather than unlimited boredom. Debord (quoted in Knabb 1981: 23–24) argued: 'The most general goal must be to extend the non-mediocre part of life, to reduce the empty moments of life as much as possible.' However, 1968 proved to be a high-water mark rather than a dress rehearsal for radical social change. In his retrospective assessment of the 'New Babylon' project written in 1980, Constant argued that the potential for even limited interventions in urban space such as the *avant-garde* 'happenings' of the 1960s had decreased:

> The material conditions for ludic actions have also deteriorated. The centres of big cities are cleared by land speculation; the population is forced to move to widely dispersed dormitory towns, dependent on car, television and supermarket, robbed of direct and spontaneous contacts [ . . . ]; in short the atmosphere and the setting for collective ludic behaviour disappears. (Reprinted in Wigley 1998: 235)

If, by 1980, ludic space seemed to be only a dream, the problems lay not only with existing social trends, but with the Situationist International's uncompromising analysis. In many respects, the Situationists echoed the tension defining Benjamin's work, suspended between his Surrealist-inspired fascination with contingency and the fragment, and his later leaning towards rationality and an almost positivist science of 'testing' under the sway of Brecht. While Debord (quoted in Knabb 1981: 50) clearly wanted to distinguish the technique of the *dérive* from the Surrealist celebration of chance, defining it as 'playful-constructive behaviour', the Situationists were limited by their oscillation between a subjective language of libidinous play and a behaviouralist language of data and effects.[20] Nevertheless, the Situationist International forms an important reference point for contemporary urbanism. Like their contemporaries such as Archigram and Constant, their attempt to articulate a different urban future remains instructive in a context where the issue of social spontaneity is no longer simply a question of urban modernization programmes, and the routinization of social life under bureaucratic capitalism, but is increasingly tied up with sophisticated technological systems monitoring urban space.

As Lyon (2001: 57) points out: 'Flexibility, mobility and speed of communication make a huge difference to the way the city is organized.' Corbusier's (1971: 179) aphorism that 'a city made for speed is made for success,' initially coined in 1924 to proselytize for the rationalization of the street, has taken on a new meaning as digital infrastructure assumes primacy in economic and social relations. Embedding devices such as cameras, motion detectors, RFIDs and other sensors in urban infrastructure, and linking them to computers and databases for analysis and feedback, creates new prospects for responsive architecture. It also raises vital questions concerning the future of public space. Roy Ascott's (1995: 39) 'smart buildings' which 'attend to our every move, our every utterance' envisions technology that not only satisfies needs as they are expressed, but *anticipates* them:

> We are not talking about simple voice commands at some crude computer interface, but about *anticipation on the part of our constructed environment*, based on our behaviour, resulting in subtle transformations of the *mise en scene* [ . . . ]. It is a matter of high speed feedback, access to massive databases, interaction with a multiplicity of minds, seeing with a thousand eyes [ . . . ].
> (Emphasis added)

As Hegel demonstrated long ago, there is a fine line between the master and the slave. The technological environment needs to know what we like, or at least what we *do*, in order to anticipate our needs. But at what point does 'anticipation' become a neo-Weberian 'iron cage' for shaping behaviour? If the horizontal networks of ubiquitous computing constitute a potential first step in the democratization of the media city, what are the implications when intelligent building, not to mention every smart appliance, compiles a personalized database as part of its optimal operation? Ascott (1995: 40) remains a keen advocate of urban transparency, a quality that is now to be achieved via technological systems rather than the glass architecture of an earlier era.[21]

> [A city] must be transparent in its structures, goals and systems of operation at all levels. Its infrastructure, like its architecture, must be 'intelligent'; and publicly intelligible, comprising systems which react to us as much as we interact with them. The principle of rapid and effective feedback at all levels should be the heart of the city's development. This means high-speed data channels crisscrossing every nook and cranny of its urban complexities. Feedback should not only work but be seen to work.

As Mitchell (2003: 29) notes, the proliferation of electronic media has reversed the traditional urban balance between the hidden and the open:

> Once, the natural condition of cities was opacity; architects created limited transparency by means of door and window openings, enfilades, open rooms and public spaces. Today, the default condition is electronic transparency, and you have to work hard to produce limited zones of privacy.

In this context Bruno Latour offers a more critical assessment of the modernist attachment to the value of transparency, and its temporal correlate of immediacy. For Latour (2005: 21), these investments are in fact political *disasters*: 'Transparency and immediacy are bad for science as well as for politics; they would make both suffocate.' If scientific knowledge which lacks awareness of its situatedness and its limits is susceptible to distortion and hubris, cities in which social interactions are governed by the precepts of perpetual contact in 'real time' lack the necessary conditions for a varied social life. Benjamin's emphasis on the importance of obstacles to vehicular circulation in sustaining the radical edge of *flânerie* before it was subsumed into accelerated practices of consumption is worth recalling. It suggests the need to recreate strategic social barriers to the rule of transparency and instantaneity in order to sustain a richer ecology of public interactions in the present.

### Mobile publics

By the 1990s, the impact of smart buildings was matched by the growing urban effects of mobile media. In what is now clearly an earlier phase of the media city, devices such as telephone and television were primarily fixed. They were usually located in either the office or the home, and in fact were pivotal to the negotiation of the gendered boundary between public and private space.[22] This phase has now given way to an era in which media technologies have become ubiquitous, mobile and scalable, generating new possibilities for social interaction in which information flows are increasingly able to act on and shape social activities as they occur. Mitchell (2003: 107) argues:

> In cities today, electronically propagated narratives flow constantly and increasingly densely. These narratives – superimposed, as they are, on real space in real time – act as feedback loops recursively transforming the very situations that produce them.

The new capacity for micro-coordination has not only exerted significant effects on social protocols among friends and acquaintances, including the negotiation of accepted notions of punctuality and presence.[23] Mobile media also have the potential to alter the dynamic of public interactions among crowds of erstwhile strangers. Mitchell (2003: 161) describes this incipient form of social activity as electronic 'swarms', while Rheingold (2002: xii) dubbed the collective actors in such situations 'smart mobs':

> Smart mobs consist of people who are able to act in concert even if they don't know each other. The people who make up smart mobs cooperate in ways never possible before because they carry devices that possess both communication and computing capabilities.

While the potential of developing new kinds of agency and cooperation in public space is enormously important, it is not an outcome which can be guaranteed by technology alone. Both Rheingold and Mitchell have a history of *boosting* new technology, and their seizure of mobile media as the next frontier reveals significant flaws. The problems in Mitchell's stance are perhaps more intractable. Mitchell largely recapitulates the *avant-garde* programme of spatial fluidity and personal mobility advocated in the 1960s by those such as Yona Friedman, Constant and Archigram:

> In the emerging wireless era, our buildings and urban environments need fewer specialized spaces built around sites of accumulation and resource availability and more versatile, hospitable, accommodating spaces that simply attract occupation and can serve diverse purposes as required. (Mitchell 2003: 159)

But, while he updates this programme to accommodate new technology, he strips it of any vision of social change. If his 'electronically supported nomadism' clearly echoes Constant's vision of the New Babylonian perpetually on the move, his primary example of so-called 'swift space management strategies' in contemporary cities strikes a markedly different tone:

> By the early 2000s, we could see the beginnings of this in the combination of electronic road pricing and electronic navigation systems for managing road real estate [ . . . ]. (Mitchell 2003: 166)

Mitchell's (2003: 57) 'electronic nomad' is very much a creature of commerce, animated less by the prospect of unpredictable social interactions than their rationalization. Wireless networks link users efficiently to services such as transport timetables, theatre tickets and parking availability. Mitchell (2003: 124) constantly presents devices such as mobile phones and PDAs as polite, reasoning servants: 'If it knows the public transportation system schedules and fares, it can figure out the best way for you to go. If it knows your interests and time constraints, it can personalize a tour for you.' This image of a thoughtful electronic servant fits his rational image of consumption, in which consumers know what they want and can afford to buy it, while producers benefit through the tracking of individual consumption patterns. Mitchell (2003: 60) extols the benefits of the hyper-coordinated market – 'the post-sedentary world represents the ultimate abstraction and mobilization of exchange capability [ . . . ]' – without considering its deeper consequences. He never questions the effects of inserting of media technologies into fundamental social bonds, such as intimate and familial relationships. Even though he acknowledges uneven access as a problem, its implications are dismissed summarily: while 'others' may worry about issues such as hierarchies of race in cyberspace, for him 'disconnection would be amputation' (Mitchell 2003: 62).

In contrast to Mitchell's vision of intelligent media faithfully serving the individual consumer, Rheingold puts more stress on the collective possibilities of 'smart mobs'. Beginning with the premise that new media, such as location-sensing wireless organizers, wireless networks and community super-computing all *enable people to act together in new ways and in situations where collective action was not possible before.* Rheingold (2002: xviii, xii) adds: 'The "killer apps" of tomorrow's mobile infocom industry won't be hardware devices or software programmes but social practices' (2002). While this focus on social relationships, and the need to reinvent the social in the context of pervasive media is welcome, Rheingold's analysis lacks awareness of fundamental political contradictions. This is most evident in his discussion of the role of 'smart mobs' in political events such as the overthrow of President Estrada in the Philippines in 2001. For Rheingold (2002: 157), 'People Power II' was simply dramatic and concrete evidence of 'the power of the mobile many'. While he cites Vincente Rafael's (2003) astute analysis of the paradoxical role mobile phones played in this event, he occludes the very political tensions that Rafael is at pains to highlight. For Rheingold, the mobile phone had two key functions in 'People Power II': first, to provide a communication network which was not susceptible to State control, and second, to coordinate massive crowds of protesters. In contrast, Rafael (2003: 400) suggests these claims for the ability of the phone to orchestrate political unity in the context of the Phillipines was largely a middle-class fantasy, symptomatic of a contemporary 'fetish of communication' predicated on the false promise of dissolving existing class divisions. Instead, he suggests that 'People Power II' actually revealed significant political instabilities and fractures, even within the middle class:

> For once heard, the masses called attention to the fragility of bourgeois claims to shape the sending and reception of messages about the proper practice of politics in the nation-state. Media politics (understood in both senses of that phrase as the politics of media systems but also politics as the inescapable event of mediation) in this context reveals the unstable workings of Filipino middle class sentiments. Unsettled in its relationship to social hierarchy, such sentiments at times redrew class divisions, at other moments anticipated their abolition, and still at others called for their reinstatement and consolidation.

Rafael's analysis highlights the Rheingold's tendency to imagine that people will act together *because* they possess new technology. But new technology has never been a sufficient condition for social change, and is in fact more likely to be integrated into existing social hierarchies. Rheingold's snappy 'smart mobs' tag rapidly acquired marketing leverage, illustrating the potential for the social possibilities of mobile networks to be reduced to schemes for viral marketing, e-commerce, and invitations for groups of strangers to perform 'wacky' gaming activities together. In order to transform public space, a deeper critique of the public uses of new media is necessary.

## Playing in public space

In their 1960 proposal to construct a labyrinth at the Amsterdam's Stedelijk Museum, the Situationists planned a three-day *dérive* through the city, employing walkie-talkies to link drifters with the mobile radio truck of the 'cartographic team'. The radical edge of such technological capabilities, which were once the prerogative of the police or military, is now far less clear. If the prevalence of mobile digital media is the condition for the profusion of 'locative' media projects in the present, it also indicates the limited political purchase of projects which claim to 'intervene' in public space simply by foregrounding the technical possibilities of mobile communication. The issue of the social potential of locative media in particular, and public space new media arts in general, came to the surface in the wake of the 'Interactive city' event at ISEA in San Jose in 2006. Common criticisms of the artworks showcased there included the fact that most projects were short term, that they emphasized technology rather than social interaction, and that they were often functioning simply as R&D for next generation telecoms.[24] At a deeper level, there was a perception that, in a society of conspicuous consumption with an emerging 'experience economy', the concept of play inherited from the Surrealists, the Lettrist International, the Situationists and others, had lost its radical potential. As one contributor rather poetically put it:

> I have visions of techno-hipsters with bluetooth headsets jammed in their ears, capturing 15-second video clips of the urban 'condition' on their phones and txting knowing messages to their hipster-doppelganger pals in line behind them on the flaneuric boulevard of derives. (Beaudry 2006)

Some of these criticisms seemed to demand far too much from what were, after all, temporary and relatively small-scale artistic interventions. Nevertheless, awareness that a project cannot be expected to single-handedly override historically sedimented urban hierarchies of race, ethnicity, gender and class should not mean abandoning all expectation. A crucial role for new media art in public space is the potential to avoid the filter of sites such as the art gallery, and thereby engage audiences who might never cross that threshold. This indicates the new function of art in the contemporary media city: not as the belated response to an already existing social world, but as an integral part of the construction of social relationships.

Taking up Sennett's metaphor of play – albeit not necessarily in the way he intended it – we need to think about uses of media which are directed to producing new forms of public relationships. Andreas Broeckmann (2000: 167) has argued:

> The challenge to the creative use of media technologies is fostering the diversity of public actors and terrains and to develop strategies of articulating the new public domains that connect physical urban spaces and the potential public sphere of the electronic networks. This public sphere will only come into being if there are complex forms of interaction, of participation and learning, that use the technical possibilities of the new networks and that allow for new and creative forms of becoming visible, becoming present, becoming active, in short, of becoming public.[25]

As Sennett and others have emphasized, public sociability is not natural; it needs to be learned, nurtured and practised. In an era in which public space is dominated by spectacular 'brandscapes' and pacified by the distributed technology of surveillance, new forms of public interaction facilitating qualities such as collective participation and unpredictable collaboration hold increasing social importance. In this context, the role of artists using new media to construct experimental interfaces in public space can assume strategic value.

One of the most striking and sustained explorations of the nature of public space in the media city has been the various 'Relational Architecture' projects undertaken by Rafael Lozano-Hemmer and his long-term collaborator, Will Bauer (see Figures 6.1, 6.2 and 6.3). I want to discuss two works which were specifically designed for public plazas. The first, *Vectorial Elevation*, was staged in Zócalo Plaza (the common name for the massive Constitution Plaza) in Mexico City from 26 December 1999 to 7 January 2000.[26] *Vectorial Elevation* consisted of eighteen powerful searchlights mounted around the plaza, with the alignment of the individual lights remotely controlled by an internet interface. Internet users could log on to the site and design a lighting configuration to be displayed in public. The light patterns changed every 6 seconds, creating an aesthetic experience in which the intervals of movement were as important as the designs themselves. The software also automatically compiled a web page archive for each user, showing their design, camera pictures of its realization in the square and providing a space for their comments on the project.

The context of the work is important to appreciate. It belonged to the genre of 'millennium events' that gripped the world in the approach to the year 2000. *Vectorial Elevation* sat alongside other events, such as the live global telecast '2000 Today'. It took place on a public site overdetermined by multiple intersections of power. The Zócalo provides an architectural nexus for the dominant stakeholders in contemporary Mexico: the massive Cathedral, the National Palace and the Supreme Court abut the elegant jewellery shops of nearby luxury hotels. Yet the plaza is more than these official icons of religious, State and economic power. As Monica Mayer (2000: 225) comments:

> But to this same *zócalo* comes feminists, gay rights organizations, religious groups, taxi drivers, policemen, street sweepers, punk rockers, nurses, Zapatistas, students, professors, and representatives of every political party, all with their proposals and demands. In the Zócalo the mass celebrates Independence Day every September 15.

Figure 6.1 *Rafael Lozano-Hemmer, 'Vectorial Elevation, Relational Architecture 4', 1999–2004 (Interactive installation at the Zócalo Square in Mexico City and at www.alzado.net. Photo by Martin Vargas.)*

151

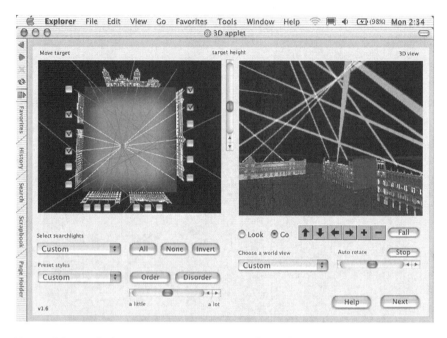

Figure 6.2  *Rafael Lozano-Hemmer, Interface from 'Vectorial Elevation, Relational Architecture 4', 1999–2004 (Interactive installation at the Zócalo Square in Mexico City and at www.alzado.net. Photo by Martin Vargas.)*

Finally, *Vectorial Elevation* drew on the history of large-scale light display. Lozano-Hemmer (2002) explicitly evoked Albert Speer's notorious 'light dome' created for a Nazi Party rally in Nuremberg in 1935, arguing: 'In Speer's spectacle of power, people were props, just like the searchlights were.' In contrast to such centrally controlled spectacles, which were designed with the aim of exerting maximum impact on the 'masses', Lozano-Hemmer aimed to use media networks to redistribute social agency in public space. As he later put it: 'I tried to introduce interactivity to transform intimidation into intimacy' (Lozano-Hemmer 2003). In contrast to what he called 'cultish extravaganzas whose effects were created to overwhelm the senses, to evoke false unity, or to provide a backdrop for mob rallies', Lozano-Hemmer's ambition was to create a 'dynamic agora' (Lozano-Hemmer 2003).

The key to realizing this ambition was facilitating widespread public participation. Instead of a spectacle mysteriously controlled from above, the work utilized the decentralized capacity of the internet to offer participants the ability to intervene, even temporarily, in a public space of great scale. Arguably, it was more successful in this endeavour at 'net' rather than 'street' level. Erkki Huhtamo (2000: 108–11) notes: 'Giving any net user the opportunity to create a massive display for a real-life public space was a gesture that radically disrupted the logic of traditional public light shows.' The internet also enabled the emergence of a politically oriented, participatory public sphere in a Habermasian sense.[27] However, while user-configuration of the searchlights via the web created a more varied and whimsical light show than an 'official' choreography would have, at street level *Vectorial Elevation* was still primarily experienced as a spectacle.

The element of participation in public space was realized more successfully in Lozano-Hemmer's *Body Movies*, first staged in 2001 at the Schouwburg Square in the centre of Rotterdam.[28] *Body Movies* utilized large-scale images, comprising over 1000 portraits taken on the streets of Rotterdam, Madrid, Mexico and Montréal, which were projected onto the façade of the Pathé Cinema building using robotically controlled projectors. However, the portraits were rendered invisible due to powerful xenon lights saturating them from ground level. It was only when people walked through the square that the silhouettes of their interposed shadows 'revealed' the projected portraits. This emphasis on the physical presence of participants' bodies plays an important role in limiting the work's appropriation as abstract spectacle. *Body Movies* was more concerned with creating a ludic public space. This shifted the nature of 'interactivity', from its common guise of choosing from a menu of often predictable consequences, to a far more open horizon in which contingency and unpredictability assumed a greater role. Instead of the logic of 'taking turns', where single users controlled the apparatus or produced representations that others could see, many people could participate in *Body Movies* at the same time. Participants could alter the scale of their shadows by moving closer to, or further away from the building, creating silhouettes ranging from 2 metre to 25 metre in height. A camera-based tracking system monitored the location of the shadows in real time. When shadows matched all the portraits in a given scene, thus revealing the entire image, the control computer immediately changed to the next set of portraits. This complex interface created a delicate balance between personal participation and collective interaction, between active engagement and reflective contemplation. While it employed 'real time' interactivity, *Body Movies* was not simply about intensifying the 'now', but enabled a more diverse set of temporalities to emerge.

Perhaps the most striking aspect of *Body Movies* was the playful engagement it sustained among groups of erstwhile strangers who came together in public space and discovered that, by enacting a collective choreography, they could affect the visual ambiance of that space. Here it is worth recalling Benjamin's argument that the radical impact of cinema in the context of the modern city depended – like architecture – on the fact that it was consumed in a 'distracted' state. Since the film image acted at the margins of conscious perception, it was able to circumvent the habitual defence shield each city dweller erected so as to protect themselves from the excessive sensory demands of urban life. *Body Movies* occupies a similar liminal terrain. Passers-by aren't sure what to make of it; the interface is striking but

Figure 6.3   *Rafael Lozano-Hemmer, 'Body Movies, Relational Architecture 6',*
*2001–06 (Large-scale interactive installation featuring over 1200*
*giant portraits that are revealed inside the shadows of passers-by.*
*First installed by V2 at the Schowburg Square in Rotterdam. Photo by*
*Jan Sprij.)*

not immediately comprehensible. Habit is suspended in favour of experimentation. Unexpected conjunctions emerge.

In contrast to the paranoia towards strangers that constitutes so much official rhetoric post 9/11, *Body Movies* celebrates the spontaneous alignments that can make genuine *public* encounters – in Sennett's terms encounters with *strangers* – so memorable. These kinds of tactical interventions into urban space provide a striking comparison to more manufactured 'media events', where the media simultaneously uses the lure of spontaneity in order to attract an audience, but generally occludes the spontaneous by imposing standardized frames in order to minimize the risk of 'nothing happening'. Rather than adhering to the cybernetic goal of informational speed and transparency, media technology in *Body Movies* becomes the basis for affective experience capable of sustaining *reflexive* public interactions. *Body Movies* takes the openness of relational space as the starting point for developing a dynamic and participatory social space. As Timothy Druckrey (2003) argues:

> It is an evocation of the kind of social space in which active participation is not a by-product, but the driving force in the creation of dynamic agora in which every position is established in an open system that ruptures hierarchies and dismantles the notion that the public is an undifferentiated mass, the media not the harbinger of a utopian global village, interactivity not the opiate of shoppers.

Art which pursues this kind of trajectory is sporadic and marginal, and may well remain so. 'Transformable', 'responsive' and 'intelligent' architecture employing sophisticated new media is more frequently used to produce spectacle and facilitate individual consumption than to critique it. While experimental zones for space creation by 'nomadic inhabitants' have been built in many cities, they tend to be limited to highly controlled situations – theme parks, shopping malls, or 'events' such as rock concerts and dance parties. Yet refusing to recognize even limited possibilities for change is to help ensure it will not occur. Lozano-Hemmer's 'limited' games might well have been ridiculed by the Situationist International, who, in their ambition for the unlimited game of the radical transformation of life, might have taken comfort in the conclusion that the situation was not yet ready for total revolution. For those interested in a less *pure* politics, changing contemporary culture demands changes in the dominant social relations sustained by technological images. Practices which forge new ways of engaging with others in public are a critical element of any such change.

## Notes

1  Venturi 1966: 133; Koolhaas 1996: 45.
2  The live global telecast '2000 Today' was a media event of Warholian duration, linking 60 countries over a 24-hour period as midnight struck around the world.
3  Similar use of large screens has now become a staple for large sporting events, including the 2002 World Cup in Korea which saw massive crowds congregate around large screens in Seoul, and the 2006 World Cup in Germany for which every host city erected large screens, and million strong crowds gathered around screens in Berlin's centre.
4  Following Walter Benjamin (2003: 3–93), who had earlier recognized *Paris Spleen* as an ur-text of modernity Berman reads two texts in particular: 'The Eyes of the Poor' (1864) and 'The Loss of Halo' (1865). Both were written at the height of 'Haussmannization' and published as *feuilleton* pieces addressing the new reading public generated by mass newspapers. 'The Eyes of the Poor' concerns the transformation of public visibility by the glass-windowed café culture of the boulevards, while 'The Loss of Halo' directly concerns the new conditions of public mobility, and the threat to life and limb of fast moving vehicles on macadamized roads.
5  The extension of mutual anonymity underlies Dupin's reasoning in Poe's (1938: 189–90) 'The Mystery of Marie Roget' (1842):

> For my own part, I should not only hold it possible, but as far more than probable, that Marie might have proceeded, at any given period, by any one of the many routes between her residence and that of her aunt, without meeting a single individual whom she knew, or by whom she was known.

6  While Sennett does not use the term 'spectacle', his analysis of the increased social passivity in public life shares common ground Debord's concept. For Debord (in Knabb 1981: 25), the very principle of spectacle is 'non-intervention'.
7  In this respect, Sennett's periodization of the rise and fall of public space is close to Habermas' account of the birth and demise of the public sphere. Habermas (1989) situates the emergence of the public sphere firmly in the

context of the decline of feudal absolutism. The waning of estate-based authorities meant that 'private people', facing a permanent administration and a standing army, needed to forge a new relation to public authority. The invention of 'civil society' was thus a response to the rise of deperson-alized State authority (see Habermas 1989: 19). However, by the mid-19th century, increasing commercial control of the press had become the 'gateway' through which privileged private interests invaded the public sphere, creating the conditions for what Habermas (1989: 195) terms its 're-feudalization'.

8  Crucially, 'playacting requires an audience of strangers to succeed, but is meaningless or even destructive among intimates' (Sennett 1977: 28–29).

9  As I noted in Chapter 2, a whole range of social practices, from photography, detective novels and physiognomy to ethology, phrenology and Bertillon measurements, emerged at this time as aids to 'reading' personal appearances in public urban space. Subject to such scrutiny, people became fearful of emitting public signs revealing their inner feelings.

10  Sennett (1977: 196) certainly points to the modern convergence between politics and performance, arguing: 'Politicians began to be judged as believable by whether or not they aroused the same belief in their personalities which actors did when on stage.' But Benjamin's analysis of the hollowing out of older political spaces such as parliaments in favour of the new media spaces such as radio and cinema offers greater purchase on this trajectory. Paralleling Sennett's emphasis on the rise of public 'intimacy', Benjamin (2003: 255) points out that *distance* is eroded above all by the rise of technological media. In contrast to Benjamin's attention to the ambivalence of the 'testing' function of modern media, discussed earlier in Chapter 3, Sennett produces a uniformly negative evaluation of their political effects. I will discuss the contemporary political role of 'intimacy' further in Chapter 8.

11  This view extended well beyond architectural circles to embrace the 'Technocracy Movement' in the USA, and apostles of rational economic planning from Thorsten Veblen to H.G. Wells.

12  Most of CIAM's principles were not put into practice until after World War II, by which time progressive architects were critiquing many of their precepts. But, as Sadler (1998: 45) notes, the principles had an after-life: 'Even as main-stream modernism was on the wane in avant-garde architectural circles, it was reaching its apogee in building production worldwide.'

13  This is certainly how Berman (1982: 164–67) treats the issue, arguing that the modernist polemic against the crowded and chaotic street is symptomatic of 20th-century attempts to displace, rather than resolve, the conflicts of modernity and tradition.

14  Giedion (1967: 822) argued:

> When Haussmann undertook the transformation of Paris, he slashed into the body of the city – as a contemporary expressed it – with sabre strokes. [ . . . ] In our period even more heroic operations are necessary. The first thing to do is to abolish the *rue corridor* with its rigid lines of buildings and its intermingling of traffic, pedestrians and residences. The fundamental condition of the contemporary city requires the restoration of liberty to all three – to traffic, to pedestrians, to residential and industrial quarters. This can be accomplished only by separating them.

15  See McQuire 1998: 235–40.

16  Some representative film *noir* titles include *Naked City, Dark City, Captive City, Panic in the Streets, City of Fear.* Writers such as Krutnik (1997) and Dimendberg (2004) have argued persuasively that *noir* emerged less from the

exigencies of Cold-War politics than from the experience of urbanization, and the profound spatial transformation of the US city caused by highway construction, suburban development and urban redevelopment.

17  This is discussed further in Chapter 8.
18  See Chapter 8.
19  In his 1960 lecture on 'Unitary Urbanism', Constant (1960: 134) underlined the historical importance of the street as 'collective living space':

> Historically, the street was more than a mere traffic artery. Its additional function, which may have been even more important than its role as thoroughfare, was as a collective living space where all the public events – markets, festivals, fairs, political demonstrations – took place, as well as encounters and contacts between smaller numbers of individuals, in short, all those activities that do not belong to the more intimate, private domain. The inn and café which sometimes spilled over into the street, were continuations of this collective space, public places where people were able to get away from the traffic on the street. The tremendous increase in traffic robbed the street of this social function. As a final refuge, there remained the café, but the street itself became a traffic route and thus a sharp dividing line between isolated units of housing. This might perhaps account for the cultural significance of the café in the last century.

20  For example, the inaugural issue of *Internationale Situationiste* defined psycho-geography as: 'The study of the specific effects of the geographic environment, consciously organised or not, on the emotions and behaviour of individuals' (reprinted in Knabb 1981: 45). The Situationist advocacy of a libidinal economy of pleasure over the capitalist economy of production drew on varied theoretical resources from Bahktin's concept of the carnivalesque, to Lefebvre's *Critique of Everyday Life* (1947, and earlier *avant-garde* movements such as Surrealism and Lettrism. Sadler (1998: 56) makes an explicit analogy between *flânerie* and the *dérive*, describing the Situationist 'drifter' as the 'new *flâneur*' who preferred the slower backwaters of old Paris to Haussmann's rationalized boulevards. He also argues that the Situationist International's stance had similar limitations to *flânerie*, particularly in its lack of engagement with the ethnic subcultures occupying the 'slower' spaces, coupled to a romantic view of their poverty.
21  See Chapter 7 below for a further discussion of glass construction.
22  Graham and Marvin (2001) point to an early AT&T ad showing a man in the office able to phone his wife to let her know he is going to be home late. This sort of image helped to consolidate the division between the 'masculine' public space of work and the 'feminine' space of the home.
23  de Souza e Silva (2004: 18) notes various studies describing the way people are considered to be 'present' at social occasions when they participate via phone.
24  Here I am drawing on internet discussion on lists such as Empyre [URL www.subtle.net/empyre/ (accessed on 18 September 2006)] and iDC [URL http://distributedcreativity.org (accessed on 19 September 2006)].
25  Inke Arms describes the ambition of the 'reactive architecture' project *Blinkenlights* designed by the Chaos Computer Club in Berlin, 2003 in similar terms: '*Blinkenlights* is not concerned with the aspect of dynamic architecture as media supported ornamentation, but precisely with the maximum possible visibility of a participatory impetus in urban space. It is concerned, in other words, with an emphatic notion of what is public' (cited in Dietz 2004).
26  *Vectorial Elevation* was subsequently staged in Vitoria-Gasteiz, Spain in 2002, in Lyon, France in December 2003, and most recently in Dublin, Ireland from 22 April and 3 May 2004 using 22 robotic searchlights. See www.alzado.net/ (accessed on 21 March 2006).

27   Lozano-Hemmer writes:

> The web pages for Vectorial Elevation were created automatically for every participant and the comments field was there so that people could personalize their design with dedications, poems, political statements, etc. Those comments fields were completely uncensored, which was quite a feat at the time because the zapatistas were quite active electronically at that time. [ . . . ] I convinced the politicians that if we censored that then the piece would become only about censorship and that they needed to stop having a paternalistic and condescending view of the general public and trust that they will send interesting texts. Sure enough we had many Zapatista messages (thank goodness for that!) but also marriage proposals, soccer scores, etc. The point being that those comments were an important aspect in the takeover of a public space. (personal communication to the author 24 March 2006)

28   *Body Movies* has subsequently been staged in Lisbon, Linz, and Liverpool in 2002, Duisburg in 2003 and Hong Kong 2006. A video archive is at www.fundacion.telefonica.com/at/rlh/video/bodymovies.html

*Part Three*

Private Space: From Glass Architecture
to Big Brother

# 7

## The Glass House

No one could possibly detect properties of beauty in large sheets of glass.

(Lucy Orrinsmith 1877)

Glass brings a new era.

(Paul Scheerbart 1914)[1]

On the eve of World War I Bruno Taut erected his famous 'Glass Pavillion' for the Werkbund Exhibition at Cologne. With exterior walls made of glass bricks, and a glass roof in the shape of a crystal, the pavilion was intended as the harbinger of a new culture. It was inscribed with aphorisms from visionary writer Paul Scheerbart including: 'We feel sorry for the brick culture', 'Coloured glass destroys hatred', and 'Glass brings a new era' (quoted in Frampton 1982: 93). Scheerbart's 1914 monograph *Glasarchitektur* exercised a major influence on many of the leading figures of the architectural *avant-garde* in Europe including Taut who, along with Adolph Behne, Walter Gropius and others, went on to form the 'Glass Chain' in 1919.[2] Scheerbart (1972) extolled the new possibilities of 'openness' inherent in glass construction:

> In order to raise our culture to a higher level, we are forced, whether we like it or not, to change our architecture. And this will be possible only if we free the rooms in which we live of their enclosed character. This, however, we can only do by introducing a glass architecture, which admits the light of the sun, of the moon, and of the stars into the rooms, not only through a few windows, but through as many walls as feasible, these to consist entirely of glass – of coloured glass.

Scheerbart's vision of iridescent glass-walled rooms could easily be aligned with the 'rational transparency' soon to be advocated by those such as de Stijl, Le Corbusier, the Bauhaus after 1923 and Soviet Constructivism. But its closing coda privileging *coloured* glass indicates its expressionist heritage. This dual alignment explains a striking feature of glass architecture: the way it was seized as a catalyst for social transformation by such a broad spectrum of architects and urban theorists.

In this chapter, I want to explore debates over the social value of transparency, particularly as they relate to changing conceptions of the private home in modern architecture. The new aesthetic of 'openness' that displaced what Scheerbart dubbed the 'enclosed character' of the room carried social and political implications that are still being played out. As those such as Arendt (1958: 28) and Habermas (1989: 9) have argued, the categories of public and private are common to both ancient and modern societies, but they appear in significantly different configurations. The expansion of the concept of privacy during the 19th century underpinned the political settlement of emerging consumer societies based around private rights and the inculcation of individual desire. However, by the late 20th century, it had become increasingly evident that the terms of this settlement were up for renegotiation. The heightened social role of electronic media networks that reached directly in the home subjected private life to new exigencies. In this chapter, I will argue that early modern debates on glass construction set the scene for a convergence between window and screen which has brought long-held assumptions about the relation of private space to modern subjectivity into question.

### Glass architecture

While glass-making techniques have been known for thousands of years, it was only in the industrial era that glass became a common construction material. Throughout most of its history, glass was so prohibitively expensive that its use was reserved for the wealthy and powerful, a privilege exemplified by the stained glass windows of medieval Cathedrals. The most common forms of domestic window – French and double-hung sashes – appeared during the Renaissance. By around 1750 glass polishing was becoming mechanized and large greenhouses began to be built from glass. Significantly, the first large-scale use of sheet glass in urban construction occurred in the Parisian Arcades from around the end of the 1820s. Iron frames sheathed in glass created the ambiguous 'interior streets' which inspired Benjamin's *Passagen-Werk*. The capacity of glass architecture to blur the boundary between interior and exterior space has since been manifested in the production of new modes of public display, but also in a new degree of visibility pertaining to private life.

Glass and iron architecture was soon adapted onto the world stage in the burgeoning circuit of international exhibitions and World's Fairs. These pseudo-religious gatherings, which Benjamin (1997: 165) aptly describes 'as places of pilgrimage to view the fetish Commodity' demanded huge structures for showcasing industrial commodities and manufacturing processes, as well as the latest scientific inventions and communication techniques. The scale of these buildings attested to the increasing desire to address the mass audience who had to be recruited to the industrial future as workers and consumers. Undoubtedly, the most famous glass structure was Joseph Paxton's Crystal Palace erected for the Great Exhibition in London in 1851. Wilson (1988: 95) notes that this pioneering structure utilized an unprecedented 400 tons of glass, amounting to fully one-third of England's total production only a decade earlier. The Crystal Palace exerted enormous influence. On a practical level, it signalled the emergence of an integrated conception of construction as a *system* which became central to modern architecture.[3] On a symbolic level, the Crystal Palace seized the popular imagination in defining an architecture of the future. Bathed in light, providing untrammelled views of their surrounds, glass structures symbolized the promise of industrial plenitude to working classes dwelling in dingy houses and polluted cities. In Nikolai Chernyshevsky's famous 1865 novel *What is to be Done?* the heroine's dream about buildings suitable for the revolutionary society to come find their prototype in the Crystal Palace: 'There is a precursor of such architecture: it is the palace of cast-iron and glass built on a hill in Sydenham'.[4] In the same manner that Lenin would reprise the novel's title for his 1902 book outlining tasks for the revolution, the image of glass construction would repeatedly assume revolutionary connotations for the European *avant-garde*.

### The politics of transparency

If Taut's 'Glass House' pavilion of 1914 was primarily a statement of the symbolic potential of glass, Adolph Behne argued that the potency of postwar glass culture had to be measured by its practical ability to generate social transformation.

> It is not the crazy caprice of a poet that glass architecture will bring a new culture. *It is a fact.* New social welfare organizations, hospitals, inventions or technical innovations and improvements – these will not bring a new culture – *but glass architecture will* [ ... ]. Therefore the European is right when he fears that glass architecture might become uncomfortable. Certainly it will be so. And that is not its least advantage. For first of all the European must be wrenched out of his cosiness. (Quoted in Frampton 1982:116–17)

Attacking the 'cosiness' of bourgeois sensibilities became a staple of the architectural *avant-garde*, which, like Behne, tended to align glass construction with the Enlightenment project of creating a rational civilization. For Behne: 'Glass architecture entails European spiritual revolution and transforms the brutish, vain animal fixed in his habits into alert, clear-headed, refined man' (quoted in Passuth 1985: 23). Such attempts to define European 'spiritual revolution' in terms of modern design aesthetics frequently assumed dubious connotations. Architectural attacks on ornament and decoration in the name of rational design were often invested with 'primitivist' projections.[5]

By the 1920s, many leading architects were producing glass designs. Walter Gropius claimed: 'glass architecture, which was just a poetic utopia not long ago, now becomes reality without constraint' (quoted in Blau and Troy 1997: 232). However, this was mostly wishful thinking. While some modern housing estates were built in Germany and the Netherlands during the 1920s, glass construction generally remained limited to key public and industrial buildings, supplemented by the occasional villa. Nevertheless, this scarcity did not prevent iconic structures such as Gropius' Dessau Bauhaus, opened in 1925 with its striking glass curtain walls, from being hailed as portents of the future. For Siegfried Giedion (quoted in Mertins 1997: 234), the blurring of interior and exterior space in Gropius' landmark building amounted to 'an epochal move away from Renaissance spatiality'. While Giedion interpreted this shift in terms of the displacement of a stable centred perspective by the dynamic point of view of a mobile observer, others invested transparency more directly with overt political connotations. In describing his (ultimately unsuccessful) design for the proposed League of Nations Building, Hannes Meyer (who succeeded Gropius as director at the Bauhaus) declared:

> If the intentions of the League of Nations are sincere, then it cannot possibly cram such a novel social organisation into the straitjacket of traditional architecture. No pillared reception rooms for wearied monarchs but hygienic workrooms for the busy representatives of their people. No back corridors for backstairs diplomacy but open glazed rooms for public negotiation of honest men. (Quoted in Frampton 1982: 134)

For Meyer, the 'hygiene' of visibility equates to honesty and healthy democracy. A similar set of connections was made in relation to the reconstruction of domestic space by Sheldon Cheney in his influential *The New World Architecture* (1930):

> Many times I have mentioned the word 'openness' as an ideal of the new home building. I use the word with more than a spatial connotation. It seems to me that there is going on a freeing process in regard to both our physical and our mental lives. While the old walled-in house, the essentially castle-refuge sort of structure, is giving way before less-confined living space, women are discarding most of their clothes, and human minds are freeing themselves slowly from old superstitions, old limiting religions, old narrowly selfish motives. This is a general coming-forth – which seems to me calculated for the better health and the greater happiness of mankind. (Cheney 1969: 272)

Faith in openness and transparency forms one of the pillars of architectural modernism. It also supports the modern political ideal of representative democracy, in which the media's role of disclosure has been enshrined in the notion of the 'fourth estate'.[6] The close connection perceived between modern media and the new architecture in promoting the emergence of the 'open' society was succinctly summed up by renowned photographer Edward Weston:

> Only with an effort can the camera be forced to lie: basically it is an honest medium: so the photographer is much more likely to approach nature in a spirit of inquiry, of communion, instead of with the saucy swagger of self-dubbed 'artists'. And contemporary vision, the new life, is based on an honest approach to all problems, be they morals or art. False fronts to buildings, false standards in morals, subterfuges and mummery of all kinds, must be, will be scrapped. (Quoted in Sontag 1979: 186)

Yet transparency in both architecture and politics remains shadowed by uncertain ends. The difference between using glass walls as a technique to displace the spatial hierarchies of the Renaissance, which was how Giedion interpreted Gropius' Bauhaus buildings, and equating untrammelled visibility with democracy, situates the political stakes of this ambivalence. Where the former plays on the uncertainty of the public/private boundary to propagate a new spatial complexity, the latter tends towards an 'overexposure' which threatens to eliminate private space entirely. While modern debates about the limits to surveillance have usually been settled with reference to the delimitation of a zone of privacy related to the home, demarcating this threshold seems increasingly problematic in the present.

## The privacy of the home

The 'enclosed character' of the bourgeois home, which was the frequent target of *avant-garde* schemes for 'modernization', needs to be located in more specific terms. The 'privacy' accorded the private home waxed in Europe as its productive and reproductive functions were increasingly removed by the growth of capitalist economies. As Habermas (1989: 154) puts it, under capitalist relations of production 'the family loses its functions in and for production'. The family dwelling's compendium of medieval functions, such as workplace and guest-house, were increasingly displaced by specialized structures such as workshops and factories, inns and hotels.[7] However, even as the home lost certain functions, it gained others, as a range of activities which previously took place in public were relocated to domestic space . The result was a substantial reconfiguration of the home's interior.

As Lewis Mumford (1973: 330) notes, the medieval dwelling lacked functionally differentiated space:

> In cities, however, this lack of internal specialization was offset by a completer development of domestic functions in public institutions. Though the house might lack a private bake-oven, there was a public one in the near-by baker's or the cook shop. Though it might lack a private bathroom, there was a munic-ipal bathhouse in the neighbourhood.

Mumford (1973: 328–29) argues that functional differentiation of the home began as early as the 13th century with the development of private bed-rooms, and then private toilets, for the wealthy. These offer 'the first hint of the nineteenth century luxury of a private toilet for every family, or the extravagant American demand for a private toilet for every bedroom'. By the 17th century, innovations in heating and lighting enabled further separation of functions. The kitchen was detached from the scullery, removing the actual cooking from the cleaning of utensils, while the social functions of the kitchen were redistributed to the living room and parlour. There was increas-ing distinction between sleeping and other activities: the dining room could no longer be used as a sleeping parlour, nor could a sleeping chamber be treated as a reception room. By the 18th century, the specialized drawing room came into existence. Where the feudal salon served 'the house' – the family and its name, irrespective of their physical location – the new salon was an identifiable room specifically for receiving guests and holding public discourse within what was otherwise regarded as private space.

The increase in functionally differentiated rooms led to the creation of a new type of interior space – the corridor – dedicated to circulation. Corridors aided the growing desire for privacy. For the first time, rooms were divided not merely by a hanging curtain, but by doors which could be closed to shut others out. As the common spaces of feudal life, such as the hall and courtyard, were diminished in favour of the expansion of distinct rooms for individual family members, the growing functional specialization of house design mirrored the class and gender roles of individual household members. Possessing a house with a range of specialized rooms became a sign of social distinction.

While this kind of functional differentiation remained the privilege of the wealthier classes, by the 19th century the desire for privacy that informed it was becoming an increasingly important part of social life. Mumford (1973: 328) posits a logical progression from the architectural to the ideological: 'Privacy in sleep; privacy in eating; privacy in religious and social ritual; finally, privacy in thought'. In similar vein, Habermas (1991: 49) argued that the quest for increased privacy manifested by the restructuring of the interior space of the home was matched by the emergence of 'interior subjectivity'. This development found cultural expression in new literary forms such as the diary and the first-person narrative, which gave the social relationships born of heightened intimacy with the conjugal family new cultural purchase. The gradual ascendancy of the psychological novel, which enjoyed an after-life as the most influential model for narrative cinema, enshrined the dominance of this interior subjectivity.[8]

The emergence of the modern sense of privacy predicated on the interior subjectivity of possessive individualism corresponds to the transformation of what Foucault designated as 'spectacular' forms of power to modern 'disciplinary' societies. As Habermas (1989: 9) notes, while European feudalism lacked the modern opposition between public and private, feudalism never-theless depended on public attributes which he dubs the *publicness of represen-tation*. This form of power was rooted in the 'double body' of the monarch – simultaneously corporeal and symbolic – in which the ruler displayed him or herself as the embodiment of higher power. [9] Great importance was placed on demonstrations of grandeur in the presence of the common people who were called upon to witness the display. These public displays not only included court ceremony, but what would now be seen as 'private' spectacles such as the monarch eating or rising from bed. As Wlewyn notes:

> [B]eginning with Versailles, the royal bedroom develops into the palace's second centre. If one finds here the bed set up like a stage, placed on a platform, a throne for lying down, separated by a barrier from the area for the spectator, this is so because in fact this room is the scene of the daily ceremonies of *lever* and *coucher*, where what is most intimate is raised to public importance. (Quoted in Habermas 1989: 10)

As society and state became more distinct, the feudal powers (monarch, Church, nobility) which had been the carriers of 'representative publicness' began to disintegrate. This created an acute problem of political legitimation, and contributed to the new configuration of public and pri-vate that characterizes political modernity. Copjec (1993: 174) frames this legitimation crisis as a problematic of *closure*:

> How, after destroying the body of the king, which formerly defined the boundary of the nation and thus closed the set of the subjects belonging to it, how then does one constitute a modern nation?

In place of the personal relations of domination which supported feudal power the more abstract mechanisms which Foucault termed disciplinary power arose. In disciplinary society the political role of the king was gradually assigned to the collective subject of 'the people', while the symbolic function of the 'representative publicness' of the royal body was replaced by the mutual lucidity of subjects. Foucault (1980: 152) underlines the radical equation of democracy with total transparency of society and self which found expression in the political philosophy of Rousseau:

> It was the dream of a transparent society, visible and legible in each of its parts, the dream of there no longer existing any zones of darkness, zones established by the privileges of royal power or the prerogatives of some corporation, zones of disorder. It was the dream that each individual, whatever position he occupied, might be able to see the whole of society, that men's hearts should communicate, their vision be unobstructed by obstacles, and that opinion of all reign over each.

In order that 'the opinion of all reign over each', disciplinary society demanded the deployment of new forms of knowledge dependent on new techniques of measuring, testing, classifying and quantifying. This was the threshold for the emergence of 'statistical society' capable of categorizing individual differences and enforcing boundaries of normality and deviance across mass urban populations.[10] It was also the basis for the abstract forms of identity which, in Copjec's (1993: 174–76) terms, enable the fictive closing of both nation and subject as a coherent 'set'. The profound transformation of the public sphere by the extension of market relations is matched by the withdrawal of 'true' identity into the intimate sphere of the family.[11] According to Ariès (1962: 402):

> It is not individualism which has triumphed but the family. But this family has advanced in proportion as sociability has retreated. It is as if the modern family has sought to take the place of the old social relationships (as these gradually defaulted) in order to preserve mankind from an unbearable moral solitude.

What Habermas (1989: 154) terms the patriarchal conjugal family was characterized by a new sense of privateness formed as the family 'withdrew in upon itself'. Its basis was the putative autonomy of the bourgeois home from the productive functions of the capitalist economy. This strict separation of home and work was, of course, a fiction. The spheres of public and private life were mutually defining, since, on the one hand, the very existence of the private sphere was underwritten by capitalist relations of production, while, on the other, the reproduction of capitalism demanded the (unpaid) labour of familial reproduction. However, the family's gradual loss of economic responsibility had created a new set of contradictions. The autonomy of the private sphere no longer arose from control over productive resources, nor from control over aspects of personal formation such as education and health care. The transfer of these responsibilities to the state, along with many other risks and issues of authority, meant that private autonomy was increasingly defined primarily by the ability to consume. The paradox that Habermas (1989: 156) emphasizes is that what is effectively the 'de-privatization' of the family was widely experienced as 'intensified privacy'. This underpinned the increasing polarization of public and private realms during the 19th century. As the private realm became the space of personal opinion divorced from public expression, and private freedom was principally manifested in choices made about consumption, the widespread exclusion of women from the formal productive economy created the specific gendering of public and private space in the modern city. The new family life lived in the interior was quite distinct from medieval forms of communal life. 'Permanent intimacy' with one's own family was paralleled by the increasing 'solitarization' of individual family members within the house.[12] Polarization of public and private realms also fed the middle-class fetishization which Benjamin (1999b: 8–9) termed 'phantasmagorias of the interior'.

> For the private individual, the place of dwelling is for the first time opposed to the place of work. The former constitutes itself as the interior. Its complement is the office. The private person, who in the office has to deal with reality, needs the domestic interior to sustain him in his illusions. This necessity is all the more pressing since he has no intention of allowing his commercial considerations to impinge on social ones. In the formation of his private environment, both are kept out. From this arise the phantasmagorias of the interior – which for the private man represent the universe. In the interior, he brings together the far away and the long ago. His living room is a box in the theatre of the world.

Benjamin emphasizes the extent to which the enclosed and apparently self-contained universe of the private home assumed a compensatory function in the context of the maturing capitalist economy. It is from this perspective that *avant-garde* proposals to 'open up' the home can assume a radical character, insofar as they strip capitalism of an erstwhile support. Yet, even as it reached an apex in 19th-century middle-class doctrines of family life, the sense of being able to sequester the private space of the home came under new challenge. Schivelbusch (1988: 174) notes the way in which new service networks, such as those supplying gas, undermined the spatial and ideological autonomy of the home. The common practice of switching the gas supply off at the street as the family had retired for the night was more a psychological than a practical safety measure. By sealing the home off from the city, it offered a symbolic restoration of familial authority. It is precisely this ability of the private dwelling to constitute an enclosed space that comes under increasing pressure from the convergence of new forms of architecture and media in the 20th century.

### Transforming the home

In 1926 the renowned Russian filmmaker Sergei Eisenstein travelled to Berlin, where his epic film *Battleship Potemkin* screened to great acclaim. Eisenstein and his regular cameraman Eduard Tisse stayed at the Hotel Hessler, a striking example of the new steel and glass architecture rapidly sprouting up in 1920s Berlin. The experience inspired him to jot down some notes for a possible film that became known as the 'Glass House' project.[13] Eisenstein discussed the project with Mary Pickford and Douglas Fairbanks when they visited Moscow in 1926, and with Le Corbusier when he arrived in 1928. In 1930 Eisenstein was in Hollywood searching for a suitable film subject to be produced by Paramount Studios. His attention was caught by an article in the *New York Times Magazine* on Frank Lloyd Wright's project for a high-rise glass tower.[14] Returning to his earlier idea, Eisenstein was inspired to write a new synopsis for the 'Glass House'.[15] Where the first version of the script was a comedy based around the moving camera's ability to perceive situations which remain invisible to the inhabitants of a glass high-rise building, this version was a psycho-social drama. It included a prologue 'Symphony of Glass' and five narrative parts dealing with the social life he imagined might be experienced in such buildings. The drama turns around the new conditions of transparency, and the fact that it is suddenly possible to see many things which were previously hidden. Part 1 is titled 'We do not see each other', because, as Eisenstein scrawls, the residents 'do not want to see each other'. Part 2 represents a change as a poet 'comes and opens our eyes'. In Part 3, the residents begin to notice each other, but 'the effect is the opposite – they put walls between each other'. The poet makes an impassioned speech which results in the formation of a 'nudiste' association. In Part 4, they begin to *use* the fact that they can see each other. But there is a 'tailor' faction opposing the 'nudistes' and 'competition becomes battle'. Part 5 details the rise of 'plots, plots, plots' and the eventual suicide of the poet. Eisenstein's notes conclude: 'Impossibility to continue like that smashing of the house'.

Although Charlie Chaplin thought the scenario wonderful, Paramount rejected it. Yet the idea persisted throughout Eisenstein's life. Former student Ivor Montagu (1969: 102) later recalled Eisenstein's fascination with the visual possibilities:

> The camera can show them [the inhabitants of the glass building] at any angle, and the richness and multiplicity of possible angles in such a set can be instantly imagined.

In 1947, the year before his death, Eisenstein returned once again to the 'Glass House' project, this time in connection with a stereoscopic film. The poet's suicide scene – first drafted only a year after Mayakovsky's suicide had signalled the terminal decline of the Soviet *avant-garde* and the intensification of Stalinist terror – is mentioned as an example of stereoscopy used for shock effect.

While his 'Glass House' film was never made, Eisenstein's identification of the new configurations of social life and sexual desire produced by the fusion of urban density with architectural transparency recur periodically in cinema, most prominently in Hitchcock's *Rear Window* (1954), which relocates Eisenstein's collective drama onto the psycho-social plane of the individual viewer-voyeur. In 1999, Dutch production house Endemol Entertainment reinvent the concept as a reality game format under the title 'The Golden Cage'. It is subsequently franchised as a successful global format under the title *Big Brother*.[16]

Around the same time that Eisenstein first conceived his 'Glass House' project in Berlin, another resident of that city, Walter Benjamin, was commencing the monumental 'Arcades' project that would occupy him for the rest of his life. The similarities between the two endeavours extend beyond the fact that both were destined to remain unfinished. Both were influenced by what Scheerbart (1972: 41) called the need to eliminate 'the enclosed character of the rooms in which we live'. In his 1929 essay on Surrealism, Benjamin extolled the revolutionary attributes of glass architecture:

> To live in a glass house is a revolutionary virtue par excellence. It is also an intoxication, a moral exhibitionism that we badly need. Discretion concerning one's own existence, once an aristocratic virtue, has become more and more an affair of petit bourgeois parvenus. (Benjamin 1999a: 209)

For Benjamin, glass architecture exemplified the radical modern break with the crowded domestic ambiance of the typical 19th-century bourgeois dwelling. In the context of widespread debates about social revolution and the stripping away of bourgeois hypocrisy, glass construction offered a potent metaphor for the total transformation demanded by revolutionary consciousness. In 'Experience and Poverty' (1933), Benjamin (1999a: 734) elaborated his position:

> If you enter a bourgeois room of the 1880s, for all the coziness it radiates, the strongest impression you receive may well be, 'You've got no business here'. And in fact you have no business in that room, for there is no spot on which the owner has not left his mark – the ornaments on the mantlepiece, the anti-macassars on the armchairs, the transparencies in the windows, the screen in front of the fire. A neat phrase from Brecht helps out here: 'Erase the traces!' is the refrain in the first poem of his *Lesebuch für Städtebewohner* [Reader for City-Dwellers].
> Erase the traces: This has now been achieved by Scheerbart, with his glass, and by the Bauhaus, with its steel. They have created rooms in which it is hard to leave traces. 'It follows from the foregoing', Scheerbart declared a good 20 years ago, 'that we can surely talk about a "culture of glass". The new glass milieu will transform humanity utterly. And now it remains only to be wished that the new glass-culture will not encounter too many enemies'.

For Benjamin (1999a: 734), at least in his more optimistic moments, glass architecture was the herald of revolution. This is exemplified by the way he invested glass itself with some unique qualities:

> It is no coincidence that glass is such a hard, smooth material to which nothing can be fixed. A cold and sober material into the bargain. Objects made of glass have no 'aura'. Glass is, in general, the enemy of secrets. It is also the enemy of possession.

In this passage, Benjamin not only aligns glass with the exposure of bourgeois hypocrisy and the negation of commodity fetishism, but, crucially, with the vector of new media. This last connection can be seen more clearly by briefly recollecting the thrust of his 'Artwork' essay, in which he attributed the destruction of the auratic properties of the work of art to the 'technical reproducibility' introduced by the camera. Destruction of aura is a function of the obliteration of 'distance', symbolized by the new potential for the camera to bring reproductions of objects 'close' to the masses. Benjamin argued that this destruction triggered an epochal shift in the social relations of the image, privileging 'use value' over 'cult value', and thereby creating the potential for reconstructing aesthetics on the basis of politics.[17] In designating glass objects as lacking 'aura', Benjamin positions glass architecture in a similar progressive role. Like the camera, the function of glass is to liquidate cultural tradition, in particular to eliminate the entrenched social relations of domestic space. Benjamin's strategic association of architectural transparency with new media such as photography and film lays the theoretical ground for understanding the relation between windows and screens which has grown more apparent in recent years. If, as Benjamin suggests, lack of aura is a function of the spatial ambiguity arising from the erosion of the distance granted by uniqueness, glass walls accentuate this condition, destabilizing the borders of the room as much as the bounds of the home.

## Walls of light

There were few more enthusiastic advocates of glass construction than Le Corbusier. *Towards a New Architecture* (1923) begins by juxtaposing the retrogression of architecture to the 'virility' of engineering, formulating the necessity of an architectural response to machine technology as a question of 'moral health'. The central problem for Corbusier (1946: 17) was that 'men live in old houses and they have not yet thought of building houses adapted to themselves'. These deficiencies are to be overcome by standardization of building materials, systematic construction, and new designs, resulting in the mass-produced 'house-tool':

> A house will no longer be this solidly-built thing which sets out to defy time and decay, and which is an expensive luxury by which wealth can be shown; it will be a tool as the motor-car is becoming a tool. (Corbusier 1946: 245)

The ambition to unite physical and moral health with modernist aesthetics pointed Corbusier (1964: 24–32) in two directions: on the one hand, towards the transformation of the interior space of the home, and, on the other, towards the rationalization of the city itself.[18] A vital aspect of his famous designation of the house as 'a machine for living in' is the provision of increased light and air: 'Daylight hardly enters your homes. Your windows are difficult to open. There are no ventilators for changing the air such as we get in any dining car' (Corbusier 1946: 89, 107). Corbusier's advocacy of the horizontal window led to a public controversy with his former mentor August Perret.[19] Perret accused younger architects, including Loos and Corbusier, of cultivating an academicism similar to the one they claimed to combat. For his part, Corbusier argued vehemently that the vertical window belonged to an obsolete mode of construction. While load-bearing walls limited the size of horizontal perforations, reinforced concrete not only allowed bigger windows but greater flexibility in their positioning.

The most interesting aspect of the controversy is not so much the preference Perret and Corbusier declared for vertical or horizontal windows respectively, but the different sense of space their argument revealed. As Reichlin notes, Perret endows the vertical window with a humanist rationale:

> The vertical window provides man with a frame; it accords with his outline [...] the vertical is the line of the upright human being, it is the line of life itself. (Quoted in Reichlin 1984: 71)

In contrast, Le Corbusier will finally justify the horizontal window by removing the argument from Perret's humanist terrain and relocating it in the new social space created by modern media. Le Corbusier begins by arguing that, compared to the horizontal window, the vertical window actually fractures the visual continuity of the exterior. Referring to his 1923 Geneva Villa (one of his earliest designs using a large horizontal window), Corbusier argued:

> A window eleven metres long brings the immensity of the outer world into the room, the unadulterated totality of a lake scene with its tempestuous moods or gleaming calm. (Le Corbusier quoted in Reichlin 1984: 72)

In order to support his contention that horizontal windows admit more light, Le Corbusier cites a photographer's table stating: '*You should expose the photographic plate 4 times less in the first room* [with horizontal windows]'. For Le Corbusier (1991: 56), this settles the argument: 'I am no longer swimming in the approximations of personal observations. I am facing sensitive photographic film that reacts to light.' The camera proves definitively what experience had merely suggested. No more need be said. But the camera's utility does not end with providing 'objective' proof as to the quantum of light. It soon becomes a powerful metaphor for the window-walled house itself. For Le Corbusier (1991: 132–33):

> When you buy a camera, you are determined to be able to take views in the twilight of Paris or the sparkling sands of an oasis; how do you manage? *You use a diaphragm.* Your window walls, your horizontal windows are all ready to be diaphragmed at will. You will let in light wherever you like.[20]

While the horizontal window allowed more light, it was only a way-station *en route* to the complete elimination of the walls. By 1930 Le Corbusier (1991: 38–40) argued:

'With reinforced concrete *you get rid of the walls completely.* [...] [I]f I want to, I can have windows on the entire surface of façade.' Removing the load-bearing function of the wall changes the nature of the house and the function of the window: 'From this emerges the true definition of the house: stages of floors [...] all around them *walls of light*' (quoted in Colomina 1994: 7). Soon Le Corbusier (1991: 65) was acknowledging that: 'The horizontal window and finally the "window wall" have brought us to a point that has nothing in common with the past'. With the window-wall, every home could potentially become a glass house. The sense of physical enclosure which had characterized the bourgeois interior was at risk of becoming a purely nostalgic point of reference.[21]

As glass takes over the walls of the house, the metaphor of the camera takes over its spatial conception. Colomina (1994: 311–12) notes the way the Corbusian house becomes a mobile box designed to frame a view.[22] Like a camera, it can be pointed anywhere to convert landscape into image. In Corbusier's (1991: 136, 139) words:

> The house is a box raised above ground, perforated all around, without interruption, by a long horizontal window. [ . . . ] It is in its right place in the rural landscape of Poissy. But in Biarritz, it would be magnificent. [ . . . ] This same house, I should set it down in a corner of the beautiful Argentine countryside; we shall have twenty houses rising from the high grass of an orchard where cows continue to graze.

This alignment between window and camera has broader resonances. If, as Reichlin (1984: 74) argues, Perret's defence of the vertical window belongs to the humanist representational space established in the Renaissance, Corbusier's advocacy of the horizontal window belongs to the gradual withdrawal of architecture from the absolute space of linear perspective. By unmooring the fixity of point of view, Corbusier's mass-produced house-machine enters the 'territory of images' that indelibly shapes modern experience. The Corbusian house functions in the manner of a view-finder, framing the landscape and submitting it to systematic classification in the manner of the postcard. From here, it is only a short step to the contemporary horizon of electronic windows capable, as Mitchell (1995: 33) puts it, of 'opening onto anything at all'.

For Le Corbusier, the importance of architectural transparency was not only aesthetic and hygienic: above all, it signified the end of superstition and irrationality. The belief that rational housing would give birth to rational society courses through his work. This politico-moral dimension returns us to the 'revolutionary virtue' of glass architecture identified by Walter Benjamin and dramatized by Sergei Eisenstein. For Corbusier, the choice was stark: ARCHITECTURE OR REVOLUTION.[23]

Others were less convinced. The point at which the 'openness' necessary for legitimate political scrutiny spills into an authoritarian demand for visibility marks a structural ambivalence inhabiting architectural and political transparency.

## Pitiless light

Criticism of glass architecture was co-extensive with its emergence. Dostoevsky's (1991: 31–32) *Notes from the Underground* (1864) mocked a glass building like the Crystal Palace as a 'chicken coop', adding: 'perhaps I am afraid of this edifice just because it is of crystal and can never be destroyed and that one could not even put one's tongue out at it even on the sly'. Cornelius Gurlitt (1888), who began his chapter on windows by citing Goethe's dying words: 'More light', complained:

> [T]he large window has joined the room too intimately to the outside world; human skill in creating large and entirely transparent panes by means of which the dividing line for the eye between the room and the outside world is blurred has increased too much for it not to have impaired the room's artistic seclusion. (Quoted in Reichlin 1984: 75)

Lucy Orrinsmith's (1978: 64–65) *The Drawing Room* (1877), suggested that 'No one could possibly detect properties of beauty in large sheets of glass', while Baillie Scott's *Houses and Gardens* (1906) lambasted the fashion for bigger windows in English suburban villas:

> Already from the outside we have been made aware of these gashes in the structure, which reveal the window arranged, like a shop is, for outside effect. [ ... ] The window is indeed furnished with all kinds of expensive dust collecting upholstering, but even this cannot cloak the glaring light. (Scott 2004: 105)

But the most damning indictment of modernist transparency was composed not by an architect, but by writer Yvgeny Zamyatin in his extraordinary novel *We*. The book's unhappy publishing history is scarcely surprising, given that it was written in 1920–21 amidst the flowering of Soviet Constructivism, and, like it, was rapidly overtaken by the socialist realist orthodoxy of Stalinism.[24] A forerunner of Orwell's *Nineteen Eighty-Four*, Zamyatin's dystopic tale is set in a futuristic city in which all buildings, and even the pavements, are entirely made of glass. As a result, personal space has largely disappeared. In its stead, life is ruled by the exigencies of the Time-Table, under the watchful eyes of authorities known as the Guardians and the Benefactor, with only two hours per day nominally set aside for personal time. Individual identity is almost totally submerged in collective belonging:

> The brisk crystal bell over my head, seven o'clock, time to get up. On the right and the left, through the glass walls, I see myself, my room, my clothes, my movements – repeated a thousand times over. This is bracing: you feel yourself a part of a great, powerful, single entity. (Zamyatin 1972: 30–31)

Zamyatin's descriptions of the organized masses seen in motion through glass walls anticipates Kracauer's concept of the 'mass ornament'. In Zamyatin's novel, the one exception to the regime of total visibility and omnipresent surveillance is sex. However, it too is rationally organized, with participants allotted specific days and times. The protagonist D narrates:

> At home I stepped hurriedly into the office, handed in my pink coupon and received the certificate permitting me to lower the shades. This right is granted only on sexual days. At all other times we live behind our transparent walls that seem woven of gleaming air – we are always visible, always washed in light. We have nothing to conceal from one another. Besides, this makes much easier the difficult and noble task of the Guardians. For who knows what might happen otherwise? Perhaps it was precisely those strange opaque dwellings of the ancients that gave rise to their paltry cage psychology. 'My (sic!) home is my castle'. What an idea! (Zamyatin 1972: 19)

Zamyatin's black science fiction, with its ironic disdain for 'paltry cage psychology', cut close to the bone in 1920s Soviet society. Already in 1919 Lenin had proclaimed : 'We recognise nothing private [ ... ] our morality is entirely subordinate to the interests of the class struggle of the proletariat' (quoted in Lyon 1994: 185–86). Zamyatin's scenario was not so far removed from certain attempts to promote collective living conditions in order to eradicate old allegiances and habits in favour of 'the new man'. A leading example was Moisei Ginzburg's architectural research which demonstrated the 'inefficiency' of bourgeois design by comparing the proportion of useful area to built volume, and instead proposed new types of functional housing. Ginzburg's 'social condenser' (1928) – a phrase which could variously refer to a building, a district, or even a whole city – aimed not only to provide shelter, but also to actively utilize space so as to influence the inhabitants towards the new way of life. Anatole Kopp (1985: 70) argues:

> The social condenser can therefore be seen as a sort of mechanism for transforming habits; for transforming former man, who was a product of the capitalist system, into that 'new man' described in all the political and Revolutionary literature of the time. [ ... ] In short, social condensers covered all the infrastructure that would lead to the collectivisation of activities which had hitherto been carried out individually.

But where Ginzburg espoused an evolutionary approach which relied on 'persuasion', other Soviet projects took on authoritarian tones. The Model Regulations for Communal Housing of 1928 specified:

> [H]ousing units should be designed for one or two people at most. They should be a place for sleeping, and for some leisure activities and intellectual work. Other premises should be provided for all other purposes. (Quoted in Kopp 1985: 80)

The assumption underpinning such regulations was that communal housing would change the coordinates of social life. According to Sabsovich, a prominent member of the Urbanists whose theories influenced many Soviet architects including the Vesnin brothers: 'The petit-bourgeois way of life will also disappear under the effect of the collectivization of the way of life' (quoted in Kopp 1985: 144). Many projects for communal housing had a striking asceticism: the collective home was often more like a collection of monastic cells designed by – and seemingly for – single young men. This was perhaps not surprising given that one aim of communal housing was the destruction of the family.[25] Nikolaev's description of 1929 hostel to house two thousand students sounds more like an army barracks, while Kopp (1985: 81) argues that Kuzmin's Time-Table for collective life published in the Constructivist magazine *SA* 'makes us think of a work camp'.

In Zamyatin's novel, the disappearance of private space assumes tragic dimensions, but not for the reasons that Eisenstein suggested. The exposure of the bourgeois interior widely seen by the modernist *avant-garde* as a precondition for social revolution has become an overexposure which eradicates not only the architectural space for individual subjectivity, but also the space for political resistance. Zamyatin's fiction recalls the thrust of Benjamin's observation about the 19th-century interior: 'The interior is not only the universe, but also the *étui* [protective covering] of the private person' (Benjamin 1999b: 6). If the perforation of this covering initiates the decomposition of an historically constituted mode of subjectivity, an essentially *political* question remains: at what point does the increased visibility the private domain erode qualities that are more than mere functions of what Benjamin dismissed as 'petit-bourgeois' sensibility?

### Two-way windows

As Zamyatin dramatized to chilling effect, the visibility of glass walls is double-edged. Colomina (1994: 8) notes:

> The picture window works two ways: it turns the outside world into an image to be consumed by those inside the house, but it also displays the image of the interior to that outside world.

Yet this reversibility was constantly elided in modern architectural discourse. Writing in 1909, Simmel (1997: 170) argued for the uni-directionality of the window: '[T]he teleological emotion with respect to the window is directed almost exclusively from inside to outside: it is there for looking out, not for looking in'. Le Corbusier took a similar stance. While an attitude of 'inwardness' may have been appropriate in the past, *la ville radiuese* would render it obsolete:

> A friend once said to me, 'No intelligent man ever looks out of his window; his window is made of ground glass; its only function is to let in light, not to look out of'. Such a feeling is only too appropriate in a congested city where the disorder is painful to witness [ . . . ]. (Le Corbusier 1971:184, 186)

In contrast, when installed in the planned city, the window-wall 'gives us the feeling of "look-outs" dominating an ordered world' (Le Corbusier 1971: 187). These 'walls of light' were the prerogative of the sovereign inhabitant looking outwards:

> *Walls of light!* Henceforth the idea of the window will be modified. Till now the function of the window was to provide light and air and to be looked through. Of these classified functions I should retain only one: that of being looked through. (Quoted in Colomina 1994: 7)

As Lacan (1977) notes, this fantasy of a window through which one sees while not being seen is symptomatic of the denial of the gaze. In Lacan's account, the window is already a gaze:

> The window, if it gets a bit dark and if I have reasons for thinking that there is someone behind it, is straight-away a gaze. From the moment that this gaze exists, I am already something other, in that I feel myself becoming an object for the gaze of others. But in this position, which is a reciprocal one, others also know that I am an object who knows himself to be seen. (1988: 215)

The reversibility of the gaze, which splits the subject in a perpetual oscillation between viewer and viewed, found a specific psycho-social architecture in cinema. The Corbusian fantasy of a one-way window through which the subject sees while not being seen echoes what Metz (1976a: 14) has termed cinema's fundamental disavowal: 'I look at it but it does not look at me looking'. Metz (1976b: 96) argues that the dominant cinematic imaginary came to be structured around its own version of the glass house, as narrative form was predicated on the transparency of the 'fourth wall':

> It is even essential [ ... ] that the actor should behave as though he were not seen (and therefore did not see his voyeur), that he should go about his ordinary business and pursue his existence as foreseen by the fiction of the film, that he should carry on with his antics in a closed room, taking the utmost care not to notice *that a glass rectangle has been set into one of the walls*, and that he lives in a kind of aquarium. [Emphasis added]

Metz's comment underlines the shared logistics of perception which joins cinema to glass architecture. This conjunction has fascinated numerous film-makers, including Eisenstein and Tati. But perhaps the most revealing exploration of its psycho-sexual tensions was Hitchcock's *Rear Window* (1954) in which the uncanny openness of the home's interior is explicitly treated as a function of the convergence of glass and media. From the beginning of the film it is made clear that the injured photojournalist Jeff (played by James Stewart and purportedly based on Magnum founder Robert Capa) is indulging in activities that are not socially sanctioned. His nurse Stella comments: 'Oh dear, we've become a race of Peeping Toms. What people ought to do is get outside their own house and look in for a change'. By the end of the film she has become an avid watcher herself. The same is true of Jeff's girl friend Lisa (Grace Kelly). Like Stella, she is initially disturbed by Jeff's voyeurism, and sceptical of his suspicions towards Therbold (Ray Burr), arguing: 'A murderer would never parade his crime in front of an open window'. However, despite her protestations, she is drawn to watching Therbold. It is only when the pair try to convince Jeff's police friend, Doyle, that Therbold is a murderer, that the ethics of what they are doing return to trouble them. But the uncertainty of this novel social terrain leads Lisa to conclude: 'I'm not much on rear window ethics.'

What is most striking in *Rear Window* is the manner in which the reversibility of the window – the reciprocity of the Lacanian gaze – attains a level of physical threat. At the very moment that the conclusive evidence of murder is revealed to both characters and spectators in a close-up shot apparently seen through Jeff's zoom lens, the murderer Therbold looks directly towards the window of Jeff's apartment. Jeff's panicked reaction, 'Turn out the light, he's seen us', functions simultaneously on two levels. While it is part of the narrative progress, it also threatens to shatter the 'glass wall' protecting the spectator's putative sovereignty. *Rear Window* dramatizes the way that glass architecture transformed the private sphere into what Habermas termed 'floodlit privacy'.[26] It also signals the manner in which this 'openness' has been intensified by the entry of new media technologies into the space of the home. If the modernist ambition to fuse the political transparency of the public sphere with the architectural transparency of domestic space already contained contradictions of the sort identified by Zamyatin, the roll out of modern media technologies further accentuated the tensions between public and private space.

In his essay for the exhibition catalogue of the landmark 'International Style' exhibition curated by Philip Johnson and Henry-Russel Hitchcock at MoMA in 1932, Lewis Mumford suggested that the impact of media technologies on the home had become a major question for architecture:

> The laying down of a new basis for housing has been, since 1914, one of the chief triumphs of modern architecture. [ ... ] With the return of entertainment to the home, through the mechanical invention of the phonograph, the radio, the motion picture, and the near prospect of television, the house has made up by gains in recreational facilities what it has lost through the disappearance of earlier household industries. Hence the proper design of the house has a new importance, in that, with greater leisure for the whole community, more time will probably be spent within its walls. (Quoted in Colomina 1994: 209–10)

While Mumford recognizes that the replacement of older productive functions with newer recreational facilities means that more time 'will probably be spent within [the home's] walls', he doesn't pose the question as to the nature of those walls, or the manner in which they are able to enclose an interior space. Today it is clear that the impact of electronic media has equalled, if not exceeded, the effect of glass architecture on private space. As the screen has become a new window, the modernist discourse of transparency has taken a new twist. Colomina (1997: 158) notes that modern architecture increasingly found itself forced to exist in a space defined by flows of images:

> This is the space of the media, of publicity. To be 'inside' this space is only to see. To be 'outside' is to be *in* the image, to be seen, whether in the press photograph, a magazine, a movie, on television, or at your window. [ ... ] But, of course, the fact that (for the most part) this audience is indeed at home is not without consequence. The private is, in this sense, now more public than the public.

In his influential study *The Organization Man* (1956), William Whyte (1969: 324) had already pointed towards the generalization of 'rear window ethics':

> Just as doors inside houses, which are sometimes said to have marked the birth of the middle class – are disappearing, so are barriers against neighbours. The picture in the picture window [ ... ] is what is going on *inside* – or what is going on inside other people's picture windows.

Whyte alerts us to the heightened interest in the intimate sphere that has since found a home as media *content*. Not only does modern media penetrate the home's space, but domestic life has itself become the subject of media attention in new ways.

This trajectory blossomed in the 1990s as webcams and 'reality television' took the exposure of private space across a new threshold. Enhanced media focus on the intimate sphere emerged precisely at the historical moment that the conjugal family was increasingly liquefied by the withdrawal of the corporatist welfare state and the growing submission of private life to market forces. The appearance of intimate relations as prime-time media content corresponds to the maturation of 'risk society'. Where the 'representative publicness' of feudal society once raised the private functions of the royal body to matters of public importance, such public attention now belongs to 'ordinary people' who gain temporary celebrity by exposing their private lives to public scrutiny.

## Notes

1 Orrinsmith 1978: 64–65; Scheerbart cited in Frampton 1982: 93.
2 The 'Glass Chain' or 'Crystal Chain' took the form of correspondence between fourteen architects and writers, including Taut who adopted the pseudonym *Glas*.
3 Frampton (1982: 34) argues: 'The Crystal Palace was not so much a particular form as it was a building process made manifest as a total system, from its initial conception, fabrication and trans-shipment, to its final erection and dismantling.'
4 Paxton's structure was moved to Sydenham in 1852, before its destruction by fire in 1936.
5 I will cite one prominent example which is all too easy to multiply. In *Towards a New Architecture* (1923), Le Corbusier (1946: 133) writes: 'Decoration [ ... ] is suited to simple races, peasants and savages [ ... ]. The peasant loves ornament and decorates his walls. The civilized man wears a well-cut suit and is the owner of easel pictures and books.'
6 Colin Rowe (1978: 4) locates social investment in transparency as a response to the horror of World War I: 'For from Woodrow Wilson's hopes for international politics to the *ville radieuse* is but the merest of steps. The crystal city and the dream of absolutely unconcealed negotiation (no playing of poker) both, alike, represented the total expulsion of evil after the purgation of war.'
7 Mumford (1973: 328) dates this development from as early as the 14th century when the emergence of milling, glass making and iron workshops marked 'the earliest break between domestic life and work, both in space and function'.
8 Habermas (1991: 50) gives literature a key role in articulating modern public and private spheres, insofar as its specific form of 'realism' created vicarious experiences that allowed 'anyone to enter into the literary action as a substitute for his own'. As Barker (1984: 52–53) points out, the new literary forms not only set the self apart from others, but imposed a new demand for self-reflection: 'The defining feature of the bourgeois discursive regime is the *in situ* control [ ... ] of the newly interiorated subject. [ ... ] Not only is it possible and necessary to narrate the outer world from an inner place, by means of a clarified and transparent instrumental language, and similarly to reflect on others as Other, but – more insidiously – the subject can now, and must, reflect on itself in the same fashion.'
9 The other face of this system of spectacular power were the forms of physical punishment, described in gruesome detail by Foucault, in which the body of miscreants were marked and rendered in the monarch's name.
10 See Chapter 2.
11 Arendt (1958: 46) points out that in classical and medieval societies public rather than private relations were the site of 'true' identity.
12 Bahrdt (1961) acutely summarizes the values incubated in the bourgeois home:

> The interiorization and cultivation of family life; a culture of life in the home that involves the conscious shaping of the most intimate material

environment; private possession of the means of education and their common use by the smallest social group; intellectual exchange as the normal and integrative form of life with one's kin; a religious life within the circle of the family, relatively independent of the Church; individual eroticism; and freedom of choice of marriage partner, which in its final stage of development grants legitimate veto power not even to the parents – all these are typical phenomena of the expansion of the private sphere and, at the same time, of bourgeois culture and morals. (Quoted in Habermas 1989: 45)

13  See Leyda and Voynow 1982: xii. Bulgakowa (2005) notes that Eisenstein visited Lang on the set of *Metropolis*, and suggests: '*The Glass House* was intended as a polemical response not only to Lang's film, but also to Bruno Taut and Mies van der Rohe's glass architecture.'
14  Bulgakowa (2005) notes he pasted the clipping into his diary and wrote: 'This is a glass sky scraper that *I* invented in Berlin.'
15  Eisenstein had already reworked the original 'glass house' idea in 1928. All following quotes in this paragraph are from the notes in Leyda and Voynow 1982: 45.
16  See Chapter 8.
17  For a more detailed discussion of this point, see McQuire 1998: 187ff.
18  Rowe (1978: 93) highlights the contradiction between what he calls Corbusier's spatially complex homes and his spatially simplistic urbanism.
19  The exchange was published in the Paris Journal in 1923 (see Reichlin 1984: 65–78). My thanks to Suzie Attiwill for drawing my attention to this essay.
20  Elsewhere, Le Corbusier (1964: 44) writes of controlling the flow of light through a 'glass wall [ … ] equipped with "diaphragms" for shutting out light at will'.
21  This trajectory was not simply a function of glass construction but was aided by the free disposition of internal volumes advocated by Loos' influential concept of the *Raumplan*.
22  Colomina (1994: 311–12) argues: 'The house is a system for taking pictures. What determines the nature of the picture is the window. [ … ] If the window is a lens, the house itself is a camera pointed at nature.'
23  This is the coda added to *Towards a New Architecture*. Corbusier's stance was based on his contention that existing conditions prevented workers from developing an understanding of industrial labour: 'We may well say, then: Architecture or demoralization – demoralization and revolution.' His solution was for the masses to claim 'their rights to a machine for living in' (see Corbusier 1946: 256, 259).
24  Although written in 1920–21, and first published in New York in 1924, *We* was not published in Russian until 1954, and even then not in Russia. Eisenstein was clearly aware of the book, but doesn't mention it in his autobiography.
25  By the 1930s destruction of the family was no longer official policy in the Soviet Union. But the moment for conceiving radical solutions to housing had also passed.
26  Strangely, given his focus on the role of the media in formation of the public sphere, Habermas barely mentions the impact of electronic media on the private sphere.

# 8

## The Digital Home

[B]lindness is still vision, vision that is no longer the possibility of seeing, but the impossibility of not seeing.

(Maurice Blanchot 1981)

I exist only insofar as I am looked at all the time.

(Slavoj Zizek 2002)[1]

### From windows to screens

In Paul Virilio's (1988: 185–97, 1991a: 69–100) evocative chronology, the history of the window is divided into three phases. The first window is simply an entrance or door: the single opening, common to cave and room, which has the primary purpose of allowing the passage of occupants. This is followed by the 'light-window' discussed in the previous chapter: a specialized opening designed to facilitate the movement of light and air rather than bodies or material objects. The 'third window', however, is an opening of a different kind: an electronic portal which initiates a radically changed relation to space. For Virilio (1991a: 79): 'The television screen is an introverted window, one which no longer opens onto adjoining space but instead faces beyond the perceptible horizon'. Virilio rightly emphasizes the extent to which the screen window *ruptures* the spatial order of its predecessors. Yet, the rupture should not be reduced too quickly to the fact that one window opens onto the 'real world', while the other opens only on to its image. Once the glass window began to cede its traditional functions of illumination and ventilation to mechanical systems of lighting and air-conditioning, its pre-eminent modern function as defined by Le Corbusier came to the fore: to frame the exterior as a *view*. With the 'picture window', the boundary between inside and outside was already effectively marked by an *image*.

The screen window accentuates this spatial ambiguity in which the outside world is apprehended as spectacle. Once electronic media such as television can provide 'real time' windows to the world, the window metaphor moves beyond the limits which have historically defined human perception.[2] In this chapter, I want to examine the way that the spatial openness of the modernist glass house has been reconfigured by the emergence of the digital home. The glass window's double function of both joining and separating – *hinging* – inside and outside has been increasingly displaced onto the ubiquitous screen, which is now asked to be the link or interface between the heterogeneous dimensions of 'home' and 'world'. But as much as electronic media offer to *screen* the world for the domestic observer – in the dual sense of projecting but also filtering – the screen home entails the subjection of domestic space to a new level of exposure. Consider, for example, the description of 'Digital Dream House', built in 2003 by entrepreneur Scott Jones:

> Keypads and touchscreens are placed around the house to provide control of audio, video, air-conditioning, heating, lighting, security, drapes and fireplace lighting. [ . . . ] The home is divided into 46 audio and video zones, 246 lighting circuits, and numerous security cameras and sensors. One can only gain entry into the master suite by touching his [sic] fingerprints against a security pad. Even the boys' tree house is wired with a T1 line (high-speed Internet access). In fact, just about the only devices that haven't been built into the network are the washing machine, the refrigerator and the toaster. No doubt, it's only a matter of time. (Schiffman 2004)

Like the Gates' House a decade earlier, the 'Digital Dream House' is presented to readers as a future which will soon be widely available. One of the most remarkable and yet unremarked features of the smart home filled with digital technology is the extent to which it is a highly surveilled space – if only because personal information is needed to access and customize the various services. If the saturation of the home with digital media not only brings into question the continued existence of private space, the fact that privacy is often relinquished voluntarily in the name of increased utility suggests its loss will not be universally mourned. In concluding the previous chapter, I suggested that the intimate sphere has now become the content of popular media and entertainment in a new way. The salient point about the global success of Endemol's reality television phenomenon *Big Brother* is not simply its fusion of the distributive function of electronic media with the design principles of glass architecture, but its promotion of a new mode for the public viewing of private life. The passage from glass architecture to *Big Brother* throws into relief the ambivalent forms of belonging which characterize social life early in the 21st century, suspended between accelerated informational and economic circulation which promise fluidity and openness, and the erosion of older identity-moulds such as the nation-state and the conjugal family.

### Static and dynamic windows

A deeper understanding of the radical nature of the screen window is facilitated by contrasting its emergence to the older representational space constructed by painting. If both classical painting and broadcast television have often been apprehended by the metaphor of the window, this is less a mark of simple continuity than of the metaphor's adaptability. While the camera utilized fundamental aspects of painting's classical system of geometric perspective, technological images also fundamentally departed this spatial paradigm. When Alberti famously described the technique of geometric perspective in the 15th century in terms of depicting forms on a plane surface as if seen through a window, he was providing an aesthetic rationale for a representational space clearly demarcated from the space of the observer.[3] The forms of visual art which emerged during the Renaissance by deploying this perspectival system, such as easel painting and free-standing sculpture, primarily aimed to depict a scenographic world in which objects and bodies were placed in a coherent space. As Panofsky (1969) underlined, this was a fundamentally *mathematical* world-view in which every part of the image enjoyed a continuous and proportional relation to every other part. Jay (1992) suggests that gradually the new spatial order came to outweigh the older symbolic order, as geometric perspective assumed pseudo-religious connotations.[4] As a result of this displacement, Renaissance art gradually abandoned its older narrative order for a new one in which individual paintings were increasingly self-sufficient 'scenes' filled with more detailed 'information'. Jay (1992: 182) argues:

> Cartesian perspectivalism was thus in league with a scientific worldview that no longer hermeneutically read the world as a divine text, but rather saw it as situated in a mathematically regular spatio-temporal order filled with natural objects that could only be observed from without by the dispassionate eye of the neutral researcher.

The space established by the Albertian window is a discrete space apparently independent from the viewer's space. It is a visual paradigm revolving around the ideal of a detached observer who sees the world as an image without being part of that image. It corresponds to what Heidegger (1977) termed the modern age of the 'world picture'. For Heidegger, the fundamental event of the modern age is precisely the Cartesian conquest of the world *as perspective*, determining a new relation between subject and object in which 'Man becomes the relational centre of that which is as such'.[5] Perspective cleared the way for rational-scientific interpretation of nature in terms of a 'ground plan' which regulates knowledge according to homogeneous dimensions of time and space.[6] It is because the world has been separated from the observer that it can be submitted to mathematics and geometry, which become the dominant matrix for both scientific knowledge and visual representation.

If the apex of this perceptual paradigm was reached in European painting between the 15th and 19th century, it is crucial to appreciate the double impact of the camera's invention. At one level, the camera extended the authority of geometric perspective by automating its production. This was a primary support for the immediate willingness of 19th-century society to invest photographic reproduction with the stamp of objective truth. However, the spatial paradigm of the detached observer who looked *through* painting's window was also profoundly challenged by 'technical repro-ducibility'. The novel ease of making – or rather, *taking* – images led to an unnerving multiplication of points of view. As early as the 1860s, photography was generating a new fluidity of visual framing. Photographic promiscuity made it progressively more difficult to maintain the authority of the relatively limited repertoire of points of view that had defined the 'realism' of painting for several centuries. The emergence of throw-away images in the 1880s, as half-tone print reproduction complemented the booming popularity of postcards, marked the threshold of a new visual terrain defined not by scarcity and fixity but over-abundance and flux. Crossing this line eventually led to the emergence of new visual forms such as collage and photomontage which were based on the re-assembly of disjunctive fragments of the visible world. By the 1920s, unusual forms of framing had become a favourite technique of *avant-garde* photographers for cultivating viewer estrangement, particularly in the context of representing the modern city. The stable subject position and centred point of view that characterized the classical observer of Alberti's painting-as-window belonged to a world which no longer seemed to exist.

Cinema effectively took the more active frame established by photography and marshalled it into dynamic narrative forms privileging multiple points of view seen by a mobile observer. As I have argued in Chapter 3, cinematic perception came to exemplify the shock aesthetic that dominated the culture of the modern city. The Renaissance model of geometric perspective had developed in concert with a humanist order of architecture in which proportion was calculated according to the fundamental measure of the human body. Hollis Frampton (1983: 189) posits a structural link between painting and other elements of the architectural order: 'Painting "assumes" architecture: walls, floors, ceilings. The illusionist painting itself may be seen as a window or doorway'. By contrast, cinema's dynamic mode of perception – 'perception conditioned by shock [*chockförmige Wahrnehmung*]' as Benjamin (2003: 328) put it – 'assumes' not the stable site of a stationary building but the variable vector of a moving vehicle.

The view through the cinematic 'window' is post-human insofar as it no longer corresponds to the embodied eye but is produced through the systematic application of technological equipment.[7] Cinema does not simply augment the perceptual capacity of the classical subject, but contributes to a technological displacement of the body as the authoritative measure of human experience. The continuous spatial envelope presumed by the Renaissance world, which conditioned the stable position of the humanist subject, increasingly finds itself displaced by what Virilio (1991b) has dubbed an 'aesthetics of disappearance'. Cinema's technological vision is integral to the modern experience in which the continuous space of Cartesian perspective gives way to the relational space of fragments that will never finally coalesce into a stable whole. The modern industrial city, powered by electricity and traversed by dynamic vehicles and media flows, is the material expression of this complex spatiality. The Corbusian villa, with its architectural 'promenade' which sought to orchestrate a series of cinema-style views, is a symptomatic response to this condition. Through mass-production, it sought to convert the modern home into a mobile frame or view-finder capable of deployment at any site. It is this uncertain terrain – this displaced or disembedded domestic space – that electronic media enter.

## Real time windows

The electronic screen is a 'real time' window. In common with the trajectory established by cinema, it offers a view which is unrestricted by the physical location of the screen or the spectator; nor is it intrinsically bound to the embodied perspective of the humanist subject. Its primary difference to the cinematic window is temporal. If the cinema window can be compared to what Duchamp once termed a 'delay in glass', insofar as it reassembles a scene that has already taken place, television is an instantaneous *relay* which shifts the screen window decisively to the present tense. Even though relatively little contemporary television is actually broadcast live, the historically novel possibility of live coverage remains central to its position in the social imaginary. Moreover, the dominance of 'real time' media has expanded with the spread of the internet. If cinema was a crucial perceptual laboratory for establishing relational space as the characteristic experience of the industrial city, the electronic screen has been the primary conduit for extending this uncertain spatiality and implanting it directly into the private home.

Writing in 1928, Paul Valéry (1964: 226) already anticipated audio–visual flows becoming an integral part of the modern home:

> Just as water gas, and electricity are brought into our houses from afar to satisfy our needs in response to minimal effort, so we shall be supplied with visual or auditory images, which will appear and disappear at a simple movement of the hand, hardly more than a sign. Just as we are accustomed, if not enslaved, to the various forms of energy that pour into our homes, we shall find it perfectly natural to receive the ultrarapid variations or oscillations that our sense organs gather in and integrate to form all that we know. I do not know whether a philosopher has ever dreamed of a company engaged in the home delivery of Sensory Reality.

While Valéry ostensibly imagines such flows becoming 'perfectly natural', his concluding remark about the 'home delivery of Sensory Reality' underlines their potential for reshaping human sense perception – and perhaps redefining 'human nature' itself. Thomas Hutchinson's influential *Here is Television, Your Window to the World*, published in 1946 as television broadcasting emerged from the shadows of war, symptomatically registers the new uncertainty affecting the relation between the spectator and what they can see. Hutchinson's chapters are structured around a comprehensive list of genres that a television viewer might expect to encounter on the small screen, from information, variety, drama and music to puppetry, live sport and news. As the title of his book suggests, he conceptualizes television primarily as a window *looking out* onto the world at large. But, almost unconsciously, Hutchinson (1946: ix) also mentions a slightly different possibility: 'the outside world can be brought into the home'. If the first trajectory belongs firmly to the Corbusian ideal of a one-way window at the service of the sovereign spectator whose identity is secured by the stable space of the home, the second indicates the extent to which 'the home delivery of Sensory Reality' might open the space of home and identity to new currents.

Hutchison does not acknowledge this second trajectory, and this neglect has been confirmed by the dominant paradigms of television research.[8] Nevertheless, my concern here is precisely the manner in which television has transformed the private sphere. As Spiegel (1992: 11–72) reminds us, the television set is itself a material object, and its arrival as a focal point in the 1950s home entailed significant reorganization of domestic space. Not only were new types and arrangements of furniture required, but competition for scarce floor space saw older entertainment staples such as the piano relegated to the nostalgic past. Television was soon implicated in the renegotiation of domestic routines, including meal times (and places), bed time, family leisure and child-care, and remains crucial to the way in which gender and generational differences are negotiated within domestic space.[9] However, there is another fundamental sense in which television alters private space, according to the reversibility characteristic of all windows. As much as it frames the world as a series of events to be watched in the home, television has helped to convert the intimate sphere into an *event* watched by others. Representations of domesticity and family life form a staple of television programming, underlining the reciprocity between the domestic space of action and the private scene of consumption. If the modern home has become the *target* for increasing amounts of advertising at least since the commercialization of radio in the 1930s, it has now literally become a *scene*: part of the screen spectacle available for everyday consumption. This conversion of private space into a scene for public viewing is a direct consequence of the 'real time' temporality of electronic media.

### And we loved *Big Brother*

As Eisenstein recognized, the modernist glass house was a scene waiting to be filmed. Or, better still, televised and webcast. Since its premiere in the Netherlands in 1999, Endemol's *Big Brother* concept, in which a group of people live together in a house over a period of months while being watched by millions of anonymous others, has extended modernist transparency beyond its previous parameters. The broad cross-cultural popularity of the format suggests that it resonates, if not a global *zeitgeist*, a condition that is extensive and pervasive.[10] The franchising of *Big Brother* not only testifies to the global nature of contemporary cultural flows; the fact that the show takes place in a television studio fashioned as a domestic dwelling is symptomatic of the ambiguous position the contemporary home occupies in the global mediascape. Both vectors are crucial in reshaping the relation between public and private space in the present.

While Endemol's *Big Brother* houses are not glass houses in a strict architectural sense, they clearly revive key aspects of Eisenstein's 'Glass House' project. Eisenstein's enthusiasm for 'the richness and multiplicity of possible angles in such a set' returns as promotional advertising extolling the number of cameras surveying the *Big Brother* houses, leaving the contestants no place to hide. Rather than glass walls, multiple cameras produce the 'virtual transparency' prototyped in highly surveilled spaces such as prisons and shopping malls. The affinity extends beyond shared technological infrastructure. As Peter Weibel (2002: 215) notes, programmes such as *Big Brother*, which involve deliberate sequestration of participants in contained spaces, recapitulate the 'prison as entertainment'.

At least some of the frisson of Endemol's creation rests on its appropriation of George Orwell's notorious vision of totalitarian society. In Orwell's (1984: 157) novel, published in 1949 on the cusp of the mainstreaming of broadcast television, it is significant that the telescreen is not a portable box like the first television sets, but a *structural* element belonging to the wall.

> The voice came from an oblong metal plaque like a dulled mirror which formed part of the surface of the right-hand wall. [ . . . ] The instrument (the telescreen, it was called) could be dimmed but there was no way of shutting it off completely.

The fact that it can be neither avoided nor shut down renders the telescreen an irreducible part of living space. Unlike the television, the Orwellian tele-screen allowed both transmission and reception. The key difference to the contemporary internet is that Orwell imagined an extremely centralized network. Rather than peer-to-peer communication, there is merely a reverse channel constructing a Benthamite panopticon with countless cells. Efficient functioning of the panoptic system, as Foucault explained so meticulously, depends upon coupling the asymmetry of the supervising gaze to uncertainty as to when supervision is actually occurring. In these structural conditions, surveillance is apt to be internalized. For Orwell (1984: 158), this psychological transformation is the primary fact of life under *Big Brother*:

> There was of course no way of knowing whether you were being watched at any moment. [ . . . ] You had to live – did live, from habit that became instinct – in the assumption that every sound you made was overheard, and except in darkness, every movement scrutinized.

Echoing Zamyatin's *We*, the result in *Nineteen Eighty-Four* is a nightmare society blighted by total loss of private space. The exception to the rule occurs when the protagonist, Winston, is able to locate an architectonic blind spot in his home:

> [F]or some reason the telescreen in the living room was in an unusual position. Instead of being placed, as was normal, in the end wall, where it could command the whole room, it was in the longer wall, opposite the window. [ . . . ] By sitting

in the alcove and keeping well back, Winston was able to remain outside the range of the telescreen [ . . . ]. It was partly the unusual geography of the room that had suggested to him the thing that he was now about to do. (Orwell 1984: 161)

This stolen private space becomes the site in which Winston's inner voice first emerges from its internal clamour, manifesting itself in that most personal undertaking characteristic of modern individuality: the writing of a diary. For Orwell, writing remains a space of conscience and personal authenticity, whereas the telescreen represents the levelled-off, lowest common denominator collective culture.[11] In Orwell's story, other cracks gradually emerge in the totality of surveillance. When Winston and his secret lover Julia find a place to meet, they rent a room in the prole quarters in the older part of the city.[12] Prole apartments are bereft of telescreens. While it remains curious that Orwell didn't see the political utility of extending the telescreen 'downward' to the proles, in the manner of radio and television broadcasting, the lack plays a strategic role in the novel. Private space opens the possibility of personal agency. According to Charrington, the old man who rents the incipient lovers a room (and is later unmasked as a member of the feared Thought Police): 'Everyone wanted a place where they could be alone occasionally' (Orwell 1984: 275).

Today it is necessary to ask: how widely is this desire still shared? In the lead-up to the second Australian series of *Big Brother* screened in 2002, 27 000 prospective contestants applied to live for 13 weeks in its glass house. How does the condition that Orwell depicted as a totalitarian nightmare transpose itself into popular entertainment in barely two generations?

### The aesthetics of boredom

As early as the 1920s, painter and film-maker Fernand Léger dreamt of a documentary film which would record the life of a man and a woman over 24 hours. Nothing should be omitted or hidden; nor should they ever become aware of the presence of the camera. While Léger's ambition pales before the megalomania of the God-like director in Peter Weir's *The Truman Show* (1998), it is revealing that he never made such a film, believing it would be 'intolerable' to watch (see Kracauer 1960: 63–64). It is worth focusing for a moment on the differences between Léger's unmade film of a day in a life, and Weir's fictional conceit about a television show which surveys an individual life over years.

While Weir's concept seems more radical in its scope, its manifestation as a film is, in fact, far more traditional. The fictional television programme in *The Truman Show* resembles 'fly-on-the-wall' documentaries of family life such *An American Family* made by the US Public Broadcasting Service in 1972, *The Family* made in the United Kingdom in 1974 and the ABC–BBC co-production *Sylvania Waters* shot in the Sydney suburbs in 1992. All these programmes used 'real people' – or rather non-professional actors playing themselves – to create multi-episode narratives focused on domestic relations in nominally private space. They were important steps in the emergence of the 'docu-drama' combining conventions of documentary film (real people and places, unobtrusive camera) with key elements of dramatic form (seriality, character-driven narrative, focus on emotions). What is most critical in this context is the fact that all these programmes were constructed through the condensation of an extended time of filming into a text comprised of what Deleuze calls 'privileged instants'. Significant moments are selected for their capacity to enhance character and storyline development, while unimportant or extraneous incidents are compressed or excluded. This narrative structure seems so obvious it is scarcely worth commenting on – except for its sharp contrast to Leger's edict that *nothing should be omitted*.

The radical edge of this demand became more apparent in the 1960s when Andy Warhol produced a series of experiments in cinematic duration which involved filming ordinary activities such as sleeping and eating in 'real time'. This led to longer projects such as *A: A Novel* (1965), with its aim to audio-tape 24 hours in Robert Olivio (aka Ondine)'s life, as well as the notorious film *The Chelsea Girls* (1966). Bosley Crowther's (1966: 3) sententious review in *The New York Times* described *The Chelsea Girls* as 'nothing more than an extensive and pretentious entertainment for voyeurs, letting them peer (I should add, quickly, for three and a half hours!) at what is presumably happening in several rooms of a New York Hotel'. Despite his dismissive tone, Crowther inadvertently hits at least one target. Duration is central to Warhol's undertaking. As Crowther's exclamation mark underlines, the film's refusal to telescope the action into a series of significant moments tests the patience of viewers and reviewers alike. It takes what Duchamp laughingly described as the most radical aspect of 1960s 'happenings' – boredom – and puts it at the centre of aesthetic experience.

Predictably, Warhol was one of the first artists to acquire a video camera.[13] Like the tape recorder which had been his constant companion for several years, video fitted his ambition for recording seemingly mundane activities over large spans of time. Unlike most film directors who see their role as making decisions about 'privileged instants', Warhol's declared ambition to be a machine found its outlet in *not* making such choices. In this regard, it is not surprising that one of his unmade projects took video surveillance as its model. In an interview in 1969, Warhol explained:

> In New York, apartments have a channel five which allows you to watch anybody who enters the front door. That will be my show: people walking past the camera. We'll call it *Nothing Special*. (Quoted in Carroll 1969: 140)

Video not only facilitated recording events of extended duration, but offered new possibilities for using media feedback to alter spatial ambiance in 'real time'. As video artist Dan Graham (1979: 62) noted:

> Video is a present-time medium. Its image can be simultaneous with its perception by/of its audience (it can be an image of its audience perceiving). The space/time it presents is continuous, unbroken and congruent to that of

the real time which is the shared time of its perceivers [ . . . ]. This is unlike film which is, necessarily, an edited representation of the past of another reality [ . . . ] for separate contemplation by unconnected individuals. [ . . . ] In a live video situation, the spectator may be included in frame at one moment or be out of frame at another moment. Film constructs a 'reality' separate and incongruent to the viewing situation; video feeds back indigenous data in the immediate, present-time environment or connects parallel time-space continua.

Through the 1970s Graham developed a striking series of artworks comprising spaces in which social interactions could be experienced 'in person' but also watched through glass walls or on co-located screens.[14] In retrospect Graham's experimental rooms with their quasi psycho-sociological experiments are both fascinating and rather unnerving. They have proved prophetic along at least two key axes: first, illustrating the capacity for 'real time' media to alter the dynamics of 'face-to-face' social interactions in the media city; and second, revealing the potential for intense scrutiny of domestic space to become a new art form.

Experiments such as Warhol's *Nothing Special* and Graham's media–architecture hybrids prefigured a new wave of art utilizing the automated video surveillance cameras which were the mainstay of the video industry prior to the commercialization of domestic camcorders in the 1980s. Virilio (1994: 47) points to the prize awarded to Michael Klier at the *Second International Video Festival* in Montbéliard in 1984 as the inauguration of 'a sort of pancinema which [ . . . ] unbeknown to us, turns our most ordinary acts into movie action'. Klier's video *Der Riese* (The Giant) was a montage of images recorded by automatic surveillance cameras on roads, airports and supermarkets in major German cities. By the end of the decade, surveillance footage was being repackaged for commercial television.[15] However, in place of the indiscriminate 'real time' duration which had interested Warhol and Graham, the television version was, rather predictably, focused on the 'privileged instants' of mishaps, accidents and emergency rescues. Nevertheless, the popularity of genres utilizing video surveillance is significant. It indicates the extent to which the presence of cameras surveying everyday life has now been routinized and normalized. This is the social context in which the *absence of the camera* can be experienced in terms of psychological loss and deprivation.

Warhol's film and video aesthetic is notoriously difficult to situate. Its 'real time' approach is antithetical to the tradition of film narrative with its overwhelming emphasis on temporal compression. It is also disjunctive to what Williams (1974) described as the 'flow' of broadcast television, since Warhol's practice extended flow far beyond the moment that television would normally switch to another segment. If Warhol's films are closest to the unblinking gaze of the automated surveillance camera, they inhabit even this space in a radical way, since raw surveillance footage lacks the data processing that unleashes its power of discrimination. These differences are all instructive. In particular, they throw into relief the way that 'live' media such as video and television bring the problem of time to the fore in a distinctive way.

As Warhol demonstrated with *The Chelsea Girls*, film already enabled the construction of media texts which are radically co-extensive with the events they ostensibly re-present. Television puts this previously marginal possibility at the centre of its mode of presentation. Despite this centrality, television has tended to limit extensive live coverage, especially outside the studio. While this has partly been for reasons of technical difficulty and cost, another factor is fear of loss of control. Extended live coverage of uncontrolled events carries the risk that viewers might be asked to embrace Warhol's *avant-garde* aesthetic of boredom. This is a risk that most television stations have been unwilling to take, particularly in the broadcast environment of spectrum scarcity where relatively few programmes compete for mass audiences. Nevertheless, live coverage is an historically proven attraction for audiences. The solution to the commercial imperative to provide the excitement of live coverage while avoiding the risk of viewer boredom has been to instigate heightened intervention in the event itself. The 'television event' must be orchestrated so that its coverage can be smoothly presented as a *live* narrative.

Outside of the studio, which has its own systems of control, intervention in the event to ensure its coherence as a live broadcast developed most rapidly in the field of sport. The combination of multi-camera coverage of the action, with interpretation provided by expert commentators and studio anchors, turns professional sport into a *structured* live event which now stands as the model for other fields, including politics and war.[16] The growth of event management, in which the view from the camera's eye takes precedence over other considerations, has come from both sides, so to speak; from broadcasters who seek control over their 'content', and from event organizers who seek to distribute their 'product' to the maximum audience.[17]

Since the launching of CNN in 1980, extended live coverage of special events has become far more common.[18] But commercial broadcasters face numerous contradictions in such undertakings. As much as television tries to avoid boredom, it frequently becomes boring precisely because of its reliance on formulaic structures and manufactured excitement to overcome its fear of the 'dead time' in which 'nothing happens'. This calculation is inevitably difficult from the broadcaster's perspective, because the only bigger sin than producing viewer boredom is missing the moment. Striking the correct balance between control over the event and anticipation of the unexpected that constitutes the fundamental *lure* of live television is the central dilemma facing programmers in a commercial environment. As Deese Schonfeld, first president of CNN, put it in 1995:

> [W]hat you want to do is have the audience want, not what you have up there now, but what they think you might have up there in the next five seconds and will miss forever if they should just turn off for a minute. You want to lock everyone in the world into the belief that the next minute, the world's greatest

catastrophe, the world's greatest joy, may occur, and if they leave CNN they will have lost that one great moment in their lives that people will talk about forever [ . . . ]. (*Naked News* 1995)

## The farming of emotions

As Benjamin and Barthes recognized half a century apart, the camera's capacity to register the contingency of social interactions is a principal attraction of photo-media. For a long time, this capacity was conceptualized as a mark of realism. However, in an era of professional public relations and pervasive information management, contingency has become a media currency in a post-realist sense. When events ranging from street encounters to school visits are routinely stage-managed as part of political or marketing campaigns, it is the momentary absence of a smoothly polished image, manifested in political gaffes and celebrity mishaps, which is read as providing access to the elusive 'real'. The unplanned and the accidental promise to take us behind the surface of the media spectacle, providing sought-after signs of authenticity.

The explosion of reality television in the late 1990s sought to exploit a similar currency. In the context of the formulaic and highly controlled narratives which constitute mainstream cinema and television programming, a new predilection for filming real people in supposedly real situations emerged. *Big Brother* has proved one of the more popular and enduring manifestations of this trend. While it is all too easy to dismiss *Big Brother*'s claims to 'realism' by pointing out all the artifices, from the extended game show structure to the participants' awareness of the cameras, this risks being a superficial response. If lack of control over pro-filmic action is still one rule of thumb for distinguishing documentary from fiction, *Big Brother* lies somewhere in between. Like televised sport, *Big Brother* is a narrative form created from a semi-controlled event. The pay-off sought by the producers and the audiences is not the drama of a contest of sporting skill, but the flashes of emotion and personal intimacy that can be captured. In short, the aim is to establish a structured situation in which a leavening of uncontrolled outcomes might occur. As Peter Abbott, Executive Producer of the Australian *Big Brother* put it:

> The whole process is one of creating an environment and then seeing what happens. And the nice thing is that it sometimes rewards you with something that is much better than what you would have imagined. (Abbott 2002)

In particular, the success of *Big Brother* depends upon the capacity of the producers to manufacture environments capable of generating emotional encounters with the ring of authenticity. Where the hunting of emotion in the world at large was once the province of authors and artists, reality television seeks to *farm* emotion through extended observation of real social interactions in controlled situations. In some respects, this shift can be traced back to the rise of the film studio and professional film acting. But its extension to non-professional actors living in hybrid environments which are simultaneously home and television studio situates the growing crisis of authenticity haunting the intimate sphere in the era of pervasive media 'testing'. As Roscoe (2001: 14) notes, there is a contradiction between wide-spread recognition of the constructed nature of life in the *Big Brother* house, and the compulsive desire to search for signs of authenticity:

> Audiences play the game of evaluating how well participants perform their role. If, as an audience, we play it well enough, we may be rewarded with a 'flicker of authenticity' – moments when the performance breaks down.

Before exploring the relation between acting and authenticity further, I want to consider the way in which the structured event of life in the *Big Brother* house becomes a nightly narrative seen on television. The process highlights significant differences between broadcast television and the internet, and suggests that the radical effect of exposing private life to public scrutiny can be easily blunted by the rush to exploit it as a commodity. When *Big Brother* is screened on prime-time television, and therefore has to compete for mass audiences, the format involves a tightly edited package of highlights compiled into an ongoing story.[19] In Australia, the 24-hour multi-camera coverage is reduced to two hours of rushes which offer building blocks for plot and character development in the half-hour nightly shows. Chris Blackburn (Australian supervising producer) notes:

> Then we have to boil it down again into some sort of storyline. The problem being that's it's not like a movie and you might get the start and the middle of a terrific story and someone just forgets to end it. So you have no control over it, you just get what you're given and you have to work around that. (Media Report 2002)

In contrast, watching *Big Brother* via the internet is tantamount to watching an entirely different phenomenon. In place of the tautly edited and smoothly narrated half-hour blocs is a far looser, less directed experi-ence.[20] Despite gestures towards enhancing 'viewer control', such as providing a menu of different camera angles, anyone who has watched *Big Brother* on the internet for any length of time will sooner or later cross the threshold into a Warholian aesthetics of boredom. Things meander. Narrative threads and character traits are far less clearly defined. Mundanity predominates. Given that boredom is a highly repressed element of broadcast television, the negative 'nothing happens' against which the dominant narrative economy of 'privileged moments' seeks to define itself, the appearance of this sort of 'real time' coverage as a popu-lar format deserves attention. Like a live broadcast of long duration, or one of Warhol's films, a real time webcast won't necessarily be watched in a focused manner. Rather, the more it tends to become part of a viewer's everyday environment, the more frequently it is 'sampled' in what Benjamin would have called a distracted manner.

## Civility and overexposure

The *Big Brother* phenomenon built on the novel social experiment constituted by the proliferation of digital webcams offering live internet coverage from private homes 24 hours a day. One of the first notable examples was Jennifer Ringley, a young Washington student who generated enormous publicity when she began to 'live life on-line' in 1996, using a digital camera to upload images of her one room dormitory to the web every two minutes. The so-called 'Jennicam' soon became a thriving enterprise attracting subscriptions – and innumerable imitators.[21] While there was undoubtedly a pornographic element to public interest in Ringley, the voyeurism extended well beyond the simple possibility of encountering nudity. Rather, the fantasy involved being able to observe the private life of a total stranger in all its minute details.

Victor Burgin (2002: 232) underlines the peculiar temporality that 'sampling' an other's life involves, arguing that the 'real striptease' was not Ringley's undressing or even the occasional bout of explicit sex, but her intermittent presence on camera. Viewers who logged on would often find only an empty room. Comparing Jenni's entrances and exits to the famous attempts by Freud's infant nephew to master a swinging cotton reel, Burgin (2002: 232) suggests:

> Jenni is in full control of her presence and absence in the room. Her mastery of her own coming and going in effect puts her in the maternal position in relation to her supplicants who log on to her website.

While viewers experience Ringley as controlling the oscillation of her presence and absence, this is not necessarily how Ringley experiences herself. It is significant that she used a webcam, rather than a video conferencing system. Ringley displayed no interest in seeing her viewers, or in letting them *hear* her. Her main contact with her audience – many of them at work, watching her student dorm via a window in the corner of their computer screen – was via email. Burgin (2002: 230) stresses the asymmetrical relation this established: 'From our side of the screen the camera is a window. From Ringley's position, her camera is a mirror'. In other words, the camera/screen apparatus was used to establish Le Corbusier's 'one-way' window. But rather than following Le Corbusier's blueprint to the letter, Jennicam inverted it. Instead of supporting the look of the sovereign spectator through the window to the world outside, Jenni put herself on display for others. It is from this perspective that Burgin (2002: 231) reads Jennicam as a transitional object in Winnicott's sense: it was deployed by Ringley as a 'plea to be noticed and approved of', and a strategy for negotiating, or failing to negotiate, what Winnicott calls the 'capacity to be alone'. For Winnicott, the capacity to be alone involves the experience of solitude while in the presence of someone else. It is precisely the parameters of such social experiences that 'real time' media situated in domestic space promise to radically alter.

When Ringley graduated and shifted from student dorm to an apartment, there was an interval during which the camera was switched off. In a radio interview she claimed: 'I felt lonely without it' (quoted in Burgin 2002: 230). When asked 'Why are you giving up your privacy like this?', Ringley (1999) responded: 'Because I don't feel I'm giving up my privacy. Just because people can see me doesn't mean it affects me – I'm still alone in my room, no matter what.'

Such a statement would have been inconceivable to George Orwell. Being alone demanded, above all, the absence of the tele-screen. When the Party member O'Brien reveals he can turn off the screen in his apartment, he immediately tells Winston and Julia: 'We are alone' (Orwell 1984: 303).[22] In contrast, contemporary forms of surveillance such as the domestic webcam are not only tolerated, but frequently sought after. As Ana Voog (2001) – one of Jennifer Ringley's imitators and creator of the website Ana-Cam – put it: 'I don't mind people watching, in fact I find it rather comforting, especially when I'm sleeping'.

As John Tagg (1988) has noted, the presence of a camera has long been accepted as a sign of accession to the status of subjecthood. The fact that 'I' am someone worth photographing or filming constitutes a peculiarly modern proof that 'I' exist as a unique individual. What has changed in recent decades is the extent to which the circulation of images of intimate social interactions is no longer contained predominantly within the personal sphere, but is routinely distributed along open media circuits. The charge of 'authentic emotion' which accrues to images of personal intimacy has become a new social currency. Giving up private space in the name of public entertainment is the reverse face of the historical process by which surveillance of public space has been normalized in the name of minimizing social risk. It constitutes a 'softer' panopticism of pleasurable viewing complementing the 'harder' mechanisms of computerized surveillance which now greatly exceed Orwell's imagination.

Ringley's webcam, like the success of *Big Brother*, also testifies to the partial reversal of the modern condition that Foucault associated with Bentham's Panopticon. In place of the fear of being observed, many people now clearly fear *not being watched*. Zizek (2002: 225) argues this indicates an 'urgent need for the fantasmatic Other's gaze serving as the guarantee of the subject's being: "I exist only insofar as I am looked at all the time".' In a context where the classical others of family, friends and acquaintances are losing their social function, Ursula Frohne (2002: 271), argues the role of reflexive self-assurance provided by the Other 'has been delegated unconsciously to the media.' As a result, Frohne (2002: 257) argues that the camera is no longer experienced as the eye of punishment, as it had been for Orwell and Foucault, but has become a means for conducting experiments in self-construction. The older paradigm of voyeuristic spectatorship which *Rear Window* exemplified has been complemented by a heightened narcissism in which new forms of self-display gain social traction.

What is at stake in this shift is not only a new degree of flexibility in self-construction but a new understanding of the level of personal detail it is acceptable to reveal in everyday social interaction. In his treatise on 'public man' published over quarter of a century ago, Richard Sennett (1978: 264) argued that

> Wearing a mask is the essence of civility. Masks permit pure sociability, detached from the circumstances of power, malaise, and private feelings of those who wear them. Civility has as its aim the shielding of others from being burdened with oneself.

For Sennett, 'civility' is an essential social art practiced by individuals exercising reciprocal self-restraint. As Zygmunt Baumann (2000: 96) glosses the concept:

> [Civility] means, first and foremost, the provision of spaces which people may share as *public personae* – without being nudged, pressed or cajoled to take off their masks and 'let themselves go', 'express themselves', confess their inner feelings and put on display their intimate thoughts, dreams and worries.

The social barometer has now swung well away from this understanding of civility in public life. One key indicator of this trend has been the rise of 'confessional' television programmes, pioneered in the United States by *Donahue* (1970–96) and *Oprah* (1986 onwards).[23] In place of Sennett's emphasis on mutual restraint as the precondition of civility, these programmes exploited growing demand for unrestrained revelation of the 'true self' in public. Expressing one's innermost feelings in public is no longer seen as placing a burden upon others, but constitutes a mark of one's personal integrity.

### Performing the authentic self

The reconstitution of the intimate sphere as media content brings new formations of identity to the fore. Contestants on *Big Brother* tend to display a form of self-conscious individuality which extends well beyond the understandable nervousness of media novices exposed to intense scrutiny.[24] Rather, this self-consciousness belongs to the heightened responsibility that reflexive individuals are asked to take for the projection of self-image.[25] However, self-construction is an ambiguous quality which is both avowed and disavowed. While most contestants are keen to be seen as 'in control' of their self-image and their social interactions – a desire which extends to an intense focus on personal appearance, body grooming and personal hygiene – there is a paradoxical desire for their personal identity to remain a 'natural' possession which demands no special effort. 'I just wanted to be myself' is the mantra contestants repeat time and again, while disdaining any notion they might be 'performing' for the cameras. At the same time, many express doubts as to whether other housemates have in fact dropped their masks, accusing them of 'playing the game' with an eye to garnering popularity with household members or the public at large. Upon leaving the house, contestants routinely evaluate their own role on the show in terms of the extent to which their 'true self' has been shown. This tends to be the nub of their satisfaction or dissatisfaction with their experience.

Nearly four decades ago, Goffmann (1969) argued that all public projections of a self inevitably contain performative aspects, as individuals adopt different 'scripts' in new situations. But pervasive media have altered the dynamics of such performances. As early as the 1920s, Vertov (1984: 125) remarked on the difficulty of capturing authentic social interactions on camera:

> In life, people very often act, and sometimes rather well. I wanted to remove that mask too. This was a very difficult task. To solve it, the camera had to penetrate into a room, into the intimate emotional experiences of people. It had to be done so that the camera would penetrate to the level on which a person reveals himself completely.

If, to Vertov, awareness of the camera compromised his survey of intimate life, it is no longer a simple matter to remove either camera or camera-consciousness. Moreover, the stakes have shifted in media cultures in which the public projection of 'personality' has assumed significant political overtones. With the rise of celebrity-based systems of mediated politics, power increasingly depends upon the convincing display of emotional qualities such as empathy and compassion. The successful politician, like the successful *Big Brother* contestant, is likely to be one who is able to pass the 'character test'. Both need to be able to *act* with conviction – which is to say, perform the 'true self' without self-consciousness. But where does performance end? For Zizek (2002: 226) the achievement of *Big Brother* is precisely the way it holds up a mirror to the lack of the real underlying our performative surface:

> In other words, what if, in our 'real lives', we already play a certain role – we are not what we are, we play ourselves? The welcome achievement of 'Big Brother' is to remind us of this uncanny fact.

The conundrum Zizek proposes is not new, but I would argue that it has assumed a new configuration in the present. To understand this twist it is worth briefly returning to Bosley Crowther's caustic review of Warhol's *The Chelsea Girls*. Crowther's categorization of the film as excessively voyeuristic ignores the high degree of awareness of those being filmed. As Joseph (2002: 240) argues in relation to Warhol's tape recordings, this self-consciousness inevitably blurs any fixed lines between reality and performance:

> An interesting problem was an interesting tape. Everybody knew that and performed for the tape. You couldn't tell which problems were real and which problems were exaggerated for the tape. Better yet the people telling you the problems couldn't decide any more if they were really having problems or if they were just performing.

Joseph's description is pertinent to the highly surveilled life lived in the *Big Brother* houses. Shifting from Crowther's presumption of the voyeuristic spectator to the perspective of the narcissistic performer establishes a rather different relation to camera and display. As Joseph (2002: 240) puts it: 'the self-conscious pro-filmic subject, narcissistically exhibiting him or herself as a means of attracting attention, is complemented by a camera whose power lies in its threat to look away'. As I've suggested above, this is precisely the threshold crossed in the passage from Orwell's *Nineteen Eighty-Four* to Endemol's *Big Brother*: the camera's power is no longer experienced in terms of the threat of visibility, but rather the indifference of invisibility. When Warhol shot *The Chelsea Girls* in 1965 this shift to narcissistic display seemed radical. In the 21st century it has become a more general condition.

The significance of *Big Brother* is not simply the dynamic of the programme itself, but what it reveals of this broader social condition. Benjamin's declared ambition to loosen the petit-bourgeois 'discretion concerning one's own existence' has been parlayed into an *overexposure* of the intimate sphere as live media content. While the new 'openness' to the public display of emotion might be read, at least in part, as the overdue insertion of women's voices and concerns into the public sphere, it also has more ambiguous affiliations. When the experience of observation by the media becomes deeply internalized, role-playing is increasingly subsumed by the roles that people think the media want to see, or will pay attention to. Ursula Frohne (2002: 256) concludes:

> As media performance comes to epitomize what is socially desirable, the longing of the audience to maneuver themselves into the images of the entertainment industry only increases. This compulsive desire to attain tele-presence, to verify and validate one's own existence – in a kind of 'screen test' – under the gaze of the media society and thereby to anchor one's cultural self-realization is characteristic of contemporary media narcissism.

The social context in which the need for constant reassurance from the Other has been increasingly delegated to media technologies is the transition to 'full modernity', in which the micro-level of the social is fully exposed to the de-territorializing forces of capitalism. As identity has increasingly lost its self-evident quality, family relations and the intimate sphere have assumed the status of a reflexive project in which gender and sexuality are more volatile elements. The contemporary desire for the perpetual presence of 'always-on' media, like the compulsive exchange of mundane and apparently trivial messages, or the acute sense of anxiety experienced in the case of separation from one's phone or computer, register the peculiar blend of anxiety and agency which characterize 'reflexive modernity'. This is the context for the wholesale subjection of social relations to what Benjamin long ago termed 'testing'. The reflective subject of Descartes' 'I think therefore I am' morphs into the reflexive subject of accelerated feedback and decisions made on the run, characterized by the short-term consciousness that Lash (2003: ix) aptly dubs 'I am I'. This is the social condition that the *Big Brother* franchise has successfully turned into prime-time drama of global proportions: a 'real life' drama dealing with the altered status of the subject living in 'real time' media culture. It is a drama belonging to the historical moment in which the increased penetration of the home by media technologies, and the increased internalization of surveillance mechanisms by home viewers, are being routinized and normalized.

*Big Brother* exemplifies the way that 'testing' via the camera can be turned into an operational concept. Competitive evaluation of the self is central to the show's drama. Weekly nominations require dissection of behavioural and character traits of housemates, while the audience votes to retain or eliminate those who are nominated.[26] Voting for or against specific housemates is not just a money-spinner for the producers, but is symptomatic of the new conditions of competitive individuation. In the era that Baumann (2000) aptly dubbed as one of 'universal comparison', individuals experience an increasingly parlous existence, not only competing with others, but constantly evaluating their own performances. Lash (2003: ix) terms this emergent subject the 'combinard':

> He puts together networks, he constructs alliances, makes deals. He must live, is forced to live in an atmosphere of risk in which knowledge and life-changes are precarious.

*Big Brother* is a drama of this contemporary life lived on the brink. The precarious nature of 'home' is no longer primarily a function of the fact that it is rented or mortgaged to the hilt (the fundamental alienation of the home under capitalism for Marx), but that your tenure now depends on the *ratings* achieved by your 'character'. Eviction is at the whim of the votes of unknown strangers. Change can happen almost instantaneously: one minute you're in, the next minute you're out. In this respect, *Big Brother* is symptomatic of the way the trope of democracy has been transformed by a radical combination of marketing and technological speed. It reflects the transition to a fully fledged image-politics in which 'character' has become a central political issue, and 'testing' means continually sampling 'public opinion', and feeding it back to the public – often using their own words – in real time.

In Orwell's *Nineteen Eighty-Four*, the functioning of the political system depended as much on citizen surveillance as on the infamous Thought Police. Endemol's *Big Brother* plays out its own policing scenario which results in the serial ejection of household members. The process, encompassing the varied fan discourses which surround it, resembles a classical Durkheimian exercise in achieving social solidarity. The communal bond is activated by the symbolic expulsion of the despised 'other'. Instead of the mythical, omnipotent patriarch who represents the face of the Party in *Nineteen Eighty-Four*, Endemol's *Big Brother* merely brings us face-to-face with ourselves and our peers.

This isn't to deny that *Big Brother* can occasionally offer glimpses of a more inclusive society.[27] The social potential of relational space lies precisely in the extent to which social relations must be actively constructed across heterogeneous spaces in which the face-to-face is imbricated with the global, and older hierarchies and forms of exclusion no longer cohere as tightly. However, in a context dominated by competitive individualism, the modern ambition for 'openness' has taken a specific turn which blunts its more radical possibilities. On *Big Brother*, friendships and co-operation bloom in the short term, only to be sacrificed to the demands of 'one winner', mirroring all too closely the contemporary social experiment in which neo-liberal economic doctrine is extended indiscriminately into the fabric of intimate life. When the self is widely experienced as a media commodity – a serial product voted on by others as part of a publicly staged test of personal popularity – the modern project of 'openness' has lost its way. The commodity self is, above all, expendable; routinely discarded or expelled in favour of a better-performing other.

Habituation of the drive to exhibit the self is the counterpart of habitual scrutiny of the other. It remains striking that the world in which the *Big Brother* format has achieved global popularity is one in which the place of the other has become an increasingly strident political issue. The pseudo-democracy of the *Big Brother* audience poll finds close parallels in the contemporary profusion of opinion polls about asylum seekers and 'border protection'.[28] The drama of serial expulsion at the heart of *Big Brother* format belongs to a context in which policies of 'border protection' increasingly pre-occupy the modern nation-state swimming the tides of globalization. Part of the process of redirecting these tides involves learning to inhabit the mediascape differently. *Big Brother* remains a fascinating social experiment precisely because it places our capacity to live with others on centre stage. But, rather than accepting the challenge of generating new models for collective existence in the context of lives routinely lived at-a-distance, *Big Brother* belongs more to the process by which private space is 'dis-embedded' – detached from the space of face-to-face connections – and reconstituted in a global network of similarly dis-embedded private spaces. New models for social existence are more likely to be closer to Warhol's films than *Big Brother* – often mundane and potentially boring, intermittently fascinating, less concerned with manufacturing controversy than with experiencing how others live. This is the promise that *Big Brother* holds up today in a distorted fashion.

## Notes

1  Blanchot 1981: 75, 90; Zizek 2002: 225.
2  For Hayles (1999: xiiii), the 'posthuman' emerges when technology is so deeply entwined with the production of identity that they can no longer meaningfully be separated.
3  The technique of symmetrical 'visual cones' was spelt out by Alberti's *De Pittura* (1435–36), as well as later treatises by Viator (1509) and Dürer (1525) among others. Alberti (1970: 28–29) wrote:

> I think every painter, if he wishes to be a great master, ought to understand clearly the similarities and the distinctions of the planes,

a thing known to very few. [ . . . ] They should know that they circumscribe the plane with their lines. When they fill the circumscribed places with colours, they should only seek to present the forms of things seen on this plane as if it were of transparent glass. Thus the visual pyramid could pass through it, placed at a definite distance with definite lights and a definite position of centre in space and in a definite place in respect to the observer.

4   Jay (1992: 180) writes:

[L]inear perspective came to symbolize a harmony between the mathematical regularities in optics and God's will. Even after the religious underpinnings of this equation were eroded, the favourable connotations surrounding the allegedly objective optical order remained powerfully in place. These positive associations had been displaced from the objects, often religious in content, depicted in earlier painting to the spatial relations of the perspectival canvas themselves.

5   As Heidegger (1977: 139) puts it: 'Through Descartes, realism is first put in the position of having to *prove* the reality of the outer world, of having to save that which is as such.'

6   Heidegger (1977: 119) argues: 'Into this ground plan of nature, as supplied with its prior stipulation, the following definitions among others have been incorporated: Motion means change of place. No motion or direction of motion is superior to any other. Every place is equal to every other. No point in time has preference over any other.'

7   Recalling Benjamin's (2003: 263) analysis: 'The equipment-free aspect of reality has here become the height of artifice, and the vision of immediate reality the Blue Flower in the land of technology.'

8   The impact of vision-at-a-distance has historically defined two primary axes for research into television: first, understanding how television 'screens' the world by imposing ideological parameters on public discourse; and second, measuring the specific 'effects' television produces on its audiences. The third major axis of television research concerns institutions.

9   See, for example, Morley 1982.

10  By 2006, the *Big Brother* format had been franchised to over 40 territories, including countries in Europe, the Americas, Asia, Australia, the Pacific, the Middle East and Africa.

11  As I will discuss below, this contrast between an imposed public mask and an ideal of personal authenticity remains central to the drama of Endemol's *Big Brother*.

12  This contrast between the modern city and an ancient dwelling or room which contains memory traces of an atavistic identity is shared by *We* and *Metropolis*, as well as *Nineteen Eighty-Four*.

13  He was given a video recorder by Norelco in 1965.

14  For example, in *Time Delay Room 1* (1974), spectators in Room A could see those in Room B live on one television monitor and on an 8-second delay on a second, while those in room B could see audience A live and themselves on delay. Spectators could walk between the two rooms, which was timed to take about 8 seconds. Graham's project resembled Vertov's use of cinematic reflexivity in some respects. While his writings often seem to accept the equivalence of embodied perception with self-presence, his experiments point elsewhere – to the continual implication of 'direct perception' with the deferred effects of memory.

15  Programmes such as *COPS*, which used surveillance footage alongside coverage of police actions premiered in 1989, while domestic counterparts such as *Australia's Funniest Home Videos* premiered in 1990.

16  A crucial threshold in the construction of the live event as media event was crossed in Leni Riefenstahl's films *Triumph of the Will* (1934) and *Olympia* (1938). See McQuire 1994, 1998.

17  As early as 1956, Anders (quoted in Weibel 2002: 210–11) argued that live broadcasting fundamentally changed the quality of 'events': 'When the event is mobile and appears in virtually countless examples, then it can be considered a serial product; and when payment is made for broadcasting the serial product, then the event becomes a commodity.'

18  Technological changes, which have made live broadcasting easier, more reliable and cheaper, have also played a role, as has the shift to a multi-channel, multi-platform mediascape.

19  In Australia, the general formula is a nightly prime-time show consisting of half an hour of edited highlights, while weekly nomination and eviction shows use edited highlights in combination with live studio action and structured live crosses to the house.

20  This distinction has become less clear over time: broadcast television is now using more live coverage, especially late at night, while the internet offers a menu of highlight clips to supplement its 'live cams'.

21  By 2001, Jennnicam was reported to attract 5 million hits per day. The site was shut down in 2003 after 7 years of operation.

22  Ironically, this constitutes a fatal invitation to openness and trust.

23  Other indicators are the popularity of highly personal talkback radio, the explosion of chatrooms and blogs on the internet, as well as the rise of reality television.

24  These comments are based on my analysis of the Australian and UK series.

25  Giddens (1991: 5) suggests that, in reflexive modernity, the self becomes a 'reflexive project': 'The reflexive project of the self, which consists in the sustaining of coherent, yet continuously revised, biographical narratives, takes place in the context of multiple choice as filtered through abstract systems. [ . . . ].' Beck (2003: 24) points to the partial and more ephemeral nature of identity in this context: 'Living a life of one's own means that standard biographies become elective biographies, do-it-yourself biographies, risk biographies, broken or broken-down biographies.'

26  These processes are themselves rapidly internalized. In the first Australian series of *Big Brother*, the contestants were uncertain as to whether or not there was an audience, while, by the sixth series, contestants displayed increased awareness of the protocols of the show, including how 'characters' are formed through selective editing, and their own roles as 'role models' to the public at large. While this sort of standardization is predictable, it also makes it increasingly harder to generate the sort of 'authentic' emotions that audiences desire.

27  Notably the way in which gay and lesbian contestants have been 'mainstreamed' in some series.

28  This cross-over became most pronounced in Australia during the 2001 Federal election campaign when, in the wake of 9/11, the conservative government was re-elected largely on a platform of preventing the entry of potential asylum seekers to Australian territory. The *Big Brother* mantra '*You* decide' was echoed by the campaign slogan '*We* decide who comes into *our* country.'

# 9

## Conclusion

In this book, I have traced the emergence of a distinctive lived environment: the media city. This passage has crossed a number of historical thresholds involving the relation between media technologies and the transformation of the city. In the mid-19th century, the invention of technological images lent the first urban modernization projects their most decisive technique for 'mapping' the new urban space. Marville's serial photography paralleled Haussmann's reconstruction of Paris, as both media and social space were submitted to the industrial logic of enhanced circulation. The reconstitution of social life by the extension of market relations and the emergence of urban spectacle counterpointed the growing apprehension of the city as a territory of images. Where the late-19th-century urban dweller might have bought a postcard as an urban souvenir, by the early 20th century they could also buy a ticket to the cinema. The broad popular appeal of film established the quintessential modern perceptual apparatus conditioned by movement. Film's mobile spectatorship facilitated the apprehension of urban space in terms of a *journey*. In the ambivalent 'shock' effects of film montage, the kaleidoscopic experience of 'big city life' found its formal counterpart. Both photography and cinema play critical roles in forging a new relation between the circulation of technological images and the transformation of modern urban experience. They lay the ground for the more profound de-territorialization set in train by the extension of electronic and digital media. The leveling of the World Trade Centre towers watched live by a global audience registered – as uncanny trauma – the tightening circuits imbricating media and city in the 21st century.

Throughout this book, I have argued that modern media are not simply forms of 'representation', in the sense of providing images that either reflect or distort a social reality already established elsewhere. Rather, I have suggested that new media platforms have consistently contributed to the formation of new modes of perception and knowledge, as well as the production of new forms and sites of social action. The articulation of photography with statistical society situates the recurrent tension between the appropriation of technological media in terms of their potential for enabling instrumental mastery over space and social action, and the other headings to which new media also point: towards the destabilization of traditional coordinates of space and subjectivity, and their possible reinvention along different lines.

This tension, which cannot finally be reduced to a simple choice of one over the other, is a mark of a fundamental ambivalence which conditions modernity.

The key departures entrained by electronic media and heightened by contemporary digital networks in the present are functions of their increased speed and ubiquity. Media no longer belong primarily to spatially bounded specialized sites such as the cinema, but are becoming mobile and pervasive. Rather than a record of past events, digital media frequently provide instantaneous feedback in 'real time'. Not only are social interactions routinely distributed across heterogeneous space-time frames, but mediation by complex technological systems has also become integral to social dynamics. The saturation of the urban environment with media technologies has accentuated the modern erosion of the nexus between place and identity, and has exercised increasingly radical effects on the stability of urban form. The hierarchy of classical urban space has given way to more radically 'open' spatial ensembles. As urban structures cede priority to seemingly immaterial flows, 'relational space' has become the dominant experience of urban life. This ascendancy belongs to the historical moment in which the active generation of social relationships is required to span the unpredictably imbricated spaces of the global and the face-to-face. If one possibility set in train by the dismantling of the old order of social space is the capacity to form new social collectivities no longer governed by modes of identity based around the exclusion of the other, another possible heading is the generalization of atomized individual existences.

The 'media city' names this historically distinctive milieu in which the complex and often contradictory currents of reflexive modernity are being lived out. Ubiquitous, customizable media correspond to the heightened demand for individuals to engage in processes of self-evaluation and self-construction across all zones of everyday life. Increasingly these endeavours are conditioned not only by abstract knowledge but also rely on complex technological systems. Smart phones, interactive interfaces, responsive architecture and intelligent environments can all too easily be aligned with the extension of commodity logic into the interstices of both public and private space. The problem is not simply the exposure of the previously private, or the increased mediation of public space. Rather, it is the all-too-frequent reduction of the social uses of new media platforms to the possibilities dictated by commercial profit and loss. Failure to imagine new publics and new forms of privacy locks the relation between public and private into an unproductive stricture of voyeurism and narcissism. If the tendency towards 'testing' by the apparatus is left unchecked in the era of digital networks, it could result in the wholesale subjection of both public life and the intimate sphere to the rule of what Benjamin once termed, only half ironically, the 'commodity-soul'.

The development of modern media has been historically intertwined with the emergence of the public sphere as a space for the mediation of State and commercial interests. The contradictions of the modern public sphere are well-known, as is the potential of 'new media' to redress some of these inadequacies by promoting greater access and reciprocal forms of interaction. But in the era of 'do-it-yourself' media, a new problem has become evident. While the public sphere of the broadcast era was undoubtedly limited, organized around structural exclusion and strategic illegibility, the massive reach of broadcast television nevertheless created a shared social space. In this context, the political imperative for marginalized groups was to achieve the threshold of 'representation' to gain a level of social agency. However, in a context where spectrum limitations have given way to media surplus, the problem is less one of being able to speak than of being heard. In the culture of personalized media and customized environments that Gitlin (1998) dubs 'public sphericules', the transversal connections linking different fora and interest groups remain relatively undeveloped. When everyone is speaking, is anyone still listening? How can the call of the other still register? How might new collectivities which cut across specialized interests form a consensus for acting? As Latour (2005: 37) describes the contradiction of contemporary global media:

> There are lots of *blogs* but no globe. And yet we are all in the same boat, or at least the same flotilla. [ . . . ] Can we make an assembly out of all the various *assemblages* in which we are already enmeshed?

In the media city, the problem of the public sphere is increasingly a problem of public space. In the context of pervasive mobile media, older forms of spatial separation, and the modes of identity and agency they have sustained, face new challenges. This is not to suggest that boundaries and limits are now somehow irrelevant. The new digital borders of access and ownership based on passwords, DRMs and the capacity to pay are as constraining as older forms of spatial exclusion, but arguably more insidious because they are so often presented as the tools for individual liberation.

In order to develop other headings, it is vital to imagine ways of deploying digital media that extend sociability rather than truncate it. This involves developing new and emergent forms of sociality based on living with others in 'media cities' where social networks are not pre-given but constructed 'on the fly' and personal relationships are routinely 'at-a-distance' as well as 'face-to-face'. In a context where basic social interactions increasingly depend on access to complex media systems, there is a need to create new spaces which are the province of broad publics rather than those who can afford 'premium networks'. There is also a need to utilize digital media to create complex modes of interaction which enable a wider array of media speeds and temporalities, so that the 'reflexive' potential of contemporary society can be deepened to include moments of reflection, negotiation and reciprocity rather than being reduced to merely the reflex response of a muscle galvanized by an electrical current. Relying on established media producers and institutions is unlikely to achieve this outcome. Explorations by contemporary artists and activists using new media in public space can yet play a critical role.

The aim of finding a new order for the media city should not be to re-solidify the 'liquid city' in the name of ostensibly stable identities and homogeneous cultures. The nexus of 'blood and soil' has had its day. Rather, the space of collective life in the context of the media city needs to be conceptualized in terms of what Lash (1999) has described as the 'groundless ground'. Living on 'groundless ground' involves developing a sense of collectivity which is no longer based on essentialist understandings of race, ethnicity, class, gender, sexuality, religion, culture or nation. Such an undertaking to live on 'the groundless ground' amounts to rethinking the terms of the social bond in the context of relational space, in which all given orderings are contingent, and the position from which any subject speaks must be actively constructed and legitimated through dialogue with others. In Derrida's terms (1997: 333), it demands a 'socius of dissociation': 'This, then, would be both the task and the wager, a preoccupation with the impossible: to give dissociation its due, but to implement it *as such* in the space of reassembly.' To adapt Langford Hughes' memorable phrase about the utopic myth of 'America': 'The city that never has been yet, And yet must be.'

# Bibliography

Abbott, P. (2002) Interviewed for The Media Report, ABC Radio National, May 23. www.abc.net.au/rn/mediareport/stories/2002/562394.htm# (accessed 20 December 2002).

Adorno, T.W. (1973) *Negative Dialectics* (trans. E.B. Ashton), New York, The Seabury Press.

Adorno, T.W. (1981–82) 'Transparencies on Film' (trans. T.Y. Levin), *New German Critique*, 24/25: 199–205.

Adorno, T.W. and Horkheimer, M. (1973) *Dialectic of Enlightenment* (trans. J. Cumming), London, Allen Lane.

Alberti, L.B. (1970) *On Painting* (trans. J.R. Spencer), New Haven, CT, Yale University Press (first published 1435–36).

Albrecht, D. (1986) *Designing Dreams: Modern Architecture in the Movies*. New York: Harper & Row in collaboration with the Museum of Modern Art.

Angel, C. (ed.) (1994) *The Films of Andy Warhol: Part II*, New York, Whitney Museum of American Art.

Appadurai, A. (1996) *Modernity at Large: Cultural Dimensions Of Globalization*, Minneapolis, MN, University of Minnesota Press.

Apollonio, U. (ed.) (1973) *Futurist Manifestos* (trans. R. Brain et al.), London, Thames and Hudson.

Aragon, L. (1994) *Paris Peasant* (trans. S. Watson), Boston, MA, Exact Change (first published 1926).

Arendt, H. (1958) *The Human Condition*, Chicago, IL, University of Chicago Press.

Ariès, P. (1962) *Centuries of Childhood: A Social History of Family Life* (trans. R. Baldick), New York, Alfred A. Knopf.

Ascott, R. (1995) 'The Architecture of Cyberception' in M. Toy (ed.), *Architects in Cyberspace*, London, Academy Editions.

Asendorf, C. (1993) *Batteries of Life: On the History of Things and Their Perception in Modernity* (trans. D. Reneau), Berkeley, CA, University of California Press.

Atkins, J. (1955) *Tomorrow Revealed*, London, Neville Spearman.

Banham, R. (1960) *Theory and Design in the First Machine Age*, London, Architectural Press.

Banham, R. (1986) 'CIAM' in V. Lampugnani (ed.), *The Thames & Hudson Encyclopaedia of Architecture*, London, Thames and Hudson.

Barber, S. (2002) *Projected Cities: Cinema and Urban Space*, London, Reaktion.

Barker, F. (1984) *The Tremulous Private Body: Essays on Subjection*, London and New York, Methuen.

Baudelaire, C. (1964) *The Painter of Modern life and Other Essays* (trans. J. Mayne), London, Phaidon (first published 1863).

Baudelaire, C. (1970) *Paris Spleen* (trans. L. Varèse), New York, New Directions (first published 1869).

Baudrillard, J. (1988) *America* (trans. C. Turner), London and New York, Verso.

Baumann, Z. (2000) *Liquid Modernity*, Cambridge, Polity Press.

Bazerman, C. (1999) *The Languages of Edison's Light*, Cambridge, MA and London, The MIT Press.

Beaudry, J. (2006) Posting 15 August to iDC list. http://distributedcreativity.org/ thread 'Interactive City: irrelevant mobile entertainment?' (accessed 19 September 2006).

Beck, U. (1992) *Risk Society: Towards a New Modernity*, London, Sage.

Beck, U. (1994) 'The reinvention of politics: towards a theory of reflexive modernization' in U. Beck, A. Giddens and S. Lash, *Reflexive Modernization* (1994), Cambridge, Polity and London, Blackwell.

Beck, U. and Beck-Gernsheim, E. (2003) *Individualization: Institutionalized Individualism and Its Social and Political Consequences*, London, Sage.

Bell, D. (ed.) (1968) *Toward the Year 2000: Work in Progress*, Boston, MA, Houghton Mifflin Co.

Benedikt, M. (ed.) (1991) *Cyberspace: First steps*. Cambridge, MA: MIT Press.

Benjamin, W. (1994) *The Correspondence of Walter Benjamin 1910–1940* (ed. G. Scholem and T.W. Adorno; trans. M.R. and E.M. Jacobson), Chicago, IL and London, University of Chicago Press.

Benjamin, W. (1996) *Selected Writings*, Vol. 1, 1913–26 (eds, M. Bullock and M.W. Jennings; trans. R. Livingstone and others), Cambridge, MA and London, Belknap Press.

Benjamin, W. (1999a) *Selected Writings*, Vol. 2, 1927–34 (eds, H. Eiland and G. Smith; trans. R. Livingstone and others), Cambridge, MA and London, Belknap Press.

Benjamin, W. (1999b) *The Arcades Project* (trans. H. Eiland and K. McLaughlin), Cambridge, MA, Belknap Press.

Benjamin, W. (2002) *Selected Writings*, Vol. 3, 1935–38 (eds, H. Eiland and M.W. Jennings; trans. E. Jephcott and others), Cambridge, MA and London, Belknap Press.

Benjamin, W. (2003) *Selected Writings*, Vol. 4, 1938–40 (eds, H. Eiland and M.W. Jennings; trans. E. Jephcott and others), Cambridge, MA and London, Belknap Press.

Berger, J. (1969) *The Moment of Cubism and Other Essays*, London, Weidenfeld and Nicolson.

Berman, M. (1982) *All that is Solid Melts into Air: The Experience of Modernity*, New York, Simon and Schuster.

Blanchot, M. (1981) *The Gaze of Orpheus* (ed. P.A. Sitney; trans. L. Davis), Barrytown, NY: Station Hill.

Blau, E. (1989) 'Patterns of fact: photography and the transformation of the early industrial city' in E. Blau and E. Kaufman (eds), *Architecture and Its Image: Four Centuries of Architectural Representation*, Montréal, Canadian Centre for Architecture.

Blau, E. and Troy, N. (eds) (1997) *Architecture and Cubism*, Montréal, Canadian Centre for Architecture and Cambridge, MA, MIT Press.

Boccioni, U. (1973) 'The plastic foundations of futurist sculpture and painting' in U. Apollonio (ed.), *Futurist Manifestos* (trans. R. Brain et al.), London, Thames and Hudson.

Bogdanovich, P. (1967) *Fritz Lang in America*, New York, Praeger.

Boyer, C. (1997) *CyberCities: Visual Perception in the Age of Electronic Communication*, New York, Princeton Architectural Press.

Brodey, W.M. (1967) 'Soft architecture: the design of intelligent environments', *Landscape*, 17:1(Autumn): 8–12.

Broeckmann, A. (2000) 'Public spheres and network interfaces' in R. Lozano-Hemmer (ed.), *Vectorial Elevation: Relational Architecture No. 4*, Mexico City, Conaculta Press, pp. 165–82.

Bukatman, S. (1995) 'The artificial infinite' in L. Cooke and P. Wollen (eds), *Visual Display: Culture Beyond Appearances*, Seattle, WA, Bay Press.

Bulgakowa, O. (2005) 'Eisenstein, the glass house and the spherical book. From the comedy of the eye to a drama of enlightenment', *Rouge* 7, www.rouge.com.au/7/eisenstein.html (accessed 21 March 2006).

Burgin, V. (2002) 'Jenni's room: exhibitionism and solitude' in T.Y. Levin, U. Frohne and P. Weibel (eds), *Ctrl Space: Rhetorics of Surveillance from Bentham to Big Brother*, Karlsruhe, ZKM Centre for Art and Media and Cambridge, MA, MIT Press.

Callas, P. (1990) 'Some liminal aspects of the technology trade', *Mediamatic*, 5–(3).

Canetti, E. (1984) *Crowds and Power* (trans, C. Stewart), London, Peregrine, (first published 1960).

Carey, J. (1989) *Communication as Culture: Essays on Media and Society*, Boston, MA: Unwin Hyman.

Carroll, P. (1969) 'What's a Wharhal?' *Playboy*, September.

Castells, M. (1996) *The Rise of the Network Society*, Cambridge, MA, Blackwell Publishers.

Cheney, S. (1969) *The New World Architecture*, New York, AMS Press (first published 1930).

Choay, F. (1969) *The Modern City: Planning in the Nineteenth Century* (trans. M. Hugo and G.R. Collins), New York, George Braziller.

Clark, T.J. (1999) *The Painting of Modern Life*, Princeton, NJ, Princeton University Press (first published 1984).

Colomina, B. (1994) *Publicity and Privacy: Modern Architecture as Mass Media*, Cambridge, MA, MIT Press.

Colomina, B. (1997) 'Where are we?' in E. Blau and N. Troy (eds), *Architecture and Cubism*, Montréal, Canadian Centre for Architecture and Cambridge, MA, The MIT Press.

Comolli, J. (1980) 'Machines of the visible' in S. Heath and T. De Lauretis (eds), *The Cinematic Apparatus*, London, Macmillan, pp. 121–43.

Conan Doyle, A. (1985) *Sherlock Holmes. Selected Stories*, New York, Avenel Books.

Conrads, U. (1970) *Programs and Manifestoes on Twentieth Century Architecture*, London, Lund Humphries.

Constant (1960) 'Unitary urbanism' reprinted in M. Wigley (1998) *Constant's New Babylon: The Hyper-Architecture of Desire*, Rotterdam, Witte de With, Center for Contemporary Art.

Constant (1973) 'The principle of disorientation' reprinted in M. Wigley (1998) *Constant's New Babylon: The Hyper-Architecture of Desire*, Rotterdam, Witte de With, Center for Contemporary Art.

Cook, P. (ed.) (1999) *Archigram*, New York, Princeton Architectural Press (first published 1972).

Copjec, J. (ed.) (1993) *Shades of Noir*, London, Verso.

Corbusier (1946) *Towards a New Architecture* (trans. F. Etchells), London, Architectural Press (first published 1923).

Corbusier (1964) *The Radiant City: Elements of a Doctrine of Urbanism to be Used as the Basis of Our Machine-Age Civilization* (trans P. Knight, E. Levieux and D. Coltman), New York, The Orion Press (first published 1935).

Corbusier (1971) *The City of Tomorrow* (trans. F. Etchells), London, The Architectural Press (translation of *Urbanisme*, first published 1924).

Corbusier (1991) *Precisions* (trans. E.S. Aujame), Cambridge, MA and London, MIT Press (first published 1930).

Crary, J. (1999) 'Untitled: (to Jan and Ron Greenberg)' in *Dan Flavin. The Architecture of Light*, New York, Guggenheim Museum; Berlin; Deutsche Guggenheim.

Crary, J. (1999) *Suspensions of Perception: Attention, Spectacle, and Modern Culture*, Cambridge, MA and London, MIT.

Crompton, D. (ed.) (1998) *Concerning Archigram . . .* , London, Archigram Archives.

Crowther, B. (1966) 'The underground overflows', *New York Times*, December 11: 3.

Davis, E. (1994) 'Agrippa, or, the apocalyptic book' in M. Dery (ed.), *Flame Wars: The Discourse of Cyberculture*, Durham, NC, Duke University Press.

Davis, F.E. (1993) 'Electrons or photons: read this before you bet on the outer limits of computing', *Wired* (Premier Issue).

Davis, M. (1990) *City of Quartz: Excavating the Future in Los Angeles*, London and New York, Verso.

Davis, M. (1992) 'Fortress Los Angeles: the militarization of urban space' in M. Sorkin (ed.), *Variations on a Theme Park. New York: Hill and Wang*, pp. 154–80.

Davis, M. (1998), *Ecology of Fear: Los Angeles and the Imagination of Disaster*, New York, Metropolitan Books.

Dayan, D. and Katz, E. (1992) *Media Events: The Live Broadcasting of History*, Cambridge, MA, Harvard University Press.

Debord, G. (1957) 'Report on the construction of situations and on the international situationist tendency's conditions of organization and action', reprinted in K. Knabb (ed. and trans.) (1981) *Situationist International Anthology*, Berkeley, CA, Bureau of Public Secrets.

Debord, G. (1994) *Society of the Spectacle*, New York, Zone Books.

Debord, G. and Wolman, G. (1956) 'Methods of detournement', reprinted in K. Knabb (ed. and trans.) (1981) *Situationist International Anthology*, Berkeley, CA, Bureau of Public Secrets.

Deleuze, G. (1992) 'Postscript on the societies of control', *October* 59 (Winter): 3–7.

Derrida, J. (1997) 'Architecture where the desire may live' in N. Leach (ed.), *Rethinking Architecture: A Reader in Cultural Theory*, New York, Routledge.

Derrida, J. (2002) *Echographies of Television: Filmed Interviews* (trans. J. Bajorek), Cambridge, Polity Press.

Dietz, S. (2004) 'Public spheres' in *Media Arts Net* www.medienkunstnetz.de/www.medienkunstnetz.de/themes/public_sphere_s/public_sphere_s/13/ (accessed 30 August 2005).

Dimendberg, E. (1997) 'From Berlin to Bunker Hill: urban space, late modernity and film noir in F. Lang and J. Losey, *M*', *Wide Angle* 19(4): 62–93.

Dimendberg, E. (2004) *Film Noir and the Spaces of Modernity*, Cambridge, MA, Harvard University Press.

Donald, J. (1999) *Imagining the Modern City*, London, Athlone.

Dostoevsky, F. (1991) *Notes from the Underground and The Grand Inquisitor* (trans. Ralph E. Matlaw), New York: Meridian (first published 1864).

Druckey, T. (2003) 'Relational architecture: the work of Rafael Lozano-Hemmer' in T. Goryucheva and E. Kluitenberg (eds), *Debates and Credits: Media/Art /Public Domain*, Amsterdam, De Balie Centre for Culture and Politics, pp. 69–72.

Dyson, E., Gilder, G., Keyworth, J. and Toffler, A. (1994) 'A magna carta for the knowledge age', *New Perspectives Quarterly*, 11 (Fall): 26–37.

Ehrenburg, I. (1976) *The Life of the Automobile* (trans. J. Neugroschel), New York, Urizen.

Einstein, A. (1920) *Relativity: The Special and General Theory. A Popular Exposition* (trans. R. Lawson), London, Methuen and Co.

Eisenstein, S. (1949) *Film Form: Essays in Film Theory* (trans. and ed. Jay Leyda), London, Harcourt Brace Jovanovich.

Eisenstein, S. (1963) *The Film Sense* (trans. J. Leyda), London, Faber and Faber.

Ellul, J. (1967) *The Technological Society* (trans. J. Wilkinson), Vintage, New York. [Translation of *La Technique: L'enjeu du siecle*, 1954].

Elssaesser, T. (ed.) (1990) *Early Cinema: Space, Frame, Narrative*, London, British Film Institute.

Elssaesser, T. (2003) 'Weimar cinema, mobile selves and anxious males: Kracauer and Eisner revisited' in D. Scheunemann (ed.), *Expressionist Film: New Perspectives*, Rochester and Suffolk, Camden House, pp. 33–71.

Engels, F. (1970) *The Housing Question*, Progress, Moscow (originally published 1872–73).

Engels, F. (1971) *The Condition of the Working Class in England* (trans. and ed. W.O. Henderson and W.H. Chaloner), Oxford, Basil Blackwell (originally published 1844).

Fear, B. (ed.) (2000) *Architecture + Film, II*, London, Wiley-Academy, 2000.

Featherstone, M. (1992) 'Postmodernism and the aestheticization of everyday life' in Lash and Friedman (eds), *Modernity and Identity*, Oxford, Blackwell.

Featherstone, M. and Burrows, R. (eds) (1995) *Cyberspace/Cyberbodies/Cyberpunk: Cultures of Technological Embodiment*, London, Sage, 1995.

Featherstone, M. and Lash, S. (1995) 'Globalization, modernity and the spatialization of social theory' in M. Featherstone, S. Lash and R. Robertson (eds), *Global Modernities*. London and Thousand Oaks, CA, Sage Publications.

Ferrarotti, F. (1994) 'Civil society as a polyarchic form: the city' in P. Kasinitz (ed.), *Metropolis: Center and Symbol of Our Times*, London, Macmillan.

Ferriss, H. (1986) *The Metropolis of Tomorrow*, New York, Princeton Architectural Press and the Avery Library, Columbia University (first published 1929).

Fierro, A. (2003) *The Glass State: The Technology of The Spectacle, 1981–1998*, Cambridge, MA, MIT Press.

Fishman, R. (1994) 'Megalopolis unbound' in P. Kasinitz (ed.), *Metropolis: Center and Symbol of our Times*, Macmillan, London.

Foucault, M. (1980) *Power/Knowledge: Selected Interviews and Other Writings, 1972–1977* (trans. and ed. C. Gordon), Brighton, Sussex, Harvester Press.

Foucault, M. (1984) 'What is Enlightenment?' in P. Rabinow (ed.), *Foucault Reader*, New York, Pantheon Books.

Frampton, H. (1983) *Circles of Confusion*, New York, Visual Studies Workshop Press.

Frampton, K. (1982) *Modern Architecture: A Critical History*, Thames and Hudson, London.

Freud, S. (1955/1919) 'The "uncanny"' in *The Standard Edition of the Complete Psychological Works of Sigmund Freud* (trans. under the general editorship of J. Strachey), vol. XVII, London, The Hogarth Press and the Institute of Psychoanalysis, pp. 219–52.

Freud, S. (1984) 'Beyond the pleasure principle' in *On Metapsychology*, vol. 11, The Pelican Freud Library (trans. as per *SE VOL XVIII 1955*), Harmondsworth, Penguin, pp. 269–338 (first published 1921).

Friedman, Y. (1999) *Structures Serving the Unpredictable*, Rotterdam, NAI Publishers.

Frisby, D. (1985) *Fragments of Modernity: Theories of Modernity in the Work of Simmel, Kracauer and Benjamin*, Cambridge and Oxford, Polity Press and Basil Blackwell.

Frohne, U. (2002) 'Media narcissism, theatricality and the internalised observer' in T.Y. Levin, U. Frohne and P. Weibel (eds), *Ctrl Space: Rhetorics Of Surveillance from Bentham to Big Brother*, Karlsruhe, ZKM Centre for Art and Media; Cambridge, MA, MIT Press.

Garfield, D. (1996) 'The next thing now, designing the 21st century museum' in *Museum News*. 75 (Jan/Feb): 34–45.

Gernsheim, H. and A. (1968) *L.J.M Daguerre*, New York, Dover.

Gibson, W. (1995) *Neuromancer*, London, HarperCollins (first published 1983).

Gibson, W. (1988) *Mona Lisa Overdrive*, London, Victor Gollanz.

Giddens, A. (1991) *Modernity and Self-identity: Self and Society in the Late Modern Age*, Cambridge, Polity Press.

Giddens, A. (1994) 'Living in a post-traditional society' in U. Beck, A. Giddens and S. Lash, *Reflexive modernization*, Cambridge and London, Polity and Blackwell.

Giedion, S. (1967) *Space, Time and Architecture: The Growth of a New Tradition*, Cambridge, MA, Harvard University Press.

Gilbert, W. (1992) 'Visions of the grail' in D.J. Kevles and L. Hood (eds), *The Code of Codes*, Cambridge, MA, Harvard University Press, pp. 83–97.

Gilroy, P. (1990) 'It ain't where you're from, it's where you're at . . . . The dialectics of diasporic identification', *Third Text*, 13 (Winter) ): 3–16.

Gitlin, T. (1998) 'Public sphere or public sphericules?' in T. Liebes and J. Curran (eds), *Media Ritual and Identity*, London, Routledge.

Gleber, A. (1999) *The Art of Taking a Walk: Flânerie, Literature Film in Weimar Culture*, Princeton, NJ, Princeton University Press.

Goffmann, E. (1969) *The presentation of self in everyday life*, London, Allen Lane.

Goncourt, E. (1962) *Pages from the Goncourt Journal* (ed. and trans. Robert Baldick), London, Oxford University Press.

Graham, D. (1979) in B. Buchloh (ed.), *Video, Architecture, Television: Writings on Video and Video Works, 1970–1978/Dan Graham*, Halifax, NS, and New York, Press of the Nova Scotia College of Art & Design and New York University Press.

Graham, D. (1997) *Architecture*. London: Architecture Association.

Graham, S. (ed.) (2004) *The Cybercities Reader*, London, Routledge.

Graham, S. and Marvin, S. (2001) *Splintering Urbanism: Networked Infrastructures, Technological Mobilities and the Urban Condition*, London, Routledge.

Greene, D. (1999) 'The ice man' in E. Holding, *Mark Fisher – Staged Architecture*, London, Wiley-Academy.

Guattari, F. (1984) *Molecular Revolution* (trans. R. Sheed), Penguin, Harmondsworth.

Gurvitch, G. (1964) *The Spectrum of Social Time*, Dordrecht.

van Haaren, H. (1966) *Constant* (trans. M. Schuchart), Amsterdam, Meulenhoff.

Habermas, J. (1989) *Structural Transformation of the Public Sphere: An Inquiry into a Category of Bourgeois Society* (trans. T. Burger with the assistance of F. Lawrence), Cambridge, MA, MIT Press.

Hacking, I. (1990) *The Taming of Chance*, Cambridge and New York, Cambridge University Press.

Hambourg, M. (1981) 'Charles Marville's old Paris' in J. Chambord (ed.), *Charles Marville: Photographs of Paris 1852–1878*, New York, French Institute and Alliance Français.

Hansen, M. (1991) *Babel and Babylon: Spectatorship in American Silent Film*, Cambridge, MA., Harvard University Press.

Hansen, M. (1993) ' "With skin and hair": Kracauer's theory of film, Marseille 1940', *Critical Inquiry* 19 (Spring): 437–69.

von Harbou, T. (no date) *Metropolis*, London, The Reader's Library.

Harvey, D. (1990) *The Condition of Postmodernity: An Enquiry into the Origins of Cultural Change*, Oxford and Cambridge, MA, Blackwell.

Harvey, D. (2003) *Paris, Capital of Modernity*, New York and London, Routledge.

Hayles, K.N. (1999) *How We Became Posthuman: Virtual Bodies in Cybernetics, Literature, and Informatics*, Chicago, IL, University of Chicago Press.

Heidegger, M. (1977) 'The age of the world picture' in *The Question Concerning Technology and Other Essays* (trans. W. Lovitt), New York, Harper and Row (originally delivered 1938).

Hookway, B. (1999) *Pandemonium: The Rise of Predatory Locales in the Postwar World*, New York and Houston, TX, Princeton Architectural Press and Rice University School of Architecture.

Huhtamo, E. (2000) 'Re-positioning vectorial elevation: media archaeological considerations' in R. Lozano-Hemmer (ed.), *Vectorial Elevation: Relational Architecture No. 4*, Mexico, City, Conaculta Press.

Hutchinson, T.H. (1946) *Here is the Television: Your Window to the World*, New York, Hastings House.

Jacobs, J. (1961) *The Death and Life of Great American Cities*, New York, Random House.

Jay, M. (1992) 'Scopic regimes of modernity' in Lash and Friedman (eds), *Modernity and Identity*, Oxford, Blackwell.

Joseph, B. (2002) 'Nothing special: Andy Warhol and the rise of surveillance' in T.Y. Levin, U. Frohne and P. Weibel (eds) *Ctrl Space: Rhetorics of Surveillance from Bentham to Big Brother*, Karlsruhe and Cambridge, MA, ZKM Centre for Art and Media and MIT Press.

Kasinitz, P. (ed.) (1994) *Metropolis: Center and Symbol of Our Times*, Macmillan, London.

Kaufman, M. (1979) 'An interview with Mikhail Kaufman', *October*, 11: 54–76.

Kenner, H. (1975) *A Homemade World: The America Modernist Writers*, New York, Morrow.

Kittler, F. (1996) 'The city is a medium', *New Literary History*, 27(4): 717–29.

Knabb, K. (ed. and trans.) (1981) *Situationist International Anthology*, Berkeley, CA, Bureau of Public Secrets.

Koolhaas, R. (1994) *Delirious New York: A Retroactive Manifesto for Manhattan*, Rotterdam, 010 Publishers.

Koolhaas, R. (1996) *Rem Koolhaas: Conversations with Students* (ed. S. Kwinter), Houston, TX and New York, Rice University School of Architecture and Princeton Architectural Press.

Koolhaas, R. (2000) 'Junk space', *OMA@work.a+u* (special edition of *Architecture and Urbanism*, May), Tokyo, a+u Publishing.

Kopp, A. (1985) *Constructivist Architecture in the USSR*, Academy, London, St Martin's Press, New York.

Kracauer, S. (1960) *Theory of Film: The Redemption of Physical Reality*, London, Oxford University Press.

Kracauer, S. (1974) *From Caligari to Hitler: A Psychological History of the German Film*, Princeton, NJ, Princeton University Press.

Kracauer, S. (1994) 'Girls and crisis' in A. Kaes, M. Jay and E. Dimendberg, *The Weimar Republic Sourcebook*, Berkeley, CA, University of California Press (first published in 1931).

Kracauer, S. (1995) *The Mass Ornament* (trans. & ed. T.Y. Levin), Cambridge, Mass. & London, England, Harvard University Press.

Kracauer, S. (2002) *Jacques Offenbach and the Paris of his Time* (trans. G. David and E. Mosbacher), Zone Books, New York (first published 1937).

Krutnik, F. (1997) 'Something more than night: tales of the *noir* city' in Clarke, D.B. (ed.) *The Cinematic City*, Routledge, London.

Kuleshov, L. (1974) *Kuleshov on Film: Writings of Lev Kuleshov* (trans. R. Levaco), Berkeley, CA, University of California Press.

Kwinter, S. (1986) 'La Città Nuova: modernity and continuity', *Zone I/II*, 80–127.

Kwinter, S. (2001) *Architectures of Time*, Cambridge, MA, MIT Press.

Lacan, J. (1977) *The Four Fundamental Concepts of Psycho-analysis* (trans. A. Sheridan and ed. A. Miller), London, Hogarth Press.

Lacan, J. (1988) *The Seminar of Jacques Lacan Book 1* (ed. J.A. Miller and trans. J. Forrester) Cambridge, Cambridge University Press.

Lamster, M. (ed.) (2000) *Architecture and film*, New York, Princeton Architectural Press.

Lash, S. (1994) 'Reflexivity and its doubles: structure, aesthetics, community' in U. Beck, A. Giddens and S. Lash, *Reflexive Modernization: Politics, Tradition and Aesthetics in the Modern Social Order*, Oxford, Polity, pp. 110–73.

Lash, S. (1999) *Another Modernity, A Different Rationality*, Oxford, Blackwell.

Lash, S. (2002a) *Critique of Information*, London, Sage.

Lash, S. (2002b) 'Informational totemism' in J. Brouwer and A. Mulder (eds), *TransUrbanism*, Rotterdam, V2: 49–64.

Lash, S. (2003) 'Foreword' in U. Beck and E. Beck-Gernsheim, *Individualization: Institutionalized Individualism and its Social and Political Consequences*, London, Sage.

Latour, B. (2005) 'From realpolitik to dingpolitik or how to make things public' in B. Latour and P. Weibel (eds), *Making Things Public: Atmospheres of Democracy*, Cambridge, MA and Karlsruhe, MIT Press and ZKM Centre for Art and Media, pp. 14–41.

Lefebvre, H. (1991) *The Production of Space* (trans. Donald Nicholson-Smith), Oxford and Cambridge, MA, Blackwell.

Lefebvre, H. (1996) *Writings on Cities* (trans and ed. E. Kofman and E. Lebas), London and Cambridge, MA, Blackwell.

Lenin, V.I. (1960) *Collected Works*, vol. 31, Moscow, Foreign Languages Publishing House.

Lenin, V.I. (1964) 'The Taylor system: man's enslavement by the machine' in *Collected Works*, vol. 20 (4th English Edition, trans. B. Isaacs and J. Fineberg), Moscow, Progress Publishers.

Lenin, V.I. (1991–98) 'Communism is Soviet power plus the electrification of the whole country' reprinted in R. Wade (ed.), *Documents of Soviet history, vol. 2, Triumph and retreat*, Gulf Breeze, FL, Academic International Press, pp. 154–57.

Levy, S. (1984) *Hackers: Heroes of the Computer Revolution*, New York: Anchor Press/Doubleday.

Leyda, J. and Voynow, Z. (1982) *Eisenstein at Work*, London, Methuen.

Lillyman, W.J., Moriarty, M.F. and Neuman, D.J. (eds) (1994) *Critical Architecture and Contemporary Culture*, New York, Oxford University Press.

Lovink, G. (2006) 'Blogging and building: The Netherlands after digitalisation' in *Zero Comments; Blogging and Critical Internet Culture*, Routledge, 2007 forthcoming.

Lozano-Hemmer, R. (ed.) (2000) *Vectorial Elevation: Relational Architecture No.4*, Mexico City, Conaculta Press.

Lozano-Hemmer, R. (2002) 'Alien relationships from public space. A winding dialogue with Rafael Lozano-Hemmer' (with Alex Adriaansens and Joke Brouwwer) in J. Brouwer and A. Mulder (eds), *TransUrbanism*, Rotterdam, V2, pp. 139–60.

Lozano-Hemmer, R. (2003) 'Introduction to relational architecture', www. lozano-hemmer.com (accessed 13 October 2003) This text is not on the rebuilt site at www.lozano-hemmer.com/eprlh.html

Lynch, K. (1960) *The Image of the City*, Cambridge, MA and MIT Press.

Lyon, D. (1994) *The Electronic Eye: The Rise of the Surveillance Society*, Cambridge, Polity Press.

Lyon, D. (2001) *Surveillance Society: Monitoring Everyday Life*, Philadelphia, Open University.

Lyon, D. (2003) *Surveillance after September 11*, Malden, MA, Polity Press in association with Blackwell.

Lyotard, J. (1984) *The Postmodern Condition: A Report on Knowledge* (trans. G. Bennington and B. Massumi), Manchester: Manchester University Press.

McLuhan, M. (1974) *Understanding Media: The Extensions of Man*, London, Abacus (first published 1964).

McQuire, S. (1994) ' "The go-for-broke game of history": the camera, the community and the scene of politics', *Arena Journal* 4: 201–27.

McQuire, S. (1997) *Crossing the Digital Threshold*, Brisbane, Australian Key Centre for Culture and Media Policy, Griffith University.

McQuire, S. (1998) *Visions of Modernity: Representation, Memory, Time and Space in the Age of the Camera*, London, Sage.

McQuire, S. (1999) 'Blinded by the (speed of) light', *Theory Culture and Society*, 16(5): 143–59.

McQuire, S. (2001) 'Space creation: lessons from the city' in V. Lynn (ed.), *Space Odysseys: Sensation and Immersion*, Sydney, Art Gallery of New South Wales, pp. 64–70.

McQuire, S. (2002) 'Space for rent in the last suburb', in A. Cavallaro, A. Johnson and D. Tofts (eds), *Prefiguring Cyberculture: An Intellectual History*, Power Publications and MIT Press, 2002, pp. 166–78.

McQuire, S. (2004) 'Slow train coming? The transition to digital distribution and exhibition in cinema', *Media International Australia*, no. 110 (February 2004): 105–19.

McQuire, S. and Papastergiadis, N. (2005a) 'After empire' in S. McQuire and N. Papastergiadis (eds), *Empires, Ruins+ Networks: The Transcultural Agenda in Art*, London and Melbourne, Rivers Orams Press and Melbourne University Press, pp. 2–10.

McQuire, S. and Papastergiadis, N. (2005b), 'From parafunctional spaces to shiny ruins' in N. Tsoutas (ed.), *Knowledge+Dialogue+Exchange: Remapping Cultural Globalisms From the South*, Artspace, Sydney, pp. 83–100.

McQuire, S. (2006) 'Technology', *Theory, Culture and Society* (special issue, New Encyclopaedia Project 'problematizing global knowledge') 25(2/3): 253–65.

Macrae, D. (2003) 'Ruttmann, rhythm, and "reality": a response to Siegfried Kracauer's interpretation of Berlin, the symphony of a great city' in

D. Scheunemann (ed.), *Expressionist Film: New Perspectives*, Rochester, NY, Camden House.

Magid, R. (1997) 'George Lucas: past, present and future', *American Cinematographer* 78(2): 48–54.

Martin, R. (2003) *The Organizational Complex: Architecture, Media and Corporate Space*, Cambridge, MA, MIT Press.

Marx, L. (2000) *The Machine in the Garden: Technology and the Pastoral Ideal in America*, New York, Oxford University Press.

Marx, K. (1863) *Theories of Surplus-Value* (Addenda I) (accessed 19 July 2006) www.marxists.org/archive/marx/works/1863/theories-surplus-value/add3.htm

Marx, K. (1973) *Grundrisse: Foundations of the Critique of Political Economy* (trans. M. Nicolaus), London, Allen Lane/NLR.

Marx, K. (1977) *Capital*, vol. 1 (trans, B. Fowkes), New York, Vintage (first published 1867).

Mayer, M. (2000) 'The Zócalo: ephemeral interventions' in R. Lozano-Hemmer (ed.), *Vectorial Elevation: Relational Architecture no. 4*, Mexico, Mexico City, Conaculta and Ediciones San Jorge, 2000.

Metz, C. (1976a) 'History/Discourse: a note on two voyeurisms', *Edinburgh '76 Magazine*.

Metz, C. (1976b) *The Imaginary Signifier. Psychoanalysis and Cinema* (trans. C. Britton et al.), Bloomington, IN, Indiana University Press.

Mills, C.W. (1951) *White collar: The American Middle Classes*, New York: Oxford University Press.

Mitchell, W. (1995) *City of Bits: Space, Place, and the Infobahn*, Cambridge, MA, MIT Press.

Mitchell, W. (2003) *ME ++ The Cyborg Self and the Networked City*, Cambridge, MA, MIT Press.

Moholy-Nagy, L. (1969) *Painting, Photography Film*, London, Lund Humphries (first published 1925).

Moholy-Nagy, L. (1947) *The New Vision: And, Abstract of an Artist*, New York, Wittenborn, Shultz.

Montagu, I. (1969) *With Eisenstein in Hollywood*, New York, International Publishers.

Morus, I. (1998) *Frankenstein's children: electricity, exhibition and experiment in early nineteenth century London*, Princeton, NJ, Princeton University Press.

Mosco, V. (2004) *The Digital Sublime: Myth, Power, and Cyberspace*, Cambridge, MA, MIT Press.

Multiplicity (2005) 'Borders: the other side of globalisation' in S. McQuire, N. Papastergiadis (eds), *Empires, Ruins + Networks: The Transcultural Agenda in Art*, Melbourne, Melbourne University Press.

Mumford, L. (1973) *The City in History*, Penguin, Harmondsworth.

Musil, R. (1979) *The Man without Qualities* (trans. E. Wilkins and E. Kaiser), London, Secker and Warburg (first published 1930–33).

Naef, W. and Sequin, J-P (1980) in B. Marbot (ed.), *After Daguerre: Masterworks of French Photography (1848–1900) from the Bibliothèque Nationale*, New York, Metropolitan Museum of Art, in association with Berger-Levrault, Paris.

*Naked News* (1995) dir: John Alexander, (part 1 of 4 part documentary United States/United Kingdom).

Negroponte, N. (1970) *The Architecture Machine*, Cambridge, MA, MIT Press.

Negroponte, N. (1975) *Soft Architecture Machines*, Cambridge, MA, MIT Press.

Neumann, D. (ed.) (1996) *Film Architecture: Set Designs from Metropolis to Blade Runner*, New York and Munich, Prestel-Verlag.

Nietzsche, F. (1998) *On the Genealogy of Morality* (trans. by M. Clark and A. Swensen), Indianapolis, IN, Hackett Publishing Company (first published 1887).

Nietzsche, F. (1968) *The Will to Power* (trans. W. Kaufmann and R.J. Hollingdale), New York, Vintage Books (first published 1901).

Novak, M. (1991) 'Liquid architectures in cyberpsace' in M. Benedikt (ed.), *Cyberspace: First Steps*, Cambridge, MA, MIT Press.

Novak, M. (1996) 'Transmitting architecture: the transphysical city', *CTheory* (online resource, accessed 11 December 2005) www.ctheory.net/articles. aspx?id=76

Nowotny, H. (1994) *Time: The Modern and Postmodern Experience* (trans. N. Plaice), Cambridge, Polity Press and Cambridge, MA, Blackwell.

Nye, D. (1990) *Electrifying America: Social Meanings of New Technology 1880–1940*, Cambridge, MA and London, MIT Press.

Nye, D. (1994) *American Technological Sublime*, Cambridge, MA, MIT Press.

Nye, D. (1997) *Narratives and Spaces: Technology and the Construction of American Culture*, Exeter, University of Exeter Press.

Orrinsmith, L. (1978) *The Drawing-Room: Its Decorations and Furniture*, London and New York: Garland (first published 1877).

Orwell, G. (1984) *Nineteen Eighty-Four*, Oxford, Clarendon Press (first published 1948).

Panofsky, E. (1969) *Renaissance and Renascences in Western Art*, New York, Harper and Row.

Papastergiadis, N. (2000) *The Turbulence of Migration: Globalization, Deterritorialization, and Hybridity*, Malden, MA : Polity Press.

Papastergiadis, N. (2005) 'Small gestures in specific places: on collaboration and the politics of art' in S. McQuire and N. Papastergiadis (eds), *Empires, Ruins + Networks: The Transcultural Agenda in Art*, London and Melbourne, Rivers Orams Press and Melbourne University Press, pp. 287–302.

Parisi, P. (1995) 'The new Hollywood', *Wired*, 3.12(1995). (On-line version: www.wired.com/wired/archive/3.12/).

Passuth, K. (1985) *Moholy-Nagy* (trans. E. Gruz et al.), London, Thames and Hudson.

Penz, F. and Thomas, M. (eds) (1997) *Cinema and Architecture: Melies, Mallet-Stevens, Multimedia*, London, BFI.

Petric, V. (1987) *Constructivism in Film*, Cambridge, MA, Cambridge University Press.

Platt, H. (1991) *The Electric City: Energy and the Growth of the Chicago Area, 1880–1930*, Chicago and London, University of Chicago Press.

Poe, E.A. (1938) *The Complete Tales and Poems of Edgar Allen Poe*, New York, Random House.

Poster, M. (1994) 'A second media age?', *Arena Journal*, 3: 49–91.

Pound, E. (1921) 'Review of Cocteau's "Poesies 1917–1920"', *The Dial* (January).

Raban, J. (1974) *Soft City*. London, Hamish Hamilton.

Rafael, V. (2003) 'The cell phone and the crowd: messianic politics in the contemporary Philippines', *Public Culture*, 15(3): 399–425.

Ranaulo, G. (2001) *Light Architecture: New Edge City*, Basel and Boston, MA, Birkhäuser.

Reichlin, B. (1984) 'The pros and cons of the horizontal window', *Daidalos*, 13: 65–78.

Rheingold, H. (1991) *Virtual Reality*, New York, Summit Books.

Rheingold, H. (1993) *The Virtual Community: Homesteading on the Electronic Frontier*, Reading, MA, Addison-Wesley.

Rheingold, H. (2002) *Smart Mobs: The Next Social Revolution*, Cambridge, MA, Perseus Publishing.

Rice, S. (1997) *Parisian Views*, Cambridge, MA, MIT Press.

Riley, T. (1995) *Light Construction*, New York, Museum of Modern Art.

Ringley, J. (1999) FAQ page at www.jennicam.org (accessed 22 April 1999).

Robinson, C. and Bletter, R. (1975) *Skyscraper Style: Art Deco New York*, Oxford, Oxford University Press.

Robinson, C. and Herschman, J. (1987) *Architecture Transformed*, Cambridge, MA and New York, MIT Press and The Architecture League of New York.

Roscoe, J. (2001) 'Real entertainment: new factual hybrid television', *Media International Australia*, 100: 9–20.

Rossi, A. (1982) *The Architecture of the City*, Cambridge, MA, MIT Press.

Rowe, C. and Koetter, F. (1978) *Collage City*, Cambridge, MA, MIT Press.

Rule, J. (1973) *Private Lives and Public Surveillance*, London: Allen Lane.

Sadler, S. (1998) *The Situationist City*. Cambridge, MA, MIT Press.

Sant'Elia, A. (1973) 'Manifesto of futurist architecture' in U. Apollonio (ed.), *Futurist Manifestos* (trans. R. Brain et al.) London, Thames and Hudson.

Sassen, S. (1991) *The Global City: New York, London, Tokyo*, Princeton, NJ, Princeton University Press.

Sassen, S. (2000) 'Spatialities and temporalities of the global: elements for a theorization', *Public Culture*, 12(1): 215–32.

Scheerbart, P. (1972) *Glass Architecture* (trans. J. Palmes), New York, Praeger (first published 1914).

Schiffmann, B. (2002) 'Digital dream house', *Forbes*, May, www.forbes. com/2002/05/17/0517home.html (accessed 12 December 2002).

Schivelbusch, W. (1986) *The Railway Journey: The Industrialization of Time and Space in the Nineteenth Century*, Berkeley, CA, University of California Press.

Schivelbusch, W. (1988) *Disenchanted Night: The Industrialization of Light in the Nineteenth Century* (trans. A. Davies), Berg, Oxford.

Schor, N. (1992) '*Cartes Postales*: representing Paris 1900', *Critical Inquiry* no. 18(Winter): 188–241.

Scott, M.H.B (2004) *Houses and Gardens. Arts and Crafts Interiors*, Suffolk, Antique Collectors' Club (first published 1906).

Sekula, A. (1989) 'Reading an archive' in B. Wallis (ed.), *Blasted Allegories: An Anthology of Writings by Contemporary Artists*, foreword by Marcia Tucker, New York, New Museum of Contemporary Art and Cambridge, MA, MIT Press.

Sennett, R. (1977) *The Fall of Public Man: On the Social Psychology of Capitalism*, Cambridge, Cambridge University Press.

Sennett, R. (1994) *Flesh and Stone: The Body and the City in Western Civilization*, New York, W.W. Norton.

Sheller, M. and Urry, J. (eds) (2006) *Mobile Technologies of the City*, London and New York, Routledge.

Shelley, M. (1985) *Frankenstein*, Harmondsworth and New York, Penguin (first published 1818).

Shiel, M. and Fitzmaurice, T. (eds) (2001) *Cinema and the City: Film and Urban Societies in a Global Context*, Oxford, Blackwell Publishing.

Short, J.R. (1991) *Imagined Country: Society, Culture and Environment*, London, Routledge.

Siegal, J. (ed.) (2002) *Mobile: The Art of Portable Architecture*, New York, Princeton Architectural Press.

Simmel, G. (1997) *Simmel on Culture* (eds. D. Frisby and M. Featherstone), London, Sage.

Soja, E. (2000) *Postmetropolis: Critical Studies of Cities and Regions*, Malden, Blackwell Publishers.

Soja, E. (2002) 'Restructuring the industrial capitalist city' in J. Brouwer and A. Mulder (eds) *Transurbanism*, Rotterdam, V2: 89–102.

Sontag, S. (1979) *On Photography*, London, Penguin.

Sorkin, M. (ed.) (1992) *Variations on a Theme Park: The New American City and the End of Public Space*, New York, Hill and Wang.

Spigel, L. (1992) *Make Room for TV: Television and the Family Ideal in Postwar America*, Chicago, IL, University of Chicago Press.

Spiller (ed.) (1998) *Architects in Cyberspace II*, London, Academy Editions.

Spuybroek, L. (2002) 'The structure of vagueness' in J. Brouwer and A. Mulder (eds), *Transurbanism*, Rotterdam, V2, pp. 65–88.

Spuybroek, L. (2004) *Nox: Machining Architecture*, London, Thames and Hudson.

Sussman, G. (1999) 'Urban congregations of capital and communications: redesigning social and spatial boundaries', *Social Text*, 17(3): 35–51.

Tabor, P. (1995) 'I am a videocam' in M. Toy (ed.), *Architects in Cyberspace*, London, Academy Editions, pp. 14–19.

Tagg, J. (1988) *The Burden of Representation: Essays on Photographies and Histories*, Basingstoke, Macmillan Education.

de Thézy, M. (1994) *Marville: Paris*, Hazan.

Thomsen, C.W. (1994) 'Mediarchitecture: stages in the evolution', *Architecture and Urbanism*, 282(March): 94–111.

Toy, M. (ed.) (1994) *Architecture & film*, London: Academy Editions.

Tschumi, B. (1981) *The Manhattan Transcripts*, London, Academy Editions.

United Nations (2004) *World Urbanization Prospects. The 2003 Revision.* Department of Economic and Social Affairs, Population Division, New York.

Vaillant, O. (1997) 'Robert Mallet-Stevens. architecture, cinema and poetics' in F. Penz and M. Thoma (eds), *Cinema & Architecture: Méliès, Mallet-Stevens, Multimedia*, London, British Film Institute, pp. 28–33.

Valéry, P. (1964) 'The conquest of ubiquity' in *Aesthetics* (trans. R. Mannheim), vol. 13 of *The Collected Works of Paul Valéry* (1956–75), New York, Pantheon.

Venturi, R. (1966) *Complexity and Contradiction in Architecture*. New York, Museum of Modern Art; Doubleday.

Vertov, D. (1978) 'Kinoki. Perevorot' *Lef* no. 3 (June/July 1923), reprinted in S.R. Feldman, *Dziga Vertov: A Guide to References and Sources*, Boston, MA, G.K. Hall.

Vertov, D. (1984) *Kino-eye: The Writings of Dziga Vertov* (trans. K. O'Brien and ed. A. Michelson), Berkeley, CA and University of California Press.

Vidler, A. (1978) 'The scenes of the street: transformations in ideal and reality 1750–1871' in S. Anderson (ed.) *On Streets*, Cambridge, MA and London, The MIT Press, pp. 29–111.

Vidler, A. (1992) *The Architectural Uncanny: Essays in the Modern Unhomely*, Cambridge, MA, MIT Press.

Virilio, P. (1986) *Speed and Politics* (trans. M. Polizzotti), New York, Semiotext(e).

Virilio, P. (1988) 'The third window' in C. Schneider and B. Wallis (eds), *Global Television*, Cambridge, MA and New York, MIT Press and Wedge Press, pp. 185–97.

Virilio, P. (1991a) *The Lost Dimension* (trans. D. Moshenberg), New York, Semiotexte.

Virilio, P. (1991b) *The Aesthetics of Disappearance* (trans. P. Beitchman), New York, Semiotext(e).

Virilio, P. (1994a) *The Vision Machine* (trans. J. Rose), London, BFI.

Virilio, P. (1995) *The Art of the Motor* (trans. J. Rose), Minneapolis, MN and London, University of Minnesota Press.

Virilio, P. and Wilson, L. (1994b) 'Cyberwar, god and television: interview with Paul Virilio', C*Theory*.

Vogel, H. (1994) *Entertainment Industry Economics: A Guide for Financial Analysis*, Cambridge, Cambridge University Press.

Voog, A. (2001) www.anacam.com.anatomy (accessed 4 December 2001).

Wade, R. (ed.) (1991–98) *Documents of Soviet History, vol. 2 Triumph and Retreat*, Gulf Breeze, FL, Academic International Press.

Weihsmann, H. (1997) 'The city in twilight: charting the genre of the "city film" 1900–1930' in F. Penz and M. Thomas (eds), *Cinema and Architecture: Melies, Mallet-Stevens, Multimedia*, London, BFI.

Wellman, B. (2001) 'Physical place and cyber place: the rise of networked individualism', *International Journal of Urban and Regional Research*, 25: 227–52.

Westin, A.F. (1967) *Privacy and Freedom*. New York, Atheneum.

Whyte, J. (2002) *Virtual Reality and the Built Environment*, Oxford, Architectural.

Whyte, W. (1969) *The Organization Man*, Harmondsworth, Penguin.

Wiener, N. (1948) *Cybernetics, or, Control and Communication in the Animal and the Machine*, Cambridge, MA, Technology Press.

Wigley, M. (1998) *Constant's New Babylon: The Hyper-Architecture of Desire*, Rotterdam, Witte de With, Center for Contemporary Art.

Williams, R. (1974) *Television, Technology and Cultural Form*, London: Fontana.

Wilson, F. (1988) 'Covering holes in the wall', *Architecture*, 77(8): 95–99.

Winnicott, D.W. (1965) 'The capacity to be alone' in *The Maturational Processes and the Facilitating Environment: Studies in the Theory of Emotional Development*, New York, International Press.

Wollen, P. (1993) 'Cinema, Americanism, the robot' in *Raiding the Icebox Reflections on Twentieth-Century Culture*, London, Verso.

Woolf, V. (1950) 'The Cinema', *The Captain's Death Bed: and Other Essays*. New York: Harcourt Brace.

Woroszylski, W. (1971) *The Life of Mayakovsky* (trans. B. Taborski), New York, Orion.

Zamyatin, Y. (1972) *We* (trans. M. Ginsburg), New York, The Viking Press.

Zizek, S. (2002) 'Big brother, or the triumph of the gaze over the eye' in Levin, Frohne and Weibel (eds), *Ctrl Space: Rhetorics of Surveillance from Bentham to Big Brother*, Cambridge, MA and Karlsruhe, MIT Press and ZKM Centre for Art and Media.

Zola, E. (1992) *The Ladies Paradise* (trans. K. Ross), Berkeley, CA, University of California Press.

Zola, E. (2000) *L'Assommoir* (The Dram Shop), trans. R. Buss, London, Penguin (originally published 1876).

# Index